Desert Paradises

CW00540588

Desert Paradises: Surveying the Landscapes of Dubai's Urban Model explores how designed landscapes can play a vital role in constructing a city's global image and legitimizing its socio-political hierarchy. Using the case study of Dubai, Bolleter explores how Dubai's rulers employ a paradisiacal image of greening the desert, in part, as a tool for political legitimization.

Bolleter also evaluates the designed landscapes of Dubai against the principles of the United Nations and the International Federation of Landscape Architects and argues that what is happening in Dubai represents a significant discrepancy between theory and practice.

This book offers a new perspective on landscape design that has until now been unexplored. It would be beneficial to academics and students of geography, landscape architecture, urban design and urban planning – particularly those with an interest in Dubai or the many cities in the region that are experiencing Dubaification.

Julian Bolleter is Deputy-Director at the Australian Urban Design Research Centre (AUDRC) at the University of Western Australia. His role includes teaching a master's programme in urban design and conducting research and design projects. Julian is a landscape architect and urban designer and has worked in Australia, the United States, the UK and the Middle East. He has published four books: *Made in Australia: The Future of Australian Cities* (with Richard Weller), *Take Me to the River: A History of Perth's Foreshore*, *Scavenging the Suburbs: Auditing Perth for One Million Infill Dwellings* and *The Ghost Cities of Australia: A Survey of New City Proposals and Their Lessons for Australia's 21st Century Development*.

Routledge Research in Landscape and Environmental Design

Series editor: Terry Clements
Associate Professor, Virginia Tech

Routledge Research in Landscape and Environmental Design is a series of academic monographs for scholars working in these disciplines and the overlaps between them. Building on Routledge's history of academic rigour and cutting-edge research, the series contributes to the rapidly expanding literature in all areas of landscape and environmental design.

Desert Paradises

Surveying the Landscapes
of Dubai's Urban Model

Julian Bolleter

Routledge
Taylor & Francis Group

LONDON AND NEW YORK

First published 2019
by Routledge
2 Park Square, Milton Park, Abingdon, Oxon OX14 4RN

and by Routledge
605 Third Avenue, New York, NY 10017

First issued in paperback 2022

Routledge is an imprint of the Taylor & Francis Group, an informa business

Publisher's Note
The publisher has gone to great lengths to ensure the quality of this reprint but points out that some imperfections in the original copies may be apparent.

British Library Cataloguing-in-Publication Data
A catalogue record for this book is available from the British Library

Library of Congress Cataloging-in-Publication Data
Names: Bolleter, Julian, author.
Title: Desert paradises : surveying the landscapes of Dubai's urban model / Julian Bolleter.
Description: Abingdon, Oxon ; New York, NY : Routledge, 2019. | Series: Routledge research in landscape and environmental design | Includes bibliographical references and index.
Identifiers: LCCN 2018058023 | ISBN 9780815355502 (hardback)
Subjects: LCSH: City planning—United Arab Emirates—Dubai. | Urban landscape architecture—United Arab Emirates—Dubai.
Classification: LCC HT169.U482 D833 2019 | DDC 307.1/2160953570—dc23
LC record available at https://lccn.loc.gov/2018058023

ISBN 13: 978-0-8153-5550-2 (hbk)
ISBN 13: 978-1-03-240159-1 (pbk)
ISBN 13: 978-1-351-12976-3 (ebk)

DOI: 10.4324/9781351129763

Typeset in Sabon
by Apex CoVantage, LLC

This book is for my mother.

Contents

Preface

In 2005, I was employed in a landscape architectural practice in Sydney, Australia. One winter's afternoon I remember a colleague showing me a render of the Palm Jumeirah development in Dubai – a project shaped like a colossal palm tree protruding out into the shallow waters of the Persian Gulf. It was mesmerizing. That afternoon I logged onto the Institute of Landscape Architects web page to see what work was available in Dubai. I saw an advert for a small company that was seeking a senior landscape architect and emailed them some folio images and a CV. I did not give the application much thought until the next morning when I received a reply that asked, 'Could you start next week?'

A month later, I was in Dubai. It was mayhem. The city was amid an unparalleled development boom. The small company I was working for, comprising only a handful of people, was designing and documenting vast projects including multi-tower podium decks, new suburban communities sprawling out into the desert, resort landscapes and key civic urban spaces (amongst others). My new boss explained that Dubai represented a fantastic opportunity for a designer, as you could make a decade of mistakes in one year (a ratio I exceeded). This was partly due to the speed of construction. Details that you designed in the morning, labourers were sometimes constructing in the afternoon. Moreover, most design practitioners (including myself) were operating with extraordinarily little in-depth knowledge of the local cultural/political milieu or desert landscapes.

This book considers what my former 29-year-old self should have known before charging into Dubai, SketchUp model in hand. More broadly, I intend that this book will contribute to a greater understanding of current landscape design practice within Dubai's environmental, societal and cultural milieu – as well as opening possibilities for future practice. While I am critical of Dubai's urban development – and the urban professions'[1] role in this – I intend this criticism in no way but constructively. The relative failings of design practitioners in Dubai are all shortcomings that were evident in my own design practice. Moreover, I do not intend to add to the already substantial pile of literature that authors have skewed towards outright denunciation of Dubai (otherwise known as 'Dubai bashing'). Nonetheless, for Dubai to prosper as an environmentally, socially and culturally enriching twenty-first-century city, the time has come for qualified critics to subject it to a detailed level of even-handed scrutiny and independent analysis. This is critical in terms not just of Dubai but also of the broader region, to which Dubai's gargantuan development companies are exporting their model of urban development.

Emirates flight EK-001 has landed in Dubai International Airport. Please now join me for a tour of the city that is reconfiguring the world.

Note

1 I use the term 'urban professions' as inclusive of urban planning and design, landscape architecture and architecture, and placemaking.

Acknowledgements

This book draws on my experience of working as a landscape architect in Dubai from 2005 to 2007 and on a related PhD, undertaken at the University of Western Australia and completed in 2010. Over the extended period from 2005 to today, many people, both in the United Arab Emirates and in Australia, have made this book possible.

First thanks go to my PhD supervisor Richard Weller, whose insights have fundamentally shaped this book. Also, to Alan Berger, Catherin Bull and James Corner for marking the PhD. I am grateful to Steven Velegrinis for photographing sites in Dubai and for reviewing the PhD in draft form. I owe a significant debt of gratitude to my sister, Amanda Bolleter, for undertaking the task of copy-editing the PhD.

Thank you to all the members of the urban professions in Dubai whom I interviewed for this book.

Thank you to peer reviewers Catherin Bull and Mohammad Gharipour for their astute reviews of an earlier draft of this book.

Thank you to the supporters of the Australian Urban Design Research Centre where I work, the Western Australian Planning Commission, the Western Australian Department of Planning, Lands and Heritage, the Department of Communities and Landcorp.

Thank you to the *Journal of Landscape Architecture*, *Landscape Research* and *LA+*, who have kindly granted permission for me to reproduce, with edits, material in this book. The original papers are:

Bolleter, J. (2009). 'Para-Scape: Landscape Architecture in Dubai', *Journal of Landscape Architecture*, vol. Spring, no. 4, pp. 28–55.
Bolleter, J. (2015). 'Charting the Potential of Landscape Urbanism in Dubai', *Landscape Research*, vol. 40, no. 5, pp. 1–22.
Bolleter, J. (2020). 'Sheikh-Down: Top-Down Placemaking in Dubai', *LA+ Interdisciplinary Journal of Landscape Architecture*, vol. 11, Spring.

Thanks also to my colleagues Chris Melsom, Anthony Duckworth-Smith, Jill Penter, Zoe Myers and Grace Oliver for their tolerance. In particular, thanks to Grace for graphic assistance.

Thanks go to my parents, Glenys and Ross, for their unwavering support.

Finally, I am grateful to my partner, Dr Sally Appleton, and my daughter, Rose Bolleter, for their patience and love.

1 Introduction

Background

By 2050, the world's urban population is expected to double, making urbanization one of the twenty-first century's most transformative trends (United Nations General Assembly 2016, p. 3). Due to this shift, cities will increasingly become the focus for population growth, economic activity, social and cultural interaction, and environmental and societal issues. Cities in this century will confront massive challenges in terms of the provision of housing, infrastructure, basic services, food, health, education, employment and natural resources, amongst many others (United Nations General Assembly 2016, p. 3). Clearly, the design of our cities will 'make or break' our planet in this twenty-first century.

Given this situation, it is important that academics (and others) critically analyze the urban models that designers and planners deploy to accommodate this vast increase in urban population. While city administrators and planners have long aspired to traditional European city models in colonial settings, increasingly the Gulf cities (and particularly Dubai) are often the city models that developers desire in rapidly urbanizing regions. A key example of this is Africa, where the urban population will almost triple in the coming 35 years (Van Noorloos & Kloosterboer 2017, p. 2). Given this situation, in this introductory chapter, I briefly introduce Dubai's development model and survey the global context that Dubai is influencing. This establishes why I believe that this book is worth reading. I set out the main research questions that direct my lines of enquiry, as well as the methods I adopt to answer these. I also define the scope of the book and clarify the terminology used so that we are all 'on the same page.'

Body

The agricultural project that started in the Fertile Crescent in ancient times has spread substantially and now covers a significant swath of the earth's surface (Morton 2015, p. 62). Some 12,500 years later, Dubai – at the opposite end of the Persian Gulf – is having a disproportionate influence on urban development patterns around the world. While Dubai is often viewed by the West as being a 'fantasy world in the desert' (Davis 2007, p. 63), readers should not underestimate its significance in the broader context. As architectural theoretician Rem Koolhaas says of Gulf cities generally: 'the emerging model of the [Gulf] city is being multiplied in a vast zone . . . . The Gulf is not reconfiguring itself, it's reconfiguring the world. This may be the final opportunity for a new blueprint of urbanism' (Koolhaas 2007, p. 7).

As this book explores, this highly influential model of urban development in Dubai has led to the destruction of both desert and sabkha ecosystems (Bolleter 2009) and has created a particularly unsustainable city that consumes vast reserves of desalinated seawater and energy (Water Footprint Calculator 2017). Moreover, the development model has created a city in which truly equitable and inclusive space is generally absent and urban form often segregates socio-economic groups into disparate urban islands (Bolleter 2009). Finally, the model has led to urban development that often trivializes traditional Emirati culture for profit (Acuto 2010; Andraos 2007). As professor of international development studies Femke van Noorloos explains:

> The Dubai model of development is the 'new global icon of imagineered urbanism,' which comes with largely unprecedented scale, implementation pace, and environmental, social, and economic impacts.
>
> (Kolo 2016, p. 162)

Despite such issues, Dubai's model of urban development is viewed by many rulers, administrators and developers in the region as a viable model that can be replicated or at least responded to. Further to this, Dubai's gargantuan development companies, such as Emaar and Dubai Holdings, are exporting the Dubai model of urban development all over the world. This is no accident, as Sheikh Mohammed explains:

> Dubai offers the countries of the central world a practical and tested development model, one that can be amended to suit the local conditions and the needs of the individual countries concerned.
>
> (Al Maktoum 2012, p. 204)

In the Gulf region, the Dubai model is spreading to Saudi Arabia, Bahrain (Rizzo 2014, p. 52), Kuwait (Moser, Swain & Alkhabbaz 2015, p. 72) and Qatar (Acuto 2010, p. 283). Farther afield, it is influencing development in China, India, Africa, Jordan, Tunisia, Morocco, Syria, Turkey, Egypt, Brazil, Baku (Rizzo 2014, p. 52), South Korea, Hong Kong (Al Maktoum 2012, p. 17), Lebanon (Abaza 2011, p. 1077), the Pilbara region of Western Australia (Sheppard 2013, p. 273) and Azerbaijan (Rizzo 2014, p. 52). Sheikh Mohammed even announced in 2017 that the United Arab Emirates (UAE) was planning to build the first city on Mars by 2117, a proposal

UAE engineers have fleshed out in a concept city about the size of Chicago (Taylor 2017).

The regional (and interplanetary!) adoption of a Dubai development model is concerning. This is particularly the case in developing countries. By way of example, in urban development in Africa, governments and developers are often diverting capital towards the construction of middle- and higher-class-oriented new cities rather than meeting the basic needs of urban dwellers elsewhere. As such, these new city developments are leading to fresh forms of spatial injustice (Van Noorloos & Kloosterboer 2017, p. 14). As a result, van Noorloos worries that the new cities will be 'unsuitable for solving Africa's urban problems, and at worst they will increase expulsions and enclosures of the poor, public funding injustice and socio-spatial segregation and fragmentation' (Van Noorloos & Kloosterboer 2017, p. 1). While it is not fair for critics to blame Dubai for all these issues, its socio-ecologically impoverishing development model compounds this situation. Moreover, even in locations where Dubai's developers are not exporting their model, the city nonetheless provides a window onto a future living and working environment increasingly dominated by neo-liberalism. The problems this book explores in Dubai are problems experienced everywhere – for instance, in Australia – writ large.

Given such emerging issues, it is critical that academics critically analyze Dubai's model of urban development and the role of the urban professions in it, so that designers and planners elsewhere understand the model for its strengths and weaknesses.

Overview of the book and methods

In tackling these issues, I have structured the book as follows. In chapter 2, 'Dubai briefing,' I seek to answer the question:

> *What are the main environmental, societal, political and economic conditions that the urban professions in Dubai navigate?*

To answer this question, I conduct a 'descriptive' research strategy (Swaffield & Deming 2011, p. 37) that draws on the related literature as well as my personal experience of working as a landscape architect in Dubai. The result is a sketch of the environmental, cultural, societal, political and economic contexts in which the urban professions deliver designed landscapes. This is valuable information because, in terms of its natural and cultural landscape, Dubai is foreign, if not hostile, to the orthodox practice of the urban professions in the West. These disjunctions become a reoccurring theme of the book, and I discuss them in subsequent chapters. This chapter also refutes the oft held conceptions of Dubai's endemic landscape as a tabula rasa passively awaiting development and of Dubai as a 'superficial' and manufactured city devoid of history (*The Guardian* in Hyde 2010, p. 68).

In chapter 3, 'Paradisiacal landscapes,' I explore the dominant designed landscape in Dubai – parascape – a verdant green landscape. The following question guides this exploration:

What societal, political, cultural and economic narratives do designed verdant landscapes in Dubai promote?

In answering this question, I deploy an 'interpretive critique' methodology (Swaffield & Deming 2011, p. 43) that reveals new perspectives upon Dubai's designed landscapes and speculates about what narratives clients of such projects may be seeking to promote.[1] I glean such understandings, in part, from a review of Dubai's Strategic Plans (Al Maktoum 2015; Government of Dubai 2014; Government of Dubai 2012) and Sheikh Mohammed's revealing book, *My Vision: Challenges in the Race for Excellence* (Al Maktoum 2012).

The central premise of the chapter is that many designed landscapes in Dubai can be defined under the rubric of parascape, a landscape that is derived, subliminally if not explicitly, from Quranic depictions of paradise (Ouis 2002). Through both its pastoral aesthetic and its religious underpinnings, this luxuriant landscape is important in constructing Dubai's global image and legitimizing its socio-political hierarchy (Ouis 2002). Moreover, it functions in a symbolic sense as redemptive, as a counterpoint to either the brutality of Dubai's desert context, the 'corruption' and socio-economic division of the city or the perceived threat of globalization within a regional culture. In this chapter, I also discuss several projects I associate with parascape – namely parks, exclusive communities, theme parks and freeway reserves.

In chapter 4, 'Urban and desert landscapes,' I survey two alternative types of designed landscape: the first that constitutes heavily place-managed urbane landscapes and the second that landscape designers have loosely based on Dubai's desert landscapes. Both provide some resistance to the dominant parascape landscape type. Two research questions drive this enquiry:

What cultural, societal and political narratives do designed urban spaces in Dubai promote?

And:

What cultural, societal and political narratives do designed xerophytic landscapes in Dubai promote?

Again, I adopt an interpretive critique methodology in answering these research questions (Swaffield & Deming 2011, p. 43). I also discuss these narratives in relation to Dubai's Strategic Plans (Al Maktoum 2015; Government of Dubai 2014; Government of Dubai 2012) and Sheikh Mohammed's book outlining his vision for Dubai (Al Maktoum 2012).

In response to the first question, I survey heavily themed and place-managed urbane projects, defined under the rubric of *urbscape*, which function to attract global tourists and capital and which conform to Sheikh Mohammed's attempt to turn Dubai into one of the 'cultural epicentres of the world' (Newman 2016). I consider several projects I associate with urbscape – namely 'old town' developments, urban waterfront developments and urban 'creative' districts – all of which contribute to achieving this goal.

In response to the second question, I survey desert-influenced, xeriphytic-designed landscapes, defined under the rubric of *xeriscape*, which respond to Dubai's hyper-arid conditions. I consider several projects I associate with xeriscape – namely new xerophytic urban districts and xeriphytic parks.

In chapter 5, 'Challenges in practice,' I pose two questions:

What environmental, societal and cultural goals should the urban professions aspire to in landscape design practice in Dubai?

And:

Do the landscapes designed by the urban professions in Dubai conform to prevailing environmental, societal and cultural goals for practice?

In answering the first question, I conduct a literature review on existing normative frameworks for assessing design practice. This review includes the United Nations Goals for Sustainable Development and the charters of the International Federation of Landscape Architects, the International Society of Architects and the International Society of City and Regional Planners. These charters, in part, reflect aspirations for sustainability, social equity and inclusiveness, and cross-cultural sensitivity.

In answering the second question, I employ an evaluative research strategy (Swaffield & Deming 2011, p. 43) that assesses the landscape design practice of the urban professions against the normative frameworks. I argue that as the 'handmaiden' of global capital, the urban professions struggle to reconcile landscape design practice with the environmental, societal and cultural aspirations of the United Nations, amongst others.

James Corner claims that Landscape Urbanism offers some of the most compelling future directions for the 'advancement of a more socially just, politically emancipating and ecologically sane mix of spatiotemporal production processes' in a world gone awry (Corner 2003, p. 62). In light of this claim, in chapter 6, 'The potential of Landscape Urbanism in Dubai,' I consider whether Landscape Urbanism theory can assist with the various challenges designers of Dubai's urban landscape face.

I structure this enquiry in relation to the question:

What aspects of Landscape Urbanism theory could the urban professions in Dubai employ in the design of environmentally, societally and culturally enriching landscapes?

In answering this question, I briefly summarize the shortfalls in current landscape design practice and theoretically 'evaluate' (Swaffield & Deming 2011, p. 42) what Landscape Urbanism could contribute. This chapter concludes with some alternative suggestions as to how practitioners could engage with Dubai's environment, societal spectrum and local culture in a bid to produce more enriching projects. The chapter, however, also acknowledges the great challenge practitioners face in terms of reconciling aspirations with practice in Dubai.

The concluding chapter, chapter 7, summarizes the key lessons of the book and provides an overview of the implications of continuing current practice, as well as the possible ramifications of exporting the Dubai model to rapidly urbanizing areas of the globe.

Scope

My decision to focus this book on the way Dubai's rulers and developers use designed landscapes (and their associated urbanism) to further certain political, economic and cultural narratives does not mean I underestimate the power of urban form/architecture alone to achieve similar ends. Rather, my decision to use designed landscapes as the 'lens' for this enquiry recognizes that a body of research already exists in relation to Dubai's architecture – Deyan Sudjic's *The Edifice of Power: The Architecture of Power* being one fine example (2005), as well as Michele Acuto's paper 'High-Rise Dubai Urban Entrepreneurialism and the Technology of Symbolic Power' (2010).

My focus on designed landscape also reflects that, in a twenty-first century global metropolis such as Dubai, the 'traditional notion of the city . . . has been largely replaced by a more polycentric and web-like sprawl' (Wall 1999, p. 234). I believe that such a characterization applies to the sprawling city of Dubai, where developers outbid one another to produce the 'lowest density villa developments in the heart of any international city' (Meydan & Sobha 2018). As such, I believe a landscape 'lens' is valid for analyzing Dubai. Finally, my decision to use designed landscape as a lens for this book reflects my training and professional experience as a landscape architect. Nonetheless, I have authored this book for wide readership and so have attempted to avoid focussing the book on landscape architectural issues alone.

Terminology

A brief note to readers regarding terminology: I use the term 'landscape designers' as inclusive of urban planners, urban designers, landscape architects, architects and placemakers – all of whom shape constructed landscapes in Dubai. I refer to these disciplines collectively as the 'urban professions,' and I discuss the operation of these disciplines in detail in the next chapter.

I refer to Dubai's rulers throughout the book. By this, I mean the Al Maktoum dynasty whose reign as rulers began in 1833. Since 2008, Sheikh Mohammed bin Rashid Al Maktoum (Sheikh Mohammed) has served as the ruler of Dubai and as vice president and prime minister of the UAE. His oldest son, Sheikh Hamdan bin Mohammed bin Rashid Al Maktoum, is Crown Prince of Dubai. Finally, Sheikh Maktoum bin Mohammed bin Rashid Al Maktoum and Sheikh Hamdan bin Rashid Al Maktoum are the deputy rulers of the Dubai emirate. On occasion, I refer to 'Dubai's ruler,' in which case I mean Sheikh Mohammed specifically.

There is some conjecture about whether 'The Gulf' is the Arabian Gulf or the Persian Gulf. To prevent exacerbating this disagreement, I refer to this shallow and warm sea as 'The Gulf.'

Conclusion

In this chapter, I have set out in brief several of the issues of the Dubai model of development, the significance of the Dubai model to the region and the globe and the research questions and methods that structure the subsequent discussions. The following chapter delves into Dubai's historical evolution and current-day operation in a bid to brief an international readership about the challenging conditions that Dubai presents to the urban professions.

Note

1 I have based this chapter on a previous journal paper (Bolleter 2009).

References and further reading

Abaza, M 2011, 'Critical Commentary: Cairo's Downtown Imagined: Dubaisation or Nostalgia?' *Urban Studies*, vol. 48, no. 6, pp. 1075–1087.

Acuto, M 2010, 'High-Rise Dubai Urban Entrepreneurialism and the Technology of Symbolic Power', *Cities*, no. 27, pp. 272–284.

Al Maktoum, MBR 2012, *My Vision: Challenges in the Race for Excellence*, Motivate Publishing, Dubai.

Al Maktoum, MBR 2015, *Dubai Strategic Plan: Highlights Dubai Government*, D Government, Dubai.

Andraos, A 2007, 'Dubai's Island Urbanism: An Archipelago of Difference for the 21st Century?' in *Vision Plus Money Plus Historical Circumstance Equals 'Cities from Zero' Unapologetic Expressions of New-Found Economic and Therefore Political Prowess in the 21st Century*, pp. 47–56. Architectural Association Publishing, London.

Bolleter, J 2009, 'Para-Scape: Landscape Architecture in Dubai', *Journal of Landscape Architecture*, vol. Spring, no. 4, pp. 28–55.

Corner, J 2003, 'Landscape Urbanism', in *Landscape Urbanism A Manual for the Machine Landscape*, pp. 58–62, Architectural Association, London.

Davis, M 2007, 'Fear and Money in Dubai', *Topos*, pp. 62–70.

Government of Dubai 2012, *Dubai 2020 Urban Masterplan*, Government of Dubai, Dubai.

Government of Dubai 2014, *2021 Dubai Plan*, Government of Dubai and Go Dubai, Dubai.

Hyde, R 2010, 'Dubai Bashing', *Al Manakh- Gulf Cont'd*, vol. 25, no. 2, p. 68.

Kolo, J 2016, 'Accidental or Envisioned Cities: A Comparative Analysis of Abu Dhabi and Dubai', in G Katodrytis & S Syed (eds), *Gulf Cities as Interfaces*, pp. 161–180, Gulf Research Centre Cambridge, Jeddah.

Koolhaas, R 2007, 'Last Chance', *Al Manakh*, vol. 12, p. 7.

Meydan & Sobha 2018, 'Mohammed Bin Rashid City: District One', *Meydan*. Available from: https://resources.lookup.ae/downloads/6585597321235058_375. pdf. [04.04].

Morton, T 2015, 'Where the Wild Things Are', *LA+*, no. Wild, pp. 60–65.

Moser, S, Swain, M & Alkhabbaz, M 2015, 'King Abdullah Economic City: Engineering Saudi Arabia's Post-Oil Future', *Cities*, no. 45, pp. 71–80.

Newman, H 2016, 'Brand Dubai: How Creative Placemaking Is Helping Put Dubai on the Cultural Map', *In Business.ae*. Available from: http://www.mediavataarme. com/index.php/industry-news/advertising/item/5200-brand-dubai-how-creative-placemaking-is-helping-put-dubai-on-the-cultural-map. [09.05].

Ouis, P 2002, 'Greening the Emirates: The Modern Construction of Nature in the United Arab Emirates', *Cultural Geographies*, no. 9, pp. 334–347.

Rizzo, A 2014, 'Rapid Urban Development and National Master Planning in Arab Gulf Countries: Qatar as a Case Study', *Cities*, no. 39, pp. 50–57.

Sheppard, E 2013, 'Thinking Through the Pilbara', *Australian Geographer*, vol. 44, no. 3, pp. 265–282.

Sudjic, D 2005, *The Edifice Complex*, Penguin Books, New York.

Swaffield, S & Deming, E 2011, 'Research Strategies in Landscape Architecture: Mapping the Terrain', *Journal of Landscape Architecture*, Spring, pp. 34–45.

Taylor, A 2017, 'The UAE's Ambitious Plan to Build a New City – on Mars', *The Washington Post*. Available from: www.washingtonpost.com/news/worldviews/ wp/2017/02/16/the-uaes-ambitious-plan-to-build-a-new-city-on-mars/?utm_ term=.2c03c9313c97. [16.08].

United Nations General Assembly 2016, 'Draft Outcome Document of the United Nations Conference on Housing and Sustainable Urban Development (Habitat III)', in Document A/CONF.

Van Noorloos, F & Kloosterboer, M 2017, 'Africa's New Cities: The Contested Future of Urbanisation', *Urban Studies*, vol. 55, no. 6, pp. 1–19.

Wall, A 1999, 'Programming the Urban Surface', in *Recovering Landscape: Essays in Contemporary Landscape Architecture*, pp. 233–250, Princeton Architectural Press, New York City.

Water Footprint Calculator 2017, 'Water Footprint Comparisons by Country', *Water Footprint Calculator*. Available from: https://www.watercalculator.org/ footprints/water-footprints-by-country/. [07.09].

2 Dubai briefing

Introduction

I have written this chapter to provide a briefing for an international reader-ship who have not visited Dubai. (See Figure 2.1.) This briefing will pro-vide the necessary information to undergird the focussed discussion about designed landscapes in Dubai, which is the focus of subsequent chapters. In this chapter, I ask the question:

> *What are the main environmental, societal, political and economic con-ditions that the urban professions in Dubai navigate?*

To answer this question, I have conducted a 'descriptive' research strat-egy (Swaffield & Deming 2011, p. 37) that incorporates a comprehensive literature review, as well as drawing on personal experience of living and working in Dubai. The early sections of the chapter detail the evolution of contemporary Dubai from a lonely port on the edge of the Rub al Khali desert, predicated on fishing, trade and smuggling, to its present status as a global metropolis. In the latter sections of this chapter, I examine contem-porary Dubai to understand its societal, political and economic features and the model of urban development its rulers (and related developers) have devised. The cultural conditions in Dubai are extreme; Dubai's population is one of the fastest growing in the world (Zaatari 2017), the local Emirati population is dwarfed by expatriates, significant division occurs between Dubai's socio-economic strata (Davis 2007) and finally the city ranks poorly in terms of greenhouse gas emissions and resource use[1] (Arcadis 2015, p. 9). These conditions present a significant challenge to the urban professions and their ethos of socially inclusive and environmentally and culturally enriching practice.

Body

The urban settlement of Dubai, which for most of its history was a small port, sits at the northern tip of the Rub al Khali desert, a vast and inhospitable

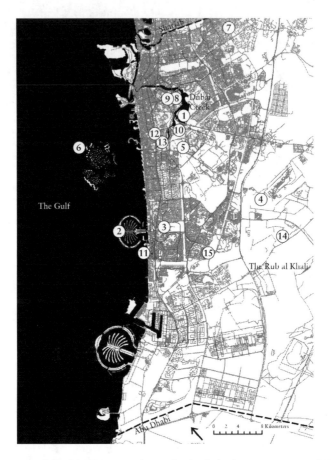

Figure 2.1 To Dubai's southeast is the Rub al Khali desert, a vast and inhospitable expanse. To Dubai's west is a warm and shallow sea known as the Persian or Arabian Gulf. For most of its history, Dubai was a small yet notorious port on Dubai Creek (at top of image).

Key to the main projects I refer to in later chapters of this book:

 1 Ras al Khor
 2 Palm Jumeirah
 3 Dubai Internet City
 4 Dubailand
 5 Sheikh Mohammed Bin Rashid City
 6 The World
 7 Holy Qu'ran Park
 8 Culture Village
 9 Al Seef
10 Dubai Design District
11 The Beach
12 Dubai City Walk
13 Opera District
14 Xeritown
15 Green Sports Hub

Source: GIS data courtesy of Trimble Maps.

expanse that covers about 600,000 square kilometres of the Arabian Peninsula. British explorer Wilfred Thesiger described the Rub al Khali desert in the following terms: 'A cloud gathers, the rain falls, men live; the cloud disperses without rain, and men and animals die' (Thesiger 1991, p. 15). Formed in the Quaternary period by Aeolian deposits associated with the Shamal,[2] the Rub al Khali consists of dunes, sometimes in 'great crescentic massifs up to 250 metres high,' which are underlain by layers of alluvial deposits and *sabkha*, an Arabic word that translates to mud[3] (Mandaville 1998, pp. 202, 203).

Despite Dubai's extremely hot summers (up to 48 degrees Celsius) and erratic rainfall (Dubai Municipality 2005), to the south-east of the small settlement of Dubai is a significant terrestrial habitat in the form of 'open desert woodland' with scattered trees and large shrubs (Parsons Harland Bartholomew 1993, pp. 10–17). This woodland principally comprises *Prosopis cineraria*, or Ghaf trees. (See Figure 2.2, top.) The Ghaf tree can survive the desert conditions by virtue of a very deep taproot that allows it to access aquifers deep beneath the desert surface (World Wildlife Fund 2006). A healthy Ghaf tree woodland sustains species such as desert hares, gazelles, oryx, foxes and falcons.

Other ecosystems of some ecological significance are sabkha landscapes that run along The Gulf coastline. These sabkha landscapes are characterized by 'a thin crust of salt and a rubbery mat of almost black algae underlain by sand, silt, or clay with a cemented hard layer of gypsum crystals' (Guba & Glennie 1998, p. 60). Sabkha areas around Dubai support salt-tolerant shrubs such as *Halopeplis perfoliata* and *Tamarix sp.* and microorganisms (Dubai Municipality 2003). (See Figure 2.2, bottom.) Moreover, the sabkha areas at the head of Dubai Creek (Ras al Khor) contain a wealth of indigenous fauna including mammals, reptiles, amphibians, fish and invertebrates. Most well known of these species is the migratory flamingo, which for time immemorial have transited through this landscape in the winter months (Dubai Municipality 2003).

Dubai's evolution

Urban settlement began in Dubai concomitant with the rise of civilization in the Fertile Crescent around 3000 BCE. Remnants of stone blocks, broken pottery, bronze and sea shells indicate the existence of a port that formed an important link in establishing economic ties between India and Iraq, two of the major civilizations in the region at that time (Dubai Museum 2009). The explorer Abu Abdullah al-Bakri mentioned Dubai in his accounts of the Gulf region in 1095. At this point and in the centuries that followed, Dubai comprised a small fishing village and port, which relied on the benefits afforded by trade and piracy for its survival. The nomadic Bedouin also used Dubai as place to obtain supplies during their journeys across the Arabian Peninsula (Thesiger 1991).

Dubai came to the attention of the Western world in the nineteenth century as British forces expanded into The Gulf. In 1820, the Sheikh of Dubai, along

Figure 2.2 Top photo: desert woodland with scattered trees and large shrubs. This woodland principally comprises *Prosopis cineraria*, or Ghaf trees; bottom photo: Sabkha terrain with salt-tolerant shrubs.

Source: Photos by the author.

with other rulers in the region, signed the 'general maritime peace treaty' with the British Government guaranteeing their protection in exchange for an exclusive relationship with Britain (Easterling 2008, p. 8). These agreements required Gulf rulers to hand over their links to the outside world to Britain and prohibited them from treaties with any other foreign power. In exchange, the British, via the Royal Navy, promised to guarantee their independence from the Ottoman and Persian empires (Easterling 2008, p. 8).

In 1901, Dubai received the first of its many twentieth-century waves of immigration when the ruler of the Persian port of Lingah, in the Bastak region of Iran, raised taxes on all local merchants (Koolhaas & AMO 2007, p. 132). The then Sheikh of Dubai, Maktoum bin Hasher Al Maktoum, grabbed the initiative and eliminated tariffs, declaring Dubai a free port and establishing Dubai's status as the predominate trading hub in the region (Al Maktoum 2012, p. 81). In doing this, Sheikh Maktoum bin Hasher Al Maktoum set the precedent for later rulers of Dubai to willingly host different cultures for economic gain (Koolhaas & AMO 2007, p. 132).

Despite such gestures, the actual settlement of Dubai underwent only modest changes in this period. (See Figure 2.3.) In 1945, British explorer Wilfred Thesiger described the historic Bastakiyah district adjacent to Dubai Creek:

> Naked children romped in the shallows, and rowing boats patrolled the creek to pick up passengers from the mouths of alleys between high

Figure 2.3 A contemporary image of Dubai's dense historic core along Dubai Creek (foreground).

Source: Photo by Kertu/Shutterstock.com.

coral houses, surmounted with square wind turrets, and pleasingly decorated plaster moulding. Behind the diversity of houses, which lined
the waterfront, were the souks, covered passageways, where merchants
sat in the gloom, cross-legged in narrow alcoves among their piled
merchandise. The souks were crowded with many races – pallid Arab
townsmen; armed Bedu, quick eyed and imperious; Negro slaves; Balu-
chis, Persians, and Indians.

(Thesiger 1991, p. 276)

The dense and labyrinthine urbanism of this core area was characterized by
residential courtyards that were framed by buildings comprised of typically
contiguous rooms, deceptively hidden entranceways to individual quarters;
the tri-fold division of space into private, controlled semi-private and public; and a clear segregation of space into male and female spheres (Abu-
Lughod 1980, p. 6).

Improvements in infrastructure, as part of a gradual campaign of
modernization, occurred during the 1950s and 1960s. In 1956, Dubai's
first concrete block house was built; however, the majority of people
were still living in traditional barastri[4] homes and drawing water from
communal wells (AMO, Reisz & Ota 2007, p. 154). In 1958, Sheikh
Rashid bin Saeed Al Maktoum (Sheikh Rashid) became the ruler of Dubai
and began to envision the transformation of Dubai's urban form. A year
later, he commissioned British architect Sir John Harris as Dubai's first
town planner. Harris planned a grid of roads throughout the desert that
grew out of Dubai's historic core and connected to major infrastructure
projects such as the airport and Port Rashid. Harris's plan was highly
praised as it took the little streets of Bastakiya and 'then drew them out,
like roots growing out quite organically . . . like a plant in a desert landscape' (Caton & Ardalan 2010, p. 46).[5] As Dubai expanded along the grid
Harris set out, the recently established Dubai Municipality introduced
new building codes outside the core area, requiring residential buildings
to be set back from plot boundaries – a stipulation that marked the end
for Dubai's traditional introspective courtyard dwellings. From then on,
builders constructed houses in the form of air-conditioned villas behind
high boundary walls and set within a garden landscape (Velegrinis &
Katodrytis 2015, p. 75).

The discovery of oil in Dubai in 1966 heralded an epoch shift in Dubai's
evolution. The massive amount of revenue generated through oil exports
soon subsumed Dubai's traditional economic mainstays of fishing and trade.
Precipitating the first major construction boom in Dubai was the oil crisis
of 1973. The crisis resulted from the decision of members of the Organization of Arab Petroleum Exporting Countries (OAPEC) to no longer ship oil
to nations that had supported Israel in its conflict with Syria and Egypt in
the Yom Kippur War. Through the ensuing turmoil, OAPEC members were
able to use their leverage over the world price-setting mechanism to increase

oil revenue. Further fuelling this boom was the realization by Dubai's then ruler, Sheikh Rashid, that constructed attractions could attract global attention. This realization was prompted by Queen Elizabeth's decision in 1972 to divert her flight to refuel in Dubai instead of Bahrain, so that she could see Dubai's recently constructed airport (AMO, Reisz & Ota 2007, p. 155). Sensing potential, Sheikh Rashid pursued the construction of a World Trade Centre for Dubai, which upon completion was the tallest building in the Middle East (AMO, Reisz & Ota 2007, p. 135). In the decades following the 1973 oil crisis, Sheikh Rashid set out to establish the infrastructure, housing and transport systems of a 'modern city.' This vision was articulated by John Harris in his successive master plans for Dubai prepared up until 1976 and later by Parsons Harland Bartholomew and Associates in their Structure Plan for the Dubai Urban Area 1993–2012 (1995).

Dubai's second, much fabled development boom began in 1997 and was initiated when Dubai's then ruler, Sheikh Maktoum bin Rashid al Maktoum (Sheikh Maktoum), allowed expatriates in special development areas to own freehold property for the first time (Easterling 2008, p. 9). Islamic investors further propagated this boom by repatriating approximately one-third of a trillion dollars' worth of investment from the United States after the September 2001 terrorist attacks (Davis 2007, p. 66). The angry reactions of many American citizens towards Islamic nations saw much of this investment redirected to financing developments in Dubai (Davis 2007, p. 66). Additionally, as a strategically located American ally, Dubai benefited from the U.S. wars with Iraq by acting as a staging post for the movement of supplies and soldiers (Davis 2007, p. 66).

With the imminent demise of Dubai's oil production capacity, the 1997–2008 development boom saw the economy geared towards trade, tourism and real estate construction as means of sustaining Dubai's economic viability. Whereas the preceding boom between 1973 and 1990 aimed to establish Dubai as a modern city, the later boom aimed to expand Dubai's global brand as synonymous with luxury and spectacle – expressed through mall culture and often extreme urban developments (Newman 2016). The Palm and The World developments, which extend into the shallow waters of The Gulf in the form of massive super graphics – best seen from space – represent the apotheosis of this global branding exercise.

In this period, Dubai's urban form increasingly fragmented into multiple mini cities within the larger city. These included Dubai Festival City, Sports City, Media City, Internet City, Healthcare City, Downtown Dubai, Dubai Marina, the Jumeirah Lakes Towers district, Knowledge Village, Humanitarian City, Mohammed bin Rashid City, Motor City and Dubai Outlet City (Velegrinis & Katodrytis 2015, p. 76; Nassar, Blackburn & Whyatt 2014, p. 50). Other mini cities also comprised exclusive, gated communities, such as Arabian Ranches, which developers delivered at typically low suburban densities. As a result, the rate of increase of Dubai's urban footprint in this period outpaced even Dubai's high population growth rate (Nassar,

Blackburn & Whyatt 2014, p. 50). Reflecting this, the total built-up area of Dubai ballooned from 5,400 hectares in 1975 to 97,700 hectares in 2015 (Zaatari 2017).

From 2009 until 2012, the effects of the Global Financial Crisis took a significant toll on Dubai's economy and its construction industry. It was estimated that urban projects valued at $670 billion US were cancelled or were 'temporarily' on hold (Liddle 2009, p. 22).[6] Commentators considered that it was difficult to put an exact figure on the scale of the meltdown because, at the time, there was 'no market. Nobody was buying, nobody was renting; there was no new business' (Liddle 2009, p. 22). Nonetheless, it was considered that house prices had dropped as much as 50 per cent from their peak in the preceding boom (Liddle 2009, p. 22).

However, in 2012 the unsettling effects of the Arab Spring on the broader region precipitated another boom for Dubai. While Dubai's ruling dynasty governs through a 'benevolent' dictatorship, its stability and relative freedoms made it attractive, particularly to many youths from Egypt, Syria and Tunisia. Across the region, the question was asked, 'Even if we can't have democracy, why can't we at least have Dubai?' (Friedman 2014). As journalist Thomas Friedman explains:

> [Dubai became the] . . . Manhattan of the Arab world – a place where young Arabs from across the region can come to realize their full potential in arts, business, media, education and technology start-ups – with world-class companies – and in their own culture, their own language, their own religious milieu, their own food preferences, music and clothing.
>
> (Friedman 2014)

Dubai's continuing reputation as a safe, relatively easy and tolerant place to live (in contrast to nearby countries such as Saudi Arabia) has also helped to fuel its attraction for expatriates from the Western world, particularly Britain (Coles & Walsh 2010, p. 1321).

In summation, Dubai has seen explosive growth since its first steps towards modernization in the 1950s – a rate of change almost unprecedented around the world (Zaatari 2017). Nonetheless, while critics accuse Dubai of being superficial, manufactured and devoid of history (Hyde 2010, p. 68), as this brief account reveals, human settlement in the geographic area of Dubai has ancient origins. I believe a similar argument pertains to the natural landscape of the region. Both Dubai's critics and proponents characterize Dubai's endemic landscape as merely a 'sand pit' awaiting being reshaped into something 'real' by the urban development process. As Sheikh Maktoum bin Rashid Al Maktoum (Sheikh Maktoum) declared, 'we will build and construct, so people will come, we will not ask people to come to an empty place' (Bantey & Heintz 2007, p. 1206). As this account reveals, the natural landscapes of Dubai are far from conveniently empty. While fragile and sparse, the endemic landscape is complex and worthy of further study. I pick this thread up in subsequent chapters.

Dubai snapshot

With the historical context established, the following section provides a snapshot of contemporary Dubai in terms of its societal, political and economic structure. This information is important because it defines the conditions that the urban professions in Dubai must navigate in the design and delivery of projects.

Societal structure

Dubai's current population is 2.1 million, and demographers predict that it will more than double to 5 million by 2027 (Zaatari 2017). Dubai's population growth to date has been driven by high immigration rather than by an increase in birth rates amongst the local population (Zaatari 2017). One result of this is that expatriates numerically dominate Emiratis. Comprising over 88 per cent of the total population (Human Rights Watch 2016), Dubai's expatriate population is proportionally one of the largest in the world. South Asian culture, represented by immigrants from India, Pakistan and Bangladesh, is the largest cultural group in Dubai; however, this often does not extend to political or societal advantage. Because of the substantial number of expatriates, Dubai's population tends to be highly mobile. As Rem Koolhaas describes, this leads to a situation where many residents feel only partial allegiance to Dubai:

> Almost everybody who lives in Dubai lives somewhere else. Because they are provisional, the inhabitants of such a city will have a radically different stake in its future. They feel a conditional loyalty.
>
> (2007, p. 195)

The mobility and conditional allegiance of (some of) Dubai's population (Koolhaas 2007, p. 195) are compounded by the number of tourists visiting each year, outstripping the actual population by a factor of nine. This trend is likely to increase in line with government-set targets for 20 million tourists visiting the city annually by 2020 (Newman 2016).

While Dubai is extremely multicultural, an elevated level of segregation occurs between socio-economic strata. This situation has even led cultural anthropologist Chad Haines to conclude that Dubai is 'inherently a racist and classist city' (Haines 2011, p. 176). Nonetheless, Dubai has successfully created spaces for diverging cultural groups without requiring significant assimilation (Kirchner & Rab 2007, p. 18). The separation of socio-economic groups (often) along cultural lines, while allowing for a 'peaceful' multicultural society, also creates conditions in which segments of the society become 'othered' from the perspective of the dominant strata of Dubai society.

While Dubai's migrant underclass also consists of South and Southeast Asian maids, nannies and other domestic and service workers (Haines 2011, p. 177), the 'others' in Dubai invariably are 'unskilled' migrant labourers housed in camps on the edge of the city – desert containment and a resultant lack of visibility being Dubai's rulers' preferred method for dealing with this 'othered' population (Smith 2010, p. 276). Often residing in extreme poverty, an Indian or Pakistani migrant labourer is likely to receive only one-sixteenth of the wage of a typical Dubai resident (Mafiwasta 2007). Migrant labourers can also face dangerous working conditions, due, in part, to being 'acutely vulnerable to forced labour' – notwithstanding some recent reforms (Human Rights Watch 2016, p. 6). According to official data, more than 30,000 Indian nationals died in Gulf states between 2005 and 2015, with stress, ill health and searing temperatures the most common causes of death (Srivastava 2017). Despite protestations from the current ruler, Sheikh Mohammed bin Rashid Al Maktoum (Sheikh Mohammed), that 'Dubai is a city where you do not feel estranged or marginalized and where nobody lives on the fringes feeling dismal' (Al Maktoum 2012, p. 151), the labourers are there to build the city in often dangerous conditions – not to inhabit it (Smith 2010, p. 276).

Because construction companies recruit a substantial number of male 'unskilled' migrant labourers to build projects, men comprise over 70 per cent of the population (Smith 2010, p. 273). This demographic imbalance results in 'corrective' measures such as the securing of residential areas and semi-public parks as 'family zones' and in the separation of (some) restaurants in Dubai into designated areas for family and 'bachelors.' Because of a severe shortage of labour accommodation, companies have sometimes rented out entire villas in residential neighbourhoods, with reports of some villas housing up to 150 labourers.

To maintain residential areas as 'safe' for families, in 2007, Dubai Municipality passed a rule that bachelors (a term that connotes labourers) could only live in apartments – not villas – and began cutting power to villas under what is called the 'One Villa, One Family' campaign (Smith 2010, p. 277). In these instances, Dubai Municipality perceives labourers as a threat to women and children and thus isolates them from otherwise 'family-friendly' neighbourhoods. This campaign also has a racial dimension in that what the Dubai Municipality was 'cleaning from view were brownskinned men' (Haines 2011, p. 177). As a result, many of these 'bachelors' have been forced to move to crowded apartments in poorer neighbourhoods, such as

Satwa or Deira, or to the neighbouring Emirate of Sharjah, which offers cheaper accommodation (Haines 2011, p. 178).

While most of Dubai's population is comprised of expatriates, the percentage of Muslims remains high because many foreign workers are from Muslim countries such as India and Pakistan. Nonetheless, Dubai's Sunni Muslim rulers (Wehrey 2013, p. 6) maintain a precarious balance between adhering to the Islamic principles held by the majority of the citizens of Dubai and the UAE and adopting a liberal attitude to the vice that fuels Dubai's attractiveness to foreign tourists and skilled labour. This fine balance is made even trickier because the authority of Dubai's rulers is also seen to stem from their adherence to Islamic values (Davidson 2008, p. 167).

The severe impact of the Global Financial Crisis on Dubai saw tensions emerge along religious lines between Western expatriates and Emiratis as economic conditions deteriorated. As the comments of a disgruntled Emirati blogger reveal:

> We are fed-up with Westerners who come here thinking they deserve an easy meal ticket. You were nothing in the West, so you came here for the houses and cars you could never get back home. You stole through taking out excessive finance that is not justified by your salaries. Then when you cannot pay, you run. Despite all of this, you still disrespect our cultural and religious values with your behaviour, dress and conduct in our malls and on our beaches. You spend all your time criticising our laws, society, and systems. Yet you could never have the lifestyle you have here back in your system. You people are no longer welcome, please go and pollute somewhere else.
>
> (In Liddle 2009, p. 22)

Such attitudes remind us of the challenge that Dubai's rulers face in terms of luring Western tourists and skilled workers who drive the economy and maintaining the allegiance of Emiratis, a proportion of whom feel that expatriates threaten their culture and way of life.

Political structure

In the UAE, just under 30 per cent of the adult population is eligible to vote (Forstenlechner, Rutledge & Salem Alnuaimi 2017). Voting is also conducted only to fill half of the posts on an advisory council (Law 2015). Within this democratically restrictive environment, Dubai officially operates under the framework of a constitutional monarchy; however, urban theoretician Mike Davis refers to the system as a 'benevolent dictatorship' (2007, p. 63). The current ruler of Dubai, Sheikh Mohammed, like his counterparts in other emirates, maintains the popularity of his unelected rule, in part, through acts of benevolence – including the provision of secure jobs, free land or housing and urban amenities such as parks. Nonetheless, the Dubai Government claims that Sheikh Mohammed governs 'for the people and not over them' (Government of Dubai 2014, p. 19) through employing '*majlis*-style' forums (public meetings) that allow for direct consultation between the ruler and his citizens (Forstenlechner, Rutledge & Salem Alnuaimi 2017). As Sheikh Mohammed explains, 'democracy should not feel threatening to us, because we have been practicing our own brand of democracy for a very long time' (Al Maktoum 2012, p. 191). Clearly, the meaning of what constitutes 'democracy' in Dubai depends on the viewer's perspective.

Nonetheless, under what Mike Davis refers to as the 'enlightened despotism' of Sheikh Mohammed (Davis 2007, p. 63), most of the newspapers are government run; in addition, Dubai's rulers censor both the Internet and television. While Dubai is liberal in comparison to its conservative neighbours, this freedom does not extend to allowing unrestricted political agitation or criticism. Sheikh Mohammed justifies censorship of the media through characterizing criticisms as inaccurate:

> I prefer to see constructive criticism in the press rather than praise. Everyone knows about achievements and we do not really need any reminders, but uncovering mistakes leads officials and decision-makers to correct them and avoid making more. I never try to impose or imply to the press what they should be writing and publishing, because media professionals know their jobs better than I do. What I always wish, however, is for criticism to be accurate and supported with content that is the result of professional research, and not originating from dubious sources, rumours or insinuations.
>
> (Al Maktoum 2012, p. 83)

Others, such as human rights activist Ahmed Mansoor, have seen another, darker face of the UAE – of which Sheikh Mohammed is the current prime minister. As he explains:

> The authorities want to silence all criticism . . . they arrest people in the middle of the night, hold them in unknown places sometimes for months at a time, use physical and psychological torture to extract confessions and then have, what the UN have called, sham trials, where they are sentenced to long jail terms.
>
> (Law 2015)

The UAE's intolerance of criticism was evident in 2016, when the government prosecuted an Emirati academic and a Jordanian journalist, among others, for exercising their right to free expression. Moreover, UAE courts recently released several Libyan nationals whom they apparently forcibly disappeared in 2015 and who had made credible allegations of torture in state security detention (Human Rights Watch 2016). This alleged mistreatment relates to the UAE's 2014 counterterrorism law that allows for the death penalty for people whose activities are found to 'undermine national unity or social peace,' neither of which is clearly defined (Human Rights Watch 2016).

Recent crackdowns to ensure 'national unity,' were undoubtedly prompted by the uprisings that rocked the Arab world in the Arab Spring (Wehrey 2013, p. xvii). In The Gulf in 2011 and 2012, rulers and government officials grew increasingly wary of the 'ripple effects' of this regional chaos, with some going so far as to warn that their normally peaceful corner of the Middle East was 'not immune from the calamity of sectarian strife' (Wehrey 2013, p. x). Despite such concerns, Sheikh Mohammed and the other rulers of the UAE have emerged unscathed out of the Arab Spring (Forstenlechner, Rutledge & Salem Alnuaimi 2017). There are two reasons for this. The first is that they are rulers whose authority stems from tribal, clan and family allegiances, and thus they do not face a crisis of legitimacy. The second is that the 'social contract' between the rulers and their citizens has so far been capable of providing enough jobs, housing and urban 'improvements' to ward off unrest (Forstenlechner, Rutledge & Salem Alnuaimi 2017).

Economic structure

The dominant economic paradigm in Dubai is neo-liberalism.[7] Social geographer David Harvey describes that the neo-liberal state 'optimizes conditions for capital accumulation no matter what the consequences are for employment or social well-being' (Harvey 2005, p. 25). In these respects, Dubai has achieved what 'neo liberal reactionaries only dream of; a paradise of free enterprise without income taxes, trade unions or opposition parties' (Davis 2007, p. 67). Dubai's leaders are unrepentant about its wholesale adoption of neo-liberal values as Saeed al-Muntafiq, one-time head of the Dubai Development and Investment Authority, attests:

> People refer to our crown prince as the chief executive officer of Dubai. It's because, genuinely he runs government as a private business for the sake of the private sector, not for the sake of the state.
>
> (Davis 2007, p. 67)

This blurs the distinction between the private and public sectors. Architect Boris Jensen refers to the conceptual negation of what constitutes the state in Dubai: 'In Dubai, the state is a private business, which per definition makes the public sphere private' (Jensen 2007, p. 153). Sheikh Mohammed also confirms this conflation:

> When we speak about the public and private sectors, we are not referring to two drivers pulling in opposite directions but are rather speaking about two drivers pulling in the same direction, working in perfect harmony to speed up the production cycle and consequently, boost the economy . . . . If they fail we will fail with them, and if they succeed, we will flourish with them.
>
> (Al Maktoum 2012, p. 137)

With a gross domestic product second only to Abu Dhabi in the UAE, commentators refer to Dubai as the lower Gulf's economic capital (Davidson 2008, p. 103). Despite initially lucrative returns from oil exports, Dubai's rulers have accepted since the mid-1980s that oil-based income alone would never be enough to maintain Dubai's economic status. This realization prompted an ongoing programme of economic diversification away from oil exports and towards real estate, retail, tourism, leisure, commerce, light manufacturing and agriculture (Davidson 2008). As a result, revenues from oil and natural gas currently account for only a small fraction of Dubai's gross domestic product. Instead, Dubai is almost completely reliant on the international exchange of capital, labour and goods for its survival (AMO, Reisz & Ota 2007, p. 76). As Rem Koolhaas's research office AMO explains:

> Dubai is halfway to everywhere. Global convergence; Chinese export hub, medical experts hub, international congresses hub, hospitality hub, floriculture hub.
>
> (AMO, Reisz & Ota 2007, p. 138)

Dubai's reliance on global investment and tourism is only gathering speed. Dubai is increasingly known for its 'world-class events and festivals' (Newman 2016). Such events are a key component of a government strategy to entice 20 million tourists to visit Dubai annually by 2020 – a level of tourism to be sustained by the city becoming one of the 'cultural epicentres of the world' (Newman 2016).

Nonetheless, beneath Dubai's official economic policies exists illicit economic activity under the control of often large criminal organizations (Davidson 2008, p. 277). Contemporary Dubai's function as a nodal point in the region for trafficking, smuggling, kidnapping, money laundering and prostitution is an expansion of its historic role as the most 'notorious port on the Arabian Sea' (Kennedy 2007, p. 407). Globally, the sex industry is estimated to produce billions of dollars in profits (Sabat 2015, p. 66). The United Arab Emirates and Dubai in particular are a destination for women and children trafficked from South and East Asia, Eastern

Europe, Africa and the Middle East for enforced servitude and exploitation in sexual terms (Central Intelligence Agency 2008). In 2008, the Central Intelligence Agency estimated that 10,000 women were victims of sex trafficking in the UAE. Further to this, women also voluntarily migrate from Africa and from South and Southeast Asia to assume employment as domestic servants but in some instances have their passports confiscated, are denied permission to leave the place of employment, or face sexual or physical abuse by their employers (Central Intelligence Agency 2008). In addition to the trafficking of people, Dubai is also regarded as being a major shipment point for drugs, given its proximity to drug-producing countries such as Pakistan and Afghanistan (Central Intelligence Agency 2008).

Dubai also has alleged terrorist connections – a former high-ranking U.S. treasury official claiming 'all roads lead to Dubai when it comes to terrorist money' (Davis 2007, p. 66). The Washington-based Centre for Advanced Defence Studies alleges that terror financiers sanctioned by the United States have used Dubai's real estate market as a haven for their profits (Associated Press 2018). It identifies $100 million US in suspicious purchases of properties in the United Arab Emirates, including million-dollar villas on the fronds of Palm Jumeirah and apartments in the Burj Khalifa, the world's tallest building (Associated Press 2018).

Dubai's 'sin city' substratum fuels tourism to the city (Sabat 2015, p. 66). It acts as a lure to attract citizens of other conservative emirates and nations in the region, such as Saudi Arabia, Qatar and Iran, who impose a restrictive lifestyle on their citizens. This dynamic was witnessed following the revolution in Iran in 1979 when Dubai became The Gulf's version of 'Miami' for many Iranian exiles (Davis 2007, p. 66). Dubai's rulers encouraged this process by granting refuge to significant numbers of exiles, many of whom became smugglers of gold, untaxed cigarettes and liquor into their restrictive homeland (Davis 2007, p. 66).

Dubai's development model

Real estate is a vital sector that drives Dubai's urban development model and in turn Dubai's economy (Davidson 2008). At the top of the development model hierarchy is Sheikh Mohammed, who is the current major shareholder of the Dubai Holding corporation ($4.57 billion US annual turnover), Dubai's largest and most powerful company with a massive portfolio of diverse interests. (See Figure 2.4.) Other companies that Sheikh Mohammed owns, or part owns, are developers such as Nakheel ($1.54 billion US annual turnover), Meraas Holding, Dubai Properties and Meydan. Through this model of entrepreneurial yet government-backed urban development, the ruling family is in control of the majority of major projects in Dubai and is able to heavily leverage these with 'state resources, power, and patronage' (Kolo 2016, p. 163).

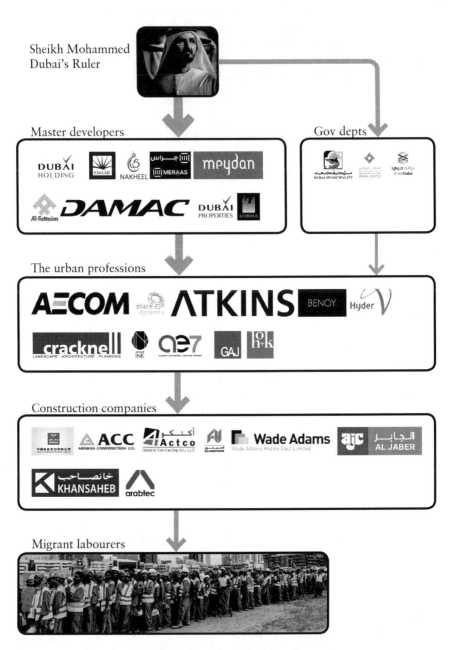

Figure 2.4 A diagrammatic summation of Dubai's hierarchical urban development model. This diagram is indicative only.

Sources: Top photo by Kertu/Shutterstock.com; bottom photo by RastoS/Shutterstock.com.

Other major real estate developers not directly owned by Sheikh Mohammed are Emaar (which specializes in resort and high-rise developments and
has a $5.83 billion US annual turnover), Al Futteim, Damac Properties and
Sobha. However, I believe Dubai's ruler still heavily influences these companies. For example, Mohamed Alabbar, chairperson of Emaar Properties,
describes Sheikh Mohammed as 'one of his inspirations,' as he elaborates:

> My teacher was Sheikh Mohammed, I worked for him for 30 years.
> From him I learned to take risks, to be responsible and I learned the art
> of delegation. You make him a promise and you deliver on it.
>
> (Bridge 2018)

Such long-term personal and professional connections mean that it is highly
likely that Sheikh Mohammed continues to exert substantial influence on
Emaar's activities through its chairperson.

Despite the confusion of the private and public sectors, a government
actor in Dubai's development model is the Dubai Municipality, the municipal organization with responsibility for delivering city services and the
maintenance of facilities. While the Dubai Municipality does not deliver
or (in some cases) approve urban projects, they do deliver and maintain
public open spaces and expansive freeway reserves. As Dubai Municipality
comes under the Government of Dubai, they are also directly answerable to
Dubai's rulers. Moreover, the director general of the Dubai Municipality,
Dawood Al Hajri, is a graduate of the Mohammed Bin Rashid Al Maktoum
Leadership Development Program (*Khaleej Times* 2018).

Another government actor in Dubai's development model is Brand Dubai,
the creative arm of the Government of Dubai Media Office. As their marketing explains, Brand Dubai utilizes street art and installations to 'enhance the
look and feel of Dubai to reflect its unique character as one of the world's
most developed, fastest growing and culturally diverse cities' and to 'communicate positive messages about Dubai's unique culture, values and identity' (Brand Dubai 2018) – and by extension Dubai's rulers. Rather than
this constituting a bottom-up, organic process, Sheikh Mohammed, to some
degree, dictates Brand Dubai's initiatives. This is not surprising because the
Dubai Media Office (Brand Dubai's parent organization) is tasked with
'driving synergies between the Government and the Media' (The Media
Office 2018). In particular, Brand Dubai aims to deliver on Sheikh Mohammed's aspirations to 'turn Dubai into an open museum, and promote aesthetic excellence and innovation, in partnership with government entities
and departments, developers, artists and designers' (Brand Dubai 2018).

Sitting beneath Dubai's real estate developers and Municipality in the
development model hierarchy are the companies who master-plan, design,
document and supervise the construction of urban projects. These include
multidisciplinary design firms like Aecom, Place Dynamix, Atkins, AE7,
Bennoy, Hyder Consulting and HOK, which typically have offices in Dubai

as well as in other global cities. These multidisciplinary firms provide services in relation to master planning, urban design, landscape architecture, architecture, interior design, engineering, placemaking and increasingly destination branding.

Competing with these global multidisciplinary firms are smaller specifically architectural or landscape architectural firms that work in Dubai from remote locations or that have minimal presence in Dubai, such as ASPECT Studios from Australia (ASPECT Studios 2018) or Martha Schwartz Partners from the United States (Waugh 2011). These practices benefit from the relative 'simplicity of transmitting digital documents' of both project imagery and specifications which are 'prepared in New York, outsourced and detailed in Mumbai, and delivered to a project manager in Dubai in days' (Katodrytis 2007, p. 43). Other landscape architecture and architecture companies have long established offices in Dubai, such as Godwin Austen Johnson, Cracknell (established in 1993) and Green Concepts Landscape Architects (~1995). These are complemented by emerging, smaller offices such as AK Design, Verdaus (2004) and desert INK (2008) (desert INK 2018; Verdaus 2018).

Building the projects designed by such firms are major construction companies such as Al Jaber ($1.06 billion US revenue), China State Construction Engineering Corporation Middle East ($3.2 billion US revenue), Arabian Construction Company ($1.1 billion US revenue), Arabtec Construction, Khansaheb Construction, Wade Adams Contracting, Al Habtoor Group and Actco General Contracting. These firms typically have projects 'on the books' worth billions of dollars in value, and the largest of the firms employ up to 40,000 people in the UAE, a substantial proportion of whom are unskilled migrant labourers (BizVibe 2018).

On the back of such labourers, the Dubai development model yields projects from the scale of the substantial 23-hectare Al Seef development on Dubai Creek up to behemoths like the 570-hectare Palm Jumeirah. The generally large size of development sites is important to maximize feasibility and profit, Mohammed Alabbar describing that 'at Emaar, we're obsessed with large sites – 37 hectares or more' (Bridge 2018). The projects themselves include large exclusive suburban developments such as Jumeriah Golf Estates, high-density waterfront precincts such as Dubai Marina or Jumeirah Beach Residences, new mixed-use precincts such as Dubai City Walk or La Mer, and mega mall developments such as Mall of the World. While large real estate firms like Emaar have emerged in Dubai, their aspirations are global. As Mohammed Alabar of Emaar explains:

> International expansion is part of our business strategy to create long-term value for our stakeholders by replicating our Dubai business model and leveraging our execution competencies in design, project

management and sales. In fact, our international land bank is over 22,600 hectares, and the value of our future projects in global markets is over $67 billion US.

(Parasie 2014)

Reflecting this, Emaar has projects in Saudi Arabia, Syria, Jordan, Lebanon, Egypt, Morocco, India, Pakistan, Turkey, the United States, Italy and Canada, in combination with emerging high-growth markets in the Middle East and North Africa regions, the Subcontinent and Southeast Asia (Parasie 2014). In Saudi Arabia, where the imperative is to create economic development for a growing population, a series of six metropolises known as the 'economic cities' are currently planned (Velegrinis & Katodrytis 2015, p. 77). The first of Saudi Arabia's new master-planned 'economic cities' is King Abdullah Economic City (KAEC), which is under construction on the Red Sea coast (Moser, Swain & Alkhabbaz 2015, p. 72). This $100 billion US project is the largest single investment to date in Saudi Arabia and far exceeds the budgets for new cities in other countries (Moser 2015). The Economic City, a subsidiary of Emaar, is privately financing and running the project (Moser, Swain & Alkhabbaz 2015, p. 73). As a public–private joint venture, KAEC is destined to become a 'city of investors, by investors, for investors' (Moser, Swain & Alkhabbaz 2015, p. 77) and a pure expression of neo-liberal values.

Dubai's development model is highly influential elsewhere in the region. Qatar, for instance, has produced a master plan for Lusail City, a 'visionary oasis built from nothing to compete as a global city' (Acuto 2010, p. 283). Kuwait's plans for the City of Silk (Madinat al Hareer), to be built opposite Kuwait City, include a 1,001-metre-high tower set to dethrone Dubai's Burj Khalifa and become the tallest in the world (Moser, Swain & Alkhabbaz 2015, p. 72). The Pearl project in Doha, in Qatar, is another example of what Elsheshtawy describes as 'Dubaification' (Rizzo 2014, p. 52). The Pearl is a series of artificial islands spanning 400 hectares. It is the first land in Qatar to be available for freehold ownership by 45,000 residents, mainly foreign nationals (Velegrinis & Katodrytis 2015, p. 76). In Bahrain, the Durrat Al Bahrain project is an array of exclusive crescent-shaped islands far from the established urban fabric of the capital city Manama (Velegrinis & Katodrytis 2015, p. 76).

In Africa, examples of Dubaification abound in Khartoum, Sudan, and in Nouakchott, Mauritania (Rizzo 2014, p. 52). These new master-planned communities have clear connections with the Gulf states, Dubai in particular, through their urban models, investors and contractors, which accept Islamic-based funding rules (Van Noorloos & Kloosterboer 2017, p. 7). These new cities are built up from scratch as comprehensively planned self-contained enclaves in the outskirts of existing cities (Van Noorloos & Kloosterboer 2017, p. 2). In other African new cities the concepts of technology, innovation and knowledge hubs is predominate, such as Konza Technology City in Kenya and King Mohammed VI Green City in Morocco (Van Noorloos & Kloosterboer 2017, p. 5). These examples stem (in part) from Dubai's Free Trade Zone model and Dubai Internet City in particular – a development that I discuss in chapter 3.

The Dubai model of development has also found expression in Egypt, in a planned new capital city, new master-planned exclusive communities on the desert fringe and the Dubaification of the existing city of Cairo (Abaza 2011, p. 1075). In these existing areas, developments advertised as 'islands of luxury' and employing privatized security guards have reputedly resulted in new patterns of spatial segregation (Abaza 2011, p. 1075). These developments visualize the influence of the taste of The Gulf 'oil monarchies' for luxurious living (Denis 2006, p. 58). For the wealthy residents of these urban islands, Cairo has become a complex of nuisances to escape from (Denis 2006, p. 53). While superficial, this brief overview provides a sense of the substantial reach and power of the Dubai development model.

Conclusion

This chapter has described Dubai's evolution and provided a snapshot of contemporary Dubai's demographic, political and economic structure – and established the broader natural and cultural milieu within which the urban professions practice in Dubai. The development model that Dubai has incubated has global reach and is extremely autocratic – with major developers connected directly or indirectly to Sheikh Mohammed – and generates vast turnover. This development machine is also relentlessly efficient in terms of producing various forms of exclusive development at a large scale.

As the following chapters explore, in terms of its environmental, societal, political and economic conditions, Dubai presents many challenges to the practice of the urban professions. Dubai's hyper-arid and often brutally hot conditions are hostile to the urban profession's reflexive creation of a green 'nature,' which becomes anything but 'natural' within the arid Dubai environment. The urban professions in Dubai find themselves adrift from the democratic, secular contexts in which they normally operate. Moreover, the autocratic rule of Sheikh Mohammed and the relative segregation of socio-economic strata in Dubai defy attempts to create inclusive and democratic open space. Dubai's bewildering array of cultures create a cross-cultural conundrum for practitioners in the urban professions who attempt to engage with the eventual users of projects. These disjunctions and challenges to practice are a reoccurring theme of this book, and I discuss them in detail in the following chapters.

Notes

1 A cultural lifestyle of 'luxury through waste' has been described as one of the chief hindrances to sustainable liveability in the region (Caton & Ardalan 2010).

2 The Shamal originates from the North, generating both significant waves and strong currents over the Gulf and scattering the aeolian sands of Iran and Iraq over Dubai (Salahudin 2006).

3 The term 'sabkha' refers to a saturated salt flat found in the Gulf (Guba & Glennie 1998). The Arabic term for 'sabkha' literally means 'mud' (Deil 1998), which could partially explain the wilfulness with which this ecology has been destroyed by development.

4 The term 'barastri' refers to a traditional method of making structures from palm fronds.

5 This was in contrast to planning in other Gulf cities such as Kuwait, where historic areas were largely demolished in the 1960s.

6 Rumours had it that, while many buildings remained empty shells, cranes were left on rooftops and moved occasionally in order to give the impression that construction was continuing (Caton & Ardalan 2010).

7 A neo-liberal system refers to a free market economy that places importance upon private enterprise and personal initiative with a minimum of interference from the state. Neo-liberal thought is that this creates the best opportunity for the progression of both the individual and the society.

References and further reading

Abaza, M 2011, 'Critical Commentary: Cairo's Downtown Imagined: Dubaisation or Nostalgia?' *Urban Studies*, vol. 48, no. 6, pp. 1075–1087.

Abu-Lughod, JL 1980, 'Contemporary Relevance of Islamic Urban Principles', *Ekistics*, vol. 47, no. 280, pp. 6–10.

Acuto, M 2010, 'High-Rise Dubai Urban Entrepreneurialism and the Technology of Symbolic Power', *Cities*, no. 27, pp. 272–284.

Al Maktoum, MbR 2012, *My Vision: Challenges in the Race for Excellence*, Motivate Publishing, Dubai.

AMO, Reisz, T & Ota, K 2007, 'Gulf Survey', *Al Manakh*, vol. 12, no. 7, pp. 70–334.

Arcadis 2015, *Sustainable Cities Index Arcadis*, Arcadis, Amsterdam.

ASPECT Studios 2018, 'Project Location Dubai', *ASPECT Studios*. Available from: www.aspect-studios.com/au/locations/dubai/. [16.06].

Associated Press 2018, 'Dubai Has Reportedly Become a Money-Laundering Paradise', *New York Post*. Available from: https://nypost.com/2018/06/12/dubai-has-reportedly-become-a-money-laundering-paradise/. [29.08].

Bantey, P & Heintz, E 2007, 'The Architecture of Elsewhere: New Urban Contexts in Dubai and Shanghai', in *Regional Architecture and Identity in the Age of Globalization Conference*, pp. 1205–1218, The Centre for the Study of Architecture in the Arab Region, Dubai.

BizVibe 2018, 'Top 10 Construction Companies in Dubai', *BizVibe*. Available from: www.bizvibe.com/blog/top-10-construction-companies-in-dubai/ [29.07].

Brand Dubai 2018, *Brand Dubai, Dubai Media Office*. Available from: www.brand dubai.com/indexen.php/. [18.08].

Bridge, S 2018, Alabar: Why the Days of Working 9–5 Are Over', *Arabian Business*. Available from: www.arabianbusiness.com/technology/396182-alabbar-why-the-days-of-working-9-5-are-over. [31.07].

Caton, S & Ardalan, N 2010, *New Arab Urbanism, the Challenge to Sustainability and Culture in the Gulf*, Harvard Kennedy School, Cambridge, MA.

Central Intelligence Agency 2008, *Central Intelligence Agency: The World Factbook*. Available from: https://www.cia.gov/library/publications/resources/the-world-factbook/index.html. [24.01].

Coles, A & Walsh, K 2010, 'From "Trucial State" to "Postcolonial" City? The Imaginative Geographies of British Expatriates in Dubai', *Journal of Ethnic and Migration Studies*, vol. 36, no. 8, pp. 1317–1333.

Davidson, C 2008, *Dubai: The Vulnerability of Success*, Columbia University Press, New York.

Davis, M 2007, 'Fear and Money in Dubai', *Topos*, pp. 62–70.

Deil, U 1998, 'Coastal and Sabkah Vegetation', in *Vegetation of the Arabian Peninsula*, pp. 209–228, Kluwer Academic Publishers, Dordrecht.

Denis, E 2006, *Cairo as Neoliberal Capital?* American University in Cairo Press, Cairo and New York.

desert INK 2018, *desert INK, Desert Group*. Available from: www.desert-ink.com/about/. [16.06].

Dubai Municipality 2003, *Ras Al Khor Wildlife Sanctuary, Brochure, Dubai Municipality*. Available from: www.panda.org/who_we_are/wwf_offices/united_arab_emirates/news/?20230/Ras-Al-Khor-Wildlife-Sanctuary.

Dubai Municipality 2005, *Climate and Environment in Dubai Statistics*, Dubai Statistics Center, Dubai.

Dubai Museum 2009, *Dubai Exhibition*, Dubai Museum, Dubai.

Easterling, K 2008, 'Extrastatecraft', *Perspecta 39 The Yale Architectural Journal: Re-Urbanism Transforming Capitals*, pp. 5–16.

Forstenlechner, I, Rutledge, E & Salem Alnuaimi, R 2017, 'The UAE, the "Arab Spring" and Different Types of Dissent', *The Middle East Policy Council*. [07.04].

Friedman, T 2014, 'Did Dubai Do It?' *New York Times*. Available from: www.nytimes.com/2014/11/19/opinion/thomas-friedman-did-dubai-do-it.html. [05.04].

Government of Dubai 2014, *2021 Dubai Plan Government of Dubai*, Go Dubai, Dubai.

Guba, I & Glennie, K 1998, 'Geology and Geomorphology', in *Vegetation of the Arabian Peninsula*, pp. 39–62, Kluwer Academic Publishers, The Netherlands.

Haines, C 2011, 'Cracks in the Façade: Landscapes of Hope and Desire in Dubai', in *Worlding Cities: Asian Experiments and the Art of Being Global*, pp. 160–181, Blackwell, Chichester.

Harvey, D 2005, *Spaces of Global Capitalism*, Verso, London.

Human Rights Watch 2016, *United Arab Emirates: Events of 2016*, Human Rights Watch, New York. Available from https://www.hrw.org/world-report/2017/country-chapters/united-arab-emirates. [06.04].

Hyde, R 2010, 'Dubai Bashing', *Al Manakh- Gulf Cont'd*, vol. 25, no. 2, p. 68.

Jensen, B 2007, *Dubai – Dynamics of Bingo Urbanism*, Architectural Publisher, Copenhagen.

Katodrytis, G 2007, 'The Dubai Experiment', *Al Manakh*, vol. 12, no. 7, pp. 38–39.

Kennedy, T 2007, 'Place Telling at Dubai Creek: Encoded Visions', in *Regional Architecture and Identity in the Age of Globalization Conference*, pp. 407–416, Centre for the Study of Architecture in the Arab Region, Dubai.

Khaleej Times 2018, 'Sheikh Mohammed Appoints New Dubai Municipality Chief', *Khaleej Times*. Available from: www.khaleejtimes.com/nation/dubai/sheikh-mohammed-appoints-new-dubai-municipality-chief-. [01.08].

Kirchner, M & Rab, S 2007, 'An Arabian Night's Fantasy, and That's OK', *Al Manakh*, vol. 12, no. 7, pp. 18–22.

Kolo, J 2016, 'Accidental or Envisioned Cities: A Comparative Analysis of Abu Dhabi and Dubai', in G Katodrytis & S Syed (eds), *Gulf Cities as Interfaces*, pp. 161–180, Gulf Research Centre Cambridge, Jeddah.

Koolhaas, R 2007, 'Frontline', *Al Manakh*, vol. 12, no. 7, pp. 194–195.

Koolhaas, R & AMO 2007, *The Gulf*, Lars Müller Publishers, Zurich.

Law, B 2015, 'United Arab Emirates: Revealing the Dark Face of the Gulf State Where Human Rights Abuses Are a Daily Occurrence', *The Guardian*. [10.04].

Liddle, R 2009, 'The Dark Side of Dubai', *The Weekend Australian Magazine*, pp. 20–25.

Mafiwasta 2007, *Facts and Figures*. Available from: www.mafiwasta.com/UAE_statistics.html.

Mandaville, J 1998, 'Vegetation of the Sands', in S Ghazanfar & M Fisher (eds), *Vegetation of the Arabian Peninsula*, pp. 191–208, Kluwer Academic Press, Dordrecht.

The Media Office 2018, *Mission, Vision, Values, Government of Dubai*. Available from: www.mediaoffice.ae/en/the-media-office/mission-vision-values.aspx. [18.08].

Moser, S, Swain, M & Alkhabbaz, M 2015, 'King Abdullah Economic City: Engineering Saudi Arabia's Post-Oil Future', *Cities*, no. 45, pp. 71–80.

Nassar, AK, Blackburn, GA & Whyatt, JD 2014, 'Developing the Desert: The Pace and Process of Urban Growth in Dubai', *Computers, Environment and Urban Systems*, vol. 45, pp. 50–62.

Newman, H 2016, 'How Creative Placemaking Is Helping Put Dubai on the Cultural Map', *Business.ae*. Available from: http://inbusiness.ae/2016/07/20/how-creative-placemaking-is-helping-put-dubai-on-the-cultural-map/. [09.05].

Parasie, N 2014, 'Q&A: Emaar's Chairman Strives for International Mix with Dubai Flavour', *The Wall Street Journal*. [31.07].

Parsons Harland Bartholomew 1995, *Structure Plan for the Dubai Urban Area 1993–2012*, Dubai Municipality Planning & Survey Department, DMPS Department, Dubai.

Rizzo, A 2014, 'Rapid Urban Development and National Master Planning in Arab Gulf Countries. Qatar as a Case Study', *Cities*, no. 39, pp. 50–57.

Sabat, M 2015, 'Spatial Regulation of the Sex Industry in New York City', *LA+*, no. Pleasure, pp. 64–71.

Salahudin, B 2006, 'The Marine Environmental Impacts of Artificial Island Construction', Master's thesis, Duke University, Durham, NC, Nicholas School of the Environment and Earth Sciences.

Smith, B 2010, 'Scared by, of, in, and for Dubai', *Social & Cultural Geography*, vol. 11, no. 3, pp. 263–283.

Srivastava, R 2017, 'Death Brings Home Reality of Indian Workers' Life in Gulf', *Reuters*. Available from: www.reuters.com/article/us-india-migration-death/death-brings-home-reality-of-indian-workers-life-in-gulf-idUSKBN1CZ034. [09.04].

Swaffield, S & Deming, E 2011, 'Research Strategies in Landscape Architecture: Mapping the Terrain', *Journal of Landscape Architecture*, Spring, pp. 34–45.

Thesiger, W 1991, *Arabian Sands*, Penguin Books, London.

Van Noorloos, F & Kloosterboer, M 2017, 'Africa's New Cities: The Contested Future of Urbanisation', *Urban Studies*, vol. 55, no. 6, pp. 1–19.

Velegrinis, S & Katodrytis, G 2015, 'Drawing on Sand: Cities in the Making', *Architectural Design*, vol. 85, no. 1, pp. 72–79.

Verdaus 2018, *Verdaus, Verdaus*. Available from: http://verdaus.com/pages/information-pages/profile.html. [16.06].

Waugh, E 2011, *Recycling Spaces: Curating the Urban Evolution*, ORO Editions, New York.

Wehrey, FM 2013, *Sectarian Politics in the Gulf: From the Iraq War to the Arab Uprisings*, Columbia University Press, New York.

World Wildlife Fund 2006, *Conserving the Tree of the Dunes*. Available from: http://wwf.panda.org/wwf_news/?60580/Conserving-the-tree-of-the-dunes. [19.02].

Zaatari, S 2017, 'Dubai Population to Double by 2027?' *Gulf News*. Available from: https://gulfnews.com/news/uae/society/dubai-population-to-double-by-2027-1.2075117. [14.05].

3   Paradisiacal landscapes

Introduction

I have aligned this chapter with the view that designed landscapes can act as 'texts' that can be 'read' and that act as communicative systems (Lindstrom, Palang & Kull 2013, p. 99). Since designed landscapes are often commissioned for powerful patrons, they provide a rich subject for scholars who seek to uncover their role in 'maintaining, elaborating, and concealing power' (Herrington 2013, p. 363) and in conveying ideologies (Egoz 2008, p. 29). This chapter highlights that Dubai's designed landscapes 'are not as innocent as they look' in that they are, wittingly or otherwise, embedded in the 'discourses of power, race and nationality' (Lindstrom, Palang & Kull 2013, p. 99). The research question that undergirds this chapter is:

> *What cultural, societal and political narratives do verdant green land-*
> *scapes in Dubai promote?*

In answering this question, I deploy an interpretive critique (Swaffield & Deming 2011, p. 43) methodology that reveals new perspectives upon Dubai's designed landscapes and that speculates about what narratives developers of such projects may be seeking to promote.[1] I glean such understandings from a review of the landscapes themselves in conjunction with Dubai's Strategic Plans (Al Maktoum 2015; Government of Dubai 2014; Government of Dubai 2012) and Sheikh Mohammed's revealing book, *My Vision: Challenges in the Race for Excellence* (Al Maktoum 2012).

The first part of this chapter explores the narratives associated with 'parascape,'[2] a manufactured, green landscape derived, subliminally if not explicitly, from Quranic depictions of paradise. Parascape originates from the conjoining of the words 'paradise' and 'scape' – the word 'scape' is described by Orff as referring to neither 'city nor landscape . . . the new post urban condition' (2001, p. 393) In this chapter, I discuss how, through both its pastoral aesthetic and its religious underpinnings, parascape functions in a highly symbolic way within Dubai's socio-political structure. In this way, this verdant yet artificial landscape acts, in part, as a means of legitimization for Dubai's unelected rulers. Through the deployment of parascape within a hyper-arid context, Dubai's rulers display their strength to their citizens, as well as create an image of a modern Islamic state. Finally, parascape also functions as a redemptive device enacted to superficially ameliorate the divisions in the city caused by rampant neo-liberalism. The second part of the chapter considers several projects – namely luxuriant parks, exclusive communities, theme parks, offshore islands and freeway reserves – that are revealing of the narratives of parascape.

Body

The concept of landscape as a source of reconciliation stretches back to the role of designed landscape in ancient cities in which the garden symbolized paradise, perhaps to assuage a settled culture for having become separated from an ancient nomadic way of life (Weller 2007, p. 6). Related narratives endure in Dubai's contemporary parascape (Bolleter 2009), a landscape that is derived, subliminally if not explicitly, from an image of paradise depicted in the Quran.[3]

Parascape narratives

In a historical and contemporary sense, the collective Emirati imagining of an idealized landscape derives partly from Quranic depictions of paradise:

> There will be green, green pastures, therein fountains of running water, fruits and palm trees, and pomegranates, maidens good and comely, houris cloistered in cool pavilions reclining upon green cushions, immortal youths who seem as if scattered pearls, adorned with brocades and bracelets of silver.
>
> (Brookes 1987, p. 13)

Paradise in the Quran constitutes a garden, and moreover the Arabic word for paradise, *jenna*, is also the word for garden. As Islam historically spread and its arts evolved, a constant aim was to render gardens as closely as possible to such Quranic descriptions, a prized garden almost always being compared to paradise[4] (Lehrman 1980, p. 32; Makhzoumi 2002, p. 220). Indeed, as Abu Bakr, arguably the successor to the Prophet Mohammad, explained, 'Three things take away sadness: water, greenery, and a beautiful face' (Doherty 2014, p. 204).

Unlike the walled introspective nature of the typical traditional Islamic courtyard garden, through increased irrigation technology, parascape in Dubai is able to encompass whole city areas, typically taking the form of swaths of turf with scatterings of palm trees (Mitchell 2016, p. 196). (See Figure 3.1.) This represents an inversion of the traditional Middle Eastern appreciation for nature as 'tamed, enclosed and ordered' to an 'outward

Figure 3.1 The parascape of Dubai's premiere park, Zabeel Park (and surrounding areas).

Sources: Top photo by Kertu/Shutterstock.com; bottom photo by the author.

movement' of 'landscape as a scene that reaches its end in the horizon' (Makhzoumi 2002, p. 222).

Sheikh Zayed bin Sultan Al Nayhan (Sheikh Zayed) instigated the initial deployment of parascape in the United Arab Emirates (UAE) in 1971, concomitantly with the formation of the nation. As president of the UAE from 1971 to 2004, Sheikh Zayed oversaw the 'miraculous' transformation of the emirate of Abu Dhabi from a 'dusty and dirt poor desert emirate into a booming city-state, a mirage like place of boulevards, towers and emerald parks' (Economist 2004, p. 90). During his reign, Sheikh Zayed oversaw the planting of over 130 million trees in the Emirate, in what he understood to be a far-sighted investment for a future in which oil had run out[5] (Economist 2004, p. 90) and as a means of combating desertification[6] (Mitchell 2016, p. 192). Sheikh Zayed's own investment in the greening project saw him personally plant trees in Abu Dhabi parks for 'his people' (Anonymous landscape architect 2009b).

Abu Dhabi, as the wealthy UAE capital, functions as a role model for the other emirates. Sheikh Zayed's transformation of Abu Dhabi undoubtedly served as a powerful model for Dubai's ruling dynasty. This greening project, as initiated by Sheikh Zayed and further propagated by Dubai's rulers,[7] including the current ruler Sheikh Mohammed, I interpret as both theological and political in nature. There is considerable evidence to suggest that this luxuriant landscape is (to a degree) a symbolic recreation of the Islamic Paradise (Ouis 2002, p. 339). John Brookes explains that the potency of the image of paradise in Islamic culture is due to the fact that the descriptions of the garden of Paradise are held up as something not only to aspire to in the afterlife but also to recreate here on earth (1987, p. 21). Thus, the greening project within Dubai takes on moral and religious overtones. The Quran itself depicts the righteousness of such an undertaking: 'If the day of reckoning comes upon any of you while he has a seedling in his hand let him plant it' (Bagader 1994, p. 2). In a similar vein, Sheikh Mohammed in his 2012 book, *My Vision*, refers to a quote from the Prophet: 'Whoever revives a barren land will be rewarded, and the effort he made in doing so will be accredited to his favour as charity whenever any creature benefits from it' (Al Maktoum 2012, p. 106).

Divinity and modernization

While parascape is a trope for divinity (Ouis 2002), it is also associated with modernization. The Dubai Municipality refers to the deployment of landscape as critical to Dubai's modernization in the 1960s and 1970s:

> The services offered were not limited to the modernization of the country's infrastructure such as roads, utilities, drainage, etc. But, they were followed by the creation of many entertaining places [parks] to meet

the necessities of modern people, provide modern features of human civilization, and to emphasize the modern image of Dubai's Emirate.

(Dubai Municipality 2001, p. 7)

Dubai's ruler's tendency to associate parascape with modernization derives, in part, from Sheikh Maktoum's personal experiences of the urban pastoral landscapes of Europe and America and his regard for these places as being 'modern' (Anonymous landscape architect 2009b). The desire of Dubai's rulers for 'modern' landscapes also stems from the period of British control over the Trucial states (1920–1970), during which the British commonly made a distinction between 'modernizing' and 'forward-looking' rulers and their 'primitive' and 'tribal' people (Kanna 2010, p. 107). By modernizing their new territories, rulers could secure British support for their rule, as well as redefine the loyalties of their respective population away from tribal solidarities and towards a national one (Amirahmadi & Razavi 1993, p. 4). Moreover, much of the parascape produced in the early years of Dubai's modernization was designed by British landscape designers who resorted to the verdant landscape models they knew well, which conformed with the expectations of Emirati clients for lush 'European' greenery (Moosavi, Makhzoumi & Grose 2016, p. 273).

Beyond acting as a symbol of modernization, parascape was also instrumental in the settlement of the UAE's nomadic Bedouin[8] population that occurred in the 1960s and 1970s. During this period, the rulers of the UAE initiated intensive settlement projects for the Bedouin, providing free state housing and associated infrastructure in a plan to control what was considered, a 'politically and spatially problematic nomadic population' (Ouis 2002, p. 335). This settling of the Bedouin was fundamental to the creation of the modern UAE nation. The current ruler of Dubai, Sheikh Mohammed, even refers to one of his proudest achievements as introducing 'gated communities to Arabia, the land of nomads and tents' (Davis 2007, p. 64).[9] While the provision of modern infrastructure and housing was a major determining factor in the settlement of the Bedouin, the rapidly forming image of Dubai as an expanded paradise garden would also have been potent. For the Bedouin – for whom greenery 'marks the difference between life and death' (Ouis 2002, p. 340) – the image of the paradise garden would have been alluring.

This ability of parascape to simultaneously sustain the narratives of divinity and modernization ensures its continuing potency within Dubai's political milieu. The greening project is ongoing in Dubai. In 1972, Dubai had just 85 hectares of green space (Nassar, Blackburn & Whyatt 2014, p. 54), a figure the Dubai Municipality projected to increase to 12,200 hectares by 2020, as part of bid to transform Dubai into a 'green paradise' by 2025. (See Figure 3.2.) This 2020 figure is substantial in that it requires a doubling of the amount of green landscape developed between 2000 and 2014 (Mitchell, 2016, p. 192). In 2016, the Dubai Municipality indicated that

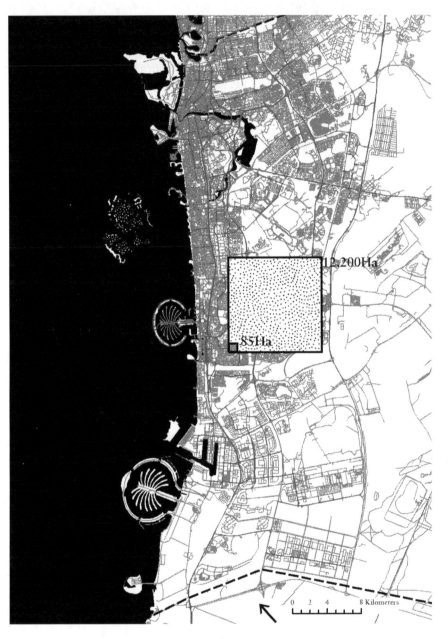

Figure 3.2 The ongoing greening project in Dubai. In 1972, Dubai had just 85 hectares of green space, a figure the Dubai Municipality project to increase to 12,200 hectares by 2020.

Source: Base GIS data courtesy of Trimble Maps.

they would invest $1.6 billion US to transform Dubai into a 'green paradise' by 2025, including $816 million US on improving and expanding the irrigation network (Mitchell, 2016, p. 192).

The Dubai Municipality couches this greening programme in terms that suggest they undertake it (in part) to seek favour from outsiders, particularly those from the West. As a statement from Director General Hussein Lootah reveals: 'We are serious about moving forward according to the expectations of the world, in line with the directives of our wise leadership' (Lootah 2014, p. 4). Clearly, Dubai's rulers and the Municipality have equated and continue to equate greening the desert with being modern and conforming aesthetically to desired Western city models.

Political legitimization

As I described in earlier chapters, Dubai operates officially under the framework of a constitutional monarchy; however, urban theoretician Mike Davis refers to the system as that of 'enlightened despotism' controlled by the current ruler, Sheikh Mohammed (Davis 2007, p. 63). The deployment of parascape is critical to the ruling dynasty's maintaining power. Since the action of greening the desert effectively has God's imprimatur, then not only are the Emirati fulfilling their Islamic duty, but their actions as political leaders are profoundly legitimized. As Sheikh Zayed himself said, 'It was through God's blessings and our determination we succeeded in transforming this desert into a green land. This encouraged us and we never looked back' (Ouis 2002, p. 338). Through their ability to conquer the desert, leaders are able to display their strong and effective leadership (Doherty 2008, p. 108) and their concern for their citizens (Ouis 2002, p. 338). While, globally, 'power is infused in the ownership of space, the resources to transform it, the process of shaping it' (Dovey 2016, p. 125), this situation becomes particularly pronounced in Dubai because of the hyper-aridity of the desert landscape and the religious underpinnings of verdant parascape.

The association of parascape with God's will both legitimizes Dubai's ruler's claims to power and makes resistance to parascape developments problematic. As Ouis describes, the discovery of oil in the UAE is often considered a 'gift from god' and thus the resulting greening of the emirates, which was facilitated by the discovery of oil, is a 'divine responsibility' and thus remains 'relatively free of criticism' (Ouis 2002, p. 339). Parascape thus legitimizes the power of the Sheikh as a benevolent and righteous leader who is performing the works of God.

Despite significant efforts towards modernization in other arenas, Dubai is still an autocracy, where any evidence of true democracy proves difficult to find. As strategic analyst Christopher Davidson describes, 'far less political reform has occurred than in neighbouring Gulf states, including even Saudi Arabia' (2008, p. 137). This situation has been maintained by Dubai's rulers through what Davidson refers to as the 'ruling bargain' (2008, p. 138).

This bargain exists between Dubai's rulers and national population and involves the buying of the populace's loyalty with distributed oil revenue and the 'careful exploitation of a range of ideological, religious, and cultural resources' (Davidson 2008, p. 138). As Sheikh Mohammed explains, 'There is a world of difference between a leadership that is based on love and respect, and one that is based on fear' (Al Maktoum 2012, p. 7), a sentiment that is 'confirmed' by offerings made as part of the ruling bargain. Parascape, with its symbolic associations of paradise, modernity and civility, becomes particularly effective as a tool for reinforcing this 'ruling bargain.'

Marginalization of desert landscape

Dubai sits near the northern end of the Rub al Khali, a vast and inhospitable desert that covers about 600,000 square kilometres of Southern Arabia. While parascape in Dubai has a certain religious authority, this deems the Rub al Khali desert, by contrast, to be contrary to God's purpose. Whereas parascape is associated with the divine, redemption, cultivation and modernity, the desert (by implication) can be associated with wilderness, savagery and the sublime. As Iraqi architect and academic Jala Makhzoumi explains:

> The duality in Middle Eastern mythological narratives between, on the one hand, the ordered, inhabited space of settlement and cultivated land and, on the other, the dangerous, unknown world of chaos, embodies the unending struggle against aridity. Mot, the god of sterility and drought, represented the world of chaos and exemplified cultural values shaped by a desert environment.
>
> (Makhzoumi 2002, p. 219)

Such associations have influenced the management of natural resources under Islamic Law. For example, there are two categories of land, *amir* (developed) and *mawat* ('dead' or undeveloped land), with a third category, *harim* (protective zones), that represents the interface of the two (Makhzoumi 2002, p. 219). Irrigators in Islamic countries have often cited verses in the Quran that present the reclamation or greening of desert areas as a sign (*ayah*) of divine beneficence, 'A sign for them is the land that is dead, we do bring it life' (36:33) (Wescoat Jr 2013, p. 9). This sensibility continues to exist in Dubai. As an organizer of a recent Dubai garden competition extolled:

> Dubai prides itself in achieving the impossible, and this garden competition is a shining example of how Dubai has defied its harsh desert location to create mesmerizing masterpieces of greenery. This is much more than a competition: it is an inspiration to the rest of the world – proving

that if we can rehabilitate the environment and grow stunning gardens in the desert, then we can heal Mother Earth everywhere else.

(Landscape Middle East 2013, p. 8)

In this reading, by producing verdant gardens, proponents believe they are 'healing' or 'rehabilitating' the problematic desert environment.

Regardless, Emiratis of Bedouin descent are also known to 'cherish the desert, its beauty and its relevance to the life and history of the Bedu people' (Anonymous landscape architect 2009b). Emiratis periodically drive out into the desert and camp for weeks with their extended families. This camping, especially apparent during the winter months, echoes the traditional Bedouin lifestyle[10] (Ouis 2002, p. 336). Nonetheless, human ecologist Pernilla Ouis describes the desert as a reminder of Emirati culture's experience of 'extreme poverty in a harsh environment,' whereas parascape represents, in part, an 'extremely affluent society with the possibility of reconstructing nature according to cultural and political desires' (2002, p. 340). This dichotomous situation magnifies the contrast between the physical experience of the lush garden and the often furnace-like conditions of the desert, a divergence that take on religious associations:

In the Quran paradise is described as a green garden with rivers and fountains, cool shades and all kinds of fruit and bounty; a place that should be contrasted with the roasting flames of hellfire.

(Ouis 2002, p. 339)

One of the implications of this polarization is the marginalization of the desert landscape when viewed in comparison to the parascape of the city. This frames the desert landscape on Dubai's urban periphery as a relative tabula rasa. Sheikh Mohammed himself characterizes the desert as a kind of nothingness:

If some of our young people think this mission [for greater development] is impossible, I would like them to open their windows and look around them . . . then I will tell them, 'Nearly all of what you see before you was created from nothing. There was nothing before but the sand of the desert.'

(Al Maktoum 2012, p. 106)

Moreover, Sheikh Mohammed declared in 2007, 'we will build and construct, so people will come, we will not ask people to come to an empty place' (Bantey & Heintz 2007, p. 1206). Typically glimpsed in the background of real estate imagery, the tabula rasa of the desert extends to the horizon, ready to passively receive the next wave of development.

The uncontested ground of the desert thus provides meagre resistance to Dubai's developers who seek to fulfil their 'interests' (Bagader 1994, p. 1).

The tabula rasa allows a blank slate for the projection of development as well as simultaneously denying the cultural claims to Dubai's landscape of the Bedouin population. I interpret this concept of emptiness as a denial of this history and the creation of a symbolic terra nullius landscape. As architectural writer Shumon Basar describes, the advantage of a desert landscape that was only ever sparsely inhabited 'is that there is no built history to contend with, no foundational forbears, no symbolic origins to tip toe around' (Basar 2007, p. 81).

Thus, while liberating development, the tabula rasa conception of the desert also legitimizes a significant lack of ecological sensitivity. This conception of the desert is also rife within the Western expatriate community in Dubai. The names given to four-wheel-drive 'adventures' such as 'dune-bashing' are evocative of the desire to conquer (and 'bash') unfamiliar and potentially hostile terrain, an act legitimized by the fact that it is 'empty' anyway (Coles & Walsh 2010, p. 1328).

Landscape architecture lecturer from the University of Sharjah[11] Tim Kennedy identifies the naming of developments in Dubai as part of a process that confirms this tabula rasa status of the desert landscape. Many of the urban developments located on Dubai's desert periphery – The Springs, The Greens, and The Meadows – 'evoke their own versions of narrative topos but with reference to other mythologies and imaginative literature' (2007, p. 411), which are without historic precedent in Dubai and completely antithetical to its desert landscape.

Redemption for the fallen city

Historically Dubai was the only deep-water port along what was known as the 'Pirate Coast' (2007, p. 65). The focus of this notorious port was the creek-side, labyrinthine districts of Deira and Bur Dubai, where dhows from as far as India and Iran would unload their cargo for sale in Dubai. Dubai's reputed function as a nodal point in the region for trafficking, smuggling, kidnapping, money laundering and prostitution I interpret as an extension of this ancient role (Central Intelligence Agency 2008; Davis 2007).

Parascape functions as a redemptive counterpoint to the desert but also, I believe, to the 'sin city' image of Dubai. The depiction of Dubai as a 'sin city' relates to the prevalence of alcohol, drugs and prostitution (Kanna 2010, p. 113), the hubris of megalomaniacal development (Sudjic 2005, p. 323) and the greed of unfettered neo-liberalism (Davis 2007), all of which contradict traditional Islamic culture. By way of example, a Saudi cleric recently sparked controversy when he issued a *fatwa* (religious edict) on his Twitter account, barring travel to Dubai because of the spread of 'immoralities' there – a *fatwa* that was later retracted after an outcry on social media (Anstey 2013). In this context, Dubai's rulers must maintain a precarious balance between allowing a lucrative underbelly of sin and vice (Davis 2007,

p. 66) and promoting a 'virtuous' image of the city within regional Islamic culture and the global marketplace (Davidson 2008, p. 135).

Parascape plays a significant role in this respect, in providing an aesthetic and symbolic redemption of the darker aspects of the 'fallen' city of Dubai. Ubiquitous date palms, ornamental plants and large swaths of irrigated turf form a backdrop to urban development (Moosavi, Makhzoumi & Grose 2016, p. 269) and obscure the city's darker side with an apparently benign landscape that, in the collective imagination, signifies innocence, nature and paradise (Corner 1999, p. 157; Ouis 2002, p. 339). While these associations may stray from the reality of what parascape in Dubai constitutes, the populace rarely challenges this construction of parascape as virtuous. Dubai Municipality's own promotional material refers to this redemptive role of landscape in the case of its 'public squares':

> Public squares are the practical manifestation of the safety and security measures accomplished by the Municipality to safeguard the youth and teenagers from corruption and dangers of playing outdoors.
>
> (Dubai Municipality 2001)

Moreover, as per the UAE's cultural traditions, parts of Dubai Municipality's park system are designated exclusively for women and children (Dubai Municipality 2001, p. 22). These areas are furnished with places 'mothers can rest and watch their children playing in the garden' (Dubai Municipality 2001, p. 22). In this respect, parascape also becomes associated with family values that counters the decadence and vice of the city. The need to designate specific park areas for women and children reflects the fact that the population of Dubai, like many other 'boomtowns' throughout history, is 70 per cent male, mostly because of the significant numbers of 'bachelors' who work in construction (Smith 2010, p. 273).

The idea that green space can have a 'salutary effect' on human nature itself (Sorkin 1992, p. 212) remains prevalent. The symbolic function of Dubai's parks (in particular) in combating 'corruption' derives from the early public parks in Europe, which proponents regarded 'offered a healthy alternative to the temptations of the inn and the tavern, with their frequent accompaniment of immorality and vice' (Ponte 1991, p. 380). Clearly, the concept of parks as spaces that can redeem an urban citizenry lingers. In the 1970s, Bahrain's first qualified doctor, Dr Ali Fakhro, suggested that greenery was needed for societal reasons because the desert impaired the temperaments of desert-dwelling people. As he warned:

> The effects on Bahrain of a reduction in the agricultural areas could be disastrous. More serious even than the economic effect of such a change could be the social one. Bahrain has been a green land all through its

history and agricultural areas have always produced a different tem-
perament of person from the deserts.

(Doherty 2014, p. 203)

While Bahrain and Dubai have their differences, in an equivalent way, parascape in Dubai serves to redeem both the city and its occupants.

Hubris and redemption

Mike Davis has referred to a 'frantic quest for hyperbole' as driving Dubai's
speculative urbanization (Marcinkoski 2015, p. 31). In Dubai, we find the
'hubristic pursuit of a global paradigm of fast-track city building, replete
with all the requisite superlatives – the largest, longest, most expensive,
tallest, and so forth –in a spectacular accumulation of luxury-driven post-
modernity' (Marcinkoski 2015, p. 31). Currently containing the tallest
building in the world, Dubai is no stranger to hubris. The dramatic shift
from Dubai's vernacular low-rise urbanism to megalomaniacal skyscrapers,
such as the Burj Khalifa, in some respects represents a problematic shift for
traditional Islamic culture. This is because the skyscraper contradicts the
traditional relationship of the Muslim to the city. John Lockerbie describes
this relationship:

> The house in Islam . . . is defined quite clearly as a sanctuary from which
> the Muslim sets out to fulfil his public obligations . . . . In contradistinc-
> tion to Western planning the hierarchy of spaces begins with the privacy
> of the interior of the house and moves out through the districts as the
> need for access to other areas requires it.
>
> (Lockerbie 2008, p. 9)

The glazed, outward-looking skyscraper dramatically contradicts the traditional Arabic courtyard dwelling and its mirroring of the 'ideal human
condition; a lack of concern with outward symbols, but space for the inner
soul to breathe and develop' (Brookes 1987, p. 21). In addition to this, the
skyscraper challenges the hierarchy of sacred and profane buildings found
in the traditional Islamic city. In such cities, the predominance of typically
low buildings with muted facades heightens the impact of the mosque on
viewers. The city's vertical structure is defined by the mosque's minarets,
which call the faithful to pray five times a day (Lockerbie 2008, p. 9) and
that represent the 'cosmic axis' (Cavendish 2004, p. 68). The replacement
of the minaret with its secular counterpart, the skyscraper, I interpret as
an attempt by Dubai's rulers to be, mythically, in the centre of the cosmic
axis (Cavendish 2004, p. 68) in which physical ascension is analogous to
spiritual ascension and thus enlightenment (Fox & Wang, p. 237). Perhaps
in reaction to the hubris implied by this inversion, Sheikh Rashid bin Saeed
al Maktoum had the first skyscraper in The Gulf – the 1979 Dubai World

Trade Centre – built with stairwells at all four corners, which was unusual for the time, because he was deeply concerned about people being trapped on upper levels during a fire (Smith 2010, p. 267).

The threat of terrorism to Dubai's skyscraper urbanism is rarely publicly articulated in Dubai; however, it runs as an undercurrent through the collective consciousness (Davis 2007, p. 66). These skyscrapers, for some, serve as a 'painful and continuing reminder of the tension between modernity and tradition' (Sudjic 2005, p. 308) and can also be interpreted as a Western imposition on Arab soil – particularly given that Dubai's high-rise architecture is typically devoid of 'reference to Arab or Muslim architectural design' (Haines 2011, p. 170). Sudjic describes that skyscrapers imposed on the Arab world can 'seem like insensitive transplants from another world with different values [that] can be seen not just as a sign of change, but its direct cause' (2005, p. 308). Dubai's Burj Khalifa is an exemplar of this situation, designed by an American company, Skidmore Owings and Merrill, and characterized by its inhuman dimension and its attempt to create an exclusive 'city within a city' (Acuto 2010, p. 280).

During the Global Financial Crisis (GFC), Dubai received a reprimand for its hubristic development practices. In the GFC, foreign investors who had lent huge sums of money to Dubai developers were now unable to get back their loans because developers could not sell their real estate products (Caton & Ardalan 2010, p. 44). Abu Dhabi guaranteed $20 billion worth of outstanding debt, but this was hardly a 'blanket bailout' (Caton & Ardalan 2010, p. 44). Each claim was reviewed independently by the Abu Dhabi Government before they made a decision as to its status, the inference being that much of Dubai's speculative development had been reckless from the perspective of its more conservative neighbour (Caton & Ardalan 2010, p. 44). The Abu Dhabi Government regarded the bailout as an opportunity to 'weed out the more untenable projects.' Clearly, Dubai had 'fallen' and was in 'disgrace' as far as Abu Dhabi was concerned (Caton & Ardalan 2010, p. 44).

It is in relation to this situation that parascape, with its ubiquitous palm trees, ornamental plants and large areas of turf (Moosavi, Makhzoumi & Grose 2016, p. 269), acts as a foil. Readers can witness this in the water-infused parascape that developers often deploy at the base of skyscrapers to reconcile them with the human scale and 'nature.' Examples of this include the luxuriant parascape at the base of the Burj Khalifa and the parascape proposed at the base of The Tower, a massive monument and new tourism development that will eclipse the Burj Khalifa when opened in 2020.

The concealment of divisions

While developers employ parascape as a foil to Dubai's megalomaniacal skyscraper development, it also ameliorates, in symbolic and aesthetic terms, the socio-economic division arising from Dubai's unfettered neo-liberalism. Indeed,

Dubai's wholesale adoption of neo-liberal ideology has resulted in a city form that primarily is structured to attract and capture the maximum flows of global capital. While other global cities aspire to similar goals, the extremely rapid evolution of Dubai and its autocratic rule have meant that this process is occurring without significant moderating influences. While global cities with historic urban centres have retrofitted their existing structure to lure global capital, Dubai's rulers have (for the most part) built the city around this enabling function. Boris Jensen, associate professor at the Department of Urbanism and Landscape at the Aahus School of Architecture, aptly describes this as 'Bingo Urbanism':

> [T]he city as gaming board seems an especially appropriate 21st century successor to the concentrically ringed city of the early 20th century. With globalization Dubai has become a pioneer of this kind of 'Bingo Urbanism' – a mosaic of monocultures in a field of business opportunities.
> (2007, p. 42)

Bingo Urbanism leads to the fragmentation of the city into what Jensen describes as 'territorially independent functioning units, which are grouped as miniature cities' (2007, p. 53). This fragmentation can be witnessed in the proliferation of discrete 'cities' that come to constitute Dubai's urban fabric. Branding consultants often tag projects with a name that signifies a village, a city, a land or a world, such as Knowledge Village, Dubailand, Humanitarian City, Industrial City, etc. Such 'urban islands' attempt to transcend their locality through their introspective natures (Basar 2007, p. 87). Compounding this fragmentation of the 'city' into a proliferation of miniature cities is the large numbers of gated communities. Since the creation of freehold land in Dubai, gated communities have flourished. In the villa housing stock, 37 per cent of dwellings are in gated freehold communities, a much higher percentage than in comparable first world cities (Unitas Consultancy 2017, p. 2). These gated communities aim for a segregation from the city in both spatial and societal terms. This segregation is at its most dramatic in The Palm and The World developments. As Jensen describes, 'The Palm is an island from which poverty has been banished' (2007, p. 67). This extreme level of segregation results in an obsession with security as the economically dominant strata of society attempt to banish the 'other.'[12]

While gated communities occur worldwide, the dominance of the urban island in Dubai is unique in that there is little connection to a centre outside of the islands. Amale Andraos, architectural professor at Princetown University, describes the islands thus:

> [They are] not dispersed suburban havens – removed yet still connected to a centre, which they either still need or have supplanted. These islands are all equal centres, self-contained nodes appearing adjacent to

one another and connected to each other by the thinnest possible road network.

(2007, p. 49)

What began as Free Trade Zones or Special Economic Zones (SEZs) have morphed into a set of models for the new metropolis (Dovey 2016, p. 149) that provide for the 'specific needs of foreign capital and expat professionals' (Davis 2007, p. 68). In comparatively recent times, SEZs in Dubai have evolved to allow business immunity from taxes, labour regulation and environmental restrictions, as well as to streamline transhipment, materials handling and duty-free retail (Easterling 2008, p. 9). Neo-liberalism has written in spatial terms its requirement for the flexibility of capital and labour in the form of the city. Dubai thus becomes a city in which prevailing economic and social forces have suppressed any sense of communal purpose, identity or responsibility and have fragmented the city into a multitude of discrete entities.

Within this unfettered neo-liberal context, parascape is employed by developers as a panacea for the fragmentation and division found within Dubai's Bingo Urbanism (Jensen 2007, p. 42), and in particular it is a cloak to conceal the fortifications, walls and security gates of discrete urban 'islands' (Jensen 2007, p. 42). Parascape conceals the brutality of the physical and societal segregation of neo-liberalism through a redemptive green layer that allows 'its occupants to believe they are actually part of a collective, refined, and enlightened society' (Corner 1999, p. 157). This belief stems from the fact that the irrigation of desert areas generally requires social cooperation and is often approached with a communitarian ethic (Wescoat Jr 2013, p. 9). The use of parascape to suggest a truly 'public' realm in this context aims to reassure citizens that they are part of a larger community regardless of the actual spatial and societal dissolution of the city into segregated worlds.

Maintaining global city status

Levitt used the term 'globalization' to describe the state of 'intense interaction and dependency of world economies' (1983). As an American economist, Levitt's reasoned definition of globalization differs significantly from that (sometimes) articulated from an Emirati viewpoint. From an Emirati perspective, entwining the concept of 'globalization' is the colonial imperialism experienced by the Trucial states during the period of Britain's colonial dominance. As Yasser Mahgoub of Kuwait University explains, in the Arab world, globalization is often regarded as another term for the imposition of Western values, and thus it is often considered a threat to Arabic Islamic culture's political, social, cultural and economic stability (Mahgoub 2007, p. 929). Thus, Emiratis sometimes make an association between globalization and Western conquest in which globalization is an imposition upon Arabic Islamic culture.

Regardless, Dubai is a global city in that it belongs to a highly competitive network of similar cities and shares greater similarities with other global cities than its own national context (Sudjic 1992, p. 3). Unsurprisingly, Sheikh Mohammed urges Emiratis to embrace globalization:

> Although some of us may prefer to turn a blind eye to the age of globalization, this is not an option; we have to embrace it wholeheartedly. We cannot ignore its effects because no matter what we do, it is here to stay. In order to bridge the huge gap between industrialized nations and ourselves, we must embrace the positive aspects of globalization, while evaluating and discarding the negative ones.
>
> (Al Maktoum 2012, p. 21)

Such arguments reflect that Dubai's economic survival is, due to the depletion of oil reserves, predicated on trapping flows of global capital through tourism, real estate development and finance (Davis 2007, p. 65; Davidson 2008, p. 135). For this reason, an unarticulated sense of fear underlies the bravado of Dubai development. Dubai constantly craves being the centre of attention, paranoid that its fading from view will herald its rapid demise. The artificial stimulation designed to 'project economic potential' (Marcinkoski 2015, p. 11) involves creating a physical spectacle measured in easily quantified superlatives (AMO, Reisz & Ota 2007, p. 222).

While the spectacle of Dubai is physical, it also has a virtual dimension in the form of the electronic imagery developers use to promote real estate projects. These hyper-realistic images promise an eternal future, and by the time developers have delivered projects, they already appear anachronistic. In this sense, Dubai appears in the global imagination as a virtual city in which the promise of the future becomes the dominant image – the ability to trap global capital being reliant on the welcoming of the 'new, just because it is a departure, and therefore an opening for profitable enterprise' (Mumford 1961, p. 414). Billboards advertise housing developments, shopping malls and theme parks, proclaiming, 'The world's most exclusive address,' 'History rising,' and 'The world has a new centre' (Bantey & Heintz 2007, p. 1212). The city becomes an electronically 'imagineered' mirage that leads the global consumer over the tabula rasa desert landscape. As Kevin Mitchell explains:

> [M]any real estate transactions are based on nothing more than sales brochures and promises. The material reality is less important than the reality that has been constructed from photorealistic images.
>
> (2007, p. 648)

Through the spectacle of the virtual, the city of Dubai gets lost part way between a physical reality and an imagined future. As opposed to the notion of the spectacle being a discrete element within the city, as readers may identify in Sydney with the spectacle of the Opera House, the situation in Dubai sees the spectacle become entire city areas. Guy Debord describes this phenomenon as:

> both the outcome and the goal of the dominant mode of production. It is not something added to the real world – not a decorative element, so to speak. On the contrary, it is the very heart of society's real unreality.
>
> (In McGlothlin 2007, p. 868)

This move from 'iconic building as spectacle' to 'city as spectacle' is evidence of a shift described by architectural historian Ole Bouman, whereby 'the inhabitants and visitors are not the city's cause, but its legitimacy and profit margin' (2007, p. 4). In Dubai, the notion of the 'city as spectacle' reaches its zenith in the urban super graphics of The Palm and The World developments, which bathe in the shallow waters of The Gulf. In these developments, the plan view of urbanism itself becomes a tool for the marketing of Dubai. The citizens of The Palm become in some respects the residents of a logo or brand rather than a city. Ayesha Al Sager, Afnan Al Rubaian and Sally Khanafer describe how the creation of the city as spectacle results in a schism between the projected 'dream' city and the real 'human' city:

> A great divide exists within our cities. It is important to note that the city in which we dwell does not follow the common typology of a city. This divides the city in half. On one half lies the dream city; a shell devoid of social cultural and psychological needs that serves the creation of purely materialistic capital. On the other half lies the human space; a city that is based on people, their daily needs and interactions.
>
> (2007, p. 8)

While the dream city becomes segregated from the 'real and the human,' a schism also forms between the city and its local physical and cultural geography. The city experiences the erosion of all fixed relations to the immediate physical and cultural landscape. Instead, 'globalised capital, electronic means of production and uniform mass culture anchor the intimate, undisciplined differentiation of traditional cities,' creating a place that is fully 'ageographic' (Sorkin 1992, p. xiii). Al Sager, Al Rubaian and Khanafer attribute the formation of this divide between the 'dream' city and the 'real' city to the shift from the organically constructed city prior to the discovery of oil (the 'real' city) to the global city whose survival relies on the attraction of global capital (the 'dream' city). While this divide occurs in several cities in the Gulf region, in Dubai Al Sager and colleagues regard that the projected dream city completely overwhelms the real city:

In Dubai, UAE, this divide [between 'dream' and 'real' city] does not seem apparent. Does the human space exist? Or is it too weak to be? Upon closer inspection, the human space begins to surface in small pockets. It is however so small in scale that the shell – the projected image of the city – completely over shadows it.

(Al Sager, Al Rubaian & Khanafer 2007, p. 10)

It is within this highly polarized landscape of global and local forces that developers deploy parascape in Dubai in two contradictory ways. Firstly, the traditional pursuit of the 'genius loci' or a 'sense of place' in landscape design and gardening has seen these actions become associated with the 'real' and 'human' side of the city (Al Sager, Al Rubaian & Khanafer 2007). While the 'global versus local' stylistic debate underlies much architectural critique in Dubai, critics rarely extend it to encompass landscape design. This is due to the (often) unquestioned association of landscape design with 'place.' In addition, parascape is organic, and thus Dubai's citizens perceive it as having an inherent connection to 'place' and thus to signify the 'real' city (as defined by Al Sager et al.).

Contrary to this understanding, parascape in Dubai remains a major player in attracting global capital and thus can also be associated with the construction and functioning of the 'dream city' as identified by Al Sager, Al Rubaian and Khanafer (2007). The use of luxuriant parascape in project branding reaches its apotheosis in Dubai, as is evident from the names of the Dubai developments, including The Greens, Emirates Hills, The Lakes, The Springs and The Meadows. In this instance, rather than providing cultural resistance to global forces, the pastoral nature of parascape evokes the global dream of 'high-class consumption and luxurious lifestyles' (Haines 2011, p. 161), as well as providing a soothing sense of familiarity to the global investor or tourist.

It is the ability of parascape to sustain these apparent contradictions between its roles as a repository of the 'real' and as a lure for global investment, which have ensured its ongoing potency in the physical and symbolic construction of Dubai.

Parascape projects

In this section, I examine specific projects that contain parascape and illustrate its cultural, societal and political narratives. Not limited to an explicit focus on usage (Forty 2000, p. 304) or on morphology (Condon 1994, p. 92), in this section I aim to position the projects in relation to the larger culture of Dubai and increase awareness of the urban professions as to the symbolic roles their projects are serving (Crewe & Forsyth 2003, p. 37). This is not to say that the pragmatic uses of projects are not important (e.g. active or passive recreation), just that the greatest lacuna for practitioners relates to the symbolic dimension of their projects.

Dubai's greening program

At a metropolitan scale, the Dubai Municipality directs the deployment of parascape through ambitious targets. In 2008, Dubai's rulers, via the Municipality, advocated for increasing so-called green space from 3.4 per cent to 8 per cent because residents could easily understand it numerically and because it meant Dubai conformed to Western standards of open space provision. As a representative of Dubai Municipality Parks Department explained:

> If we are a global city, if we like to call ourselves a global city then we should not have less than 8% green area to compare ourselves to any other city around the world. To see what other cities are doing around the world and to be equal to them.
>
> (2008)

Later, in 2014, a representative from the Dubai Municipality indicated that by 2020, the amount of green space in Dubai would increase to 12,200 hectares, a massive increase from 85 hectares in 1972 (Nassar, Blackburn & Whyatt 2014, p. 54). This 2020 figure is substantial in that it requires a doubling of the amount of green landscape developed between 2000 and 2014 (Mitchell 2016, p. 192). In 2016, the Dubai Municipality indicated that $1.6 billion US would be invested in an effort to transform Dubai into a 'green paradise' by 2025, including $816 million US on improving and expanding the irrigation network (Mitchell 2016, p. 192). More recently, in 2018, representatives from the Municipality indicated it had 'intensified its efforts to beautify, decorate, and plant the city' (Landscape Middle East 2018, p. 6), through greening its parks, streets and freeways.

Municipality parks

The apotheosis of the greening programme is the Dubai Municipality managed park system. Typically, the Municipality parks, which are comprised of 'large public parks,' 'residential parks' and 'city centre parks' (Dubai Municipality 2001), consist of vast swaths of irrigated turf and lush shrub plantings and scatterings of trees, often *Phoenix dactylifera* date palms. Parascape is extremely 'thirsty.' In summer, a date palm requires approximately 128 litres of freshwater per day and a square metre of turf 15 litres per day. Parascape is undoubtedly a contributor to UAE the having the highest rate of water consumption in the world at 550 litres of water per day per capita. (See Figure 3.3.)

Complementing this luxuriant, pastoral landscape is an assortment of curvilinear walking paths, jogging paths, playgrounds, seating and shade structures. Expatriates and Emiratis often use these parks for family picnics and barbeques, walking, jogging and informal games of football. The Dubai

Figure 3.3 A migrant maintenance worker at Zabeel Park, with irrigated parascape
in the background.

Source: Photo by the author.

Municipality defines the park system as constituting 'the creation of recreational facilities for everyone' (Dubai Municipality 2001, p. 7). While billed
as for 'everyone,' they primarily intend them to be family areas. In this
respect, the Municipality parks realize Sheikh Mohammed's intention to
'provide nurturing environments' for children (Government of Dubai 2014,
p. 11).

To maintain this family-friendly atmosphere, the Dubai Municipality
fences the Municipality parks and charges an entry fee of up to $1.5 US
for entry. This fee, in conjunction with the substantial distance between
the parks and worker accommodation on the urban periphery, is enough
to discourage Dubai's underclass of effectively single male migrant workers from entering. Among these labourers, there is reputedly a 'very high
level of sexual frustration' (Davidson 2008, p. 193), which I believe the
Dubai Municipality is intent on banishing from family-orientated parks.[13]
In Dubai, decency policing is about keeping 'men,' usually 'bachelors,'
from harassing women in public (Smith 2010, p. 272), and the fencing of
parks certainly reflects this policy. Moreover, in public places, families seek
to maintain as much distance as they can from any unaccompanied, unre-
lated males (Abu-Gazzeh, p. 275). Reflecting this practice, there have been

demands for women-only parks in the UAE, as this excerpt from a letter to the *Gulf Daily News* indicates:

> Please, there should be a lady's park. I have been to many parks where families hang around, but I think that there should be one just for ladies . . . . A park where women can freely take a morning walk or exercise, will be most appreciated.
>
> (In Doherty 2011, p. 195)

The Dubai Municipality close several parks in Dubai to men on select week-days; however, there are no exclusively women-and-children-only parks.

The fencing of the Municipality parks also means they are not effective sites for political demonstration, such protests occurring (when rarely they do) on Dubai's major streets. Significantly, the Arab Spring in Cairo was fermented in urban spaces such as Tahrir Square, which lacked legible edges, comprised adjoining spaces and had no real beginning or end, with no way for authorities to completely control access (AlSayyad & Guvenc 2015, p. 2022). This ambiguous, interconnected public space that enables contestation simply does not exist in Dubai. A collective yet clearly circumscribed semi-public space such as a Municipality park simply cannot serve that purpose (Carbonell 2016, p. 239).

While the Municipality have fenced Dubai's pastoral parks and in so doing precluded demonstrations, the parks do evoke democratic ideals that manifest in a symbolic sense. That the Municipality parks evoke democratic public space, in the collective imagination, is due to their resemblance to well-known pastoral landscapes such as Hyde Park in London. It is, per-haps, these associations that sustain the image of the municipal parks as 'being for everyone' (Dubai Municipality 2001, p. 7) when the reality is quite different.

Finally, the provision of the municipal parks I interpret as an attempt by Dubai's rulers to boost their 'ideological, religious, and cultural legitimacy' (Davidson 2008, p. 167). As policy expert Christopher Davidson describes, if certain charitable donations can enhance the reputation of Dubai's rulers by emphasizing their generosity, then Emiratis will be 'far more accepting of the autocratic ruling bargain, safe in the knowledge that their guardians are at least well intentioned and benevolent' (Davidson 2008, p. 167). Thus, while the Municipality park system carries democratic associations, its provision also further legitimizes the rule of an autocratic leader.

Holy Quran Park

The narrative of parascape reaches its purest expression in Dubai Munici-pality's 64-hectare, $7 million US Holy Quran Park, which was com-pleted in 2015 (Landscape Middle East 2014, p. 4) (See Figure 3.4.). The Municipality commissioned the park in a bid to introduce visitors to the 'miracles' of Quran. The Quranic theming takes the form of swaths of plant species mentioned in the Quran including figs, pomegranates, olives, corn, and vineyards, amongst many others. The park also includes an air-conditioned tunnel to reveal the wonders of the 'Holy book.' Finally the Municipality commissioned a lake in the centre of the park to 'give a look and real feel of an oasis surrounded by fascinating trees and sands for the visitors' (Landscape Middle East 2014, p. 4). Such heavily themed park elements are complemented by generic facilities such as entrance and administration buildings, children's play areas, an outside theatre, fountains, a running and cycling track and a sandy walking track (Landscape Middle East 2014, p. 4).

While Dubai's rulers, via the Municipality, partly directed the park towards an Emirati audience, they also aimed to lure Islamic tourists from around the world. As Hussein Lootah, director general of Dubai Municipality, explains:

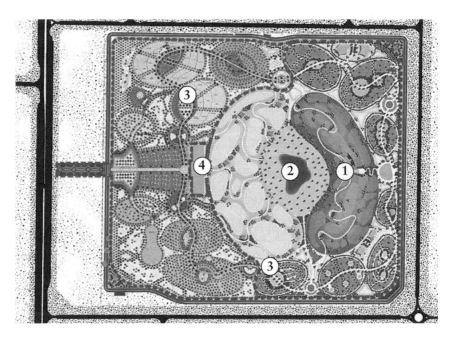

Figure 3.4 The Holy Quran Park portrays Dubai's ruling dynasty as performing the 'works of god' and, as such, acts to legitimize their rule in a profound way.

Key:
1 Artificial landform with air-conditioned tunnel revealing the wonders of the 'Holy book'
2 Artificial lake
3 Walking track
4 Glass house containing plant specimens

Source: Plan by the Dubai Municipality.

The Holy Quran Park is one of the most prestigious projects of the civic body, and not only the UAE, but also the entire tourist world is waiting to visit the park without patience.

(Landscape Middle East 2014, p. 4)

While a sincere gesture, the Holy Quran Park could also be an attempt by Dubai's rulers to tap into the lucrative Islamic tourist market. An example of this is the Muslim pilgrimage to Mecca in Saudi Arabia (the *Hajj*), which economic experts have estimated will generate over $150 billion US annually by 2022 (Al-Thaqafi 2017). Regardless, more than any other parascape project, the Holy Quran Park portrays Dubai's ruling dynasty as performing the 'works of god' and, as such, acts to legitimize their rule in a profound way.

Exclusive communities

Parascape also forms the backdrop of exclusive communities that sate the demands of Dubai's well-heeled citizens for both exclusivity and luxury. (See Figure 3.5.) These exclusive gated communities consist of a cornucopia of lush vegetation and water features concentrated in private parks, gardens, golf courses, community centres and streetscapes.

Figure 3.5 Dubai Hills development, a model of luxury.

Source: Photo by the author.

While Dubai's ruler seeks to 'market its unique melting pot of cultures and nationalities,' such exclusive urbanism results from 'demand-oriented planning' that creates exclusive 'comfort zones' for wealthy expatriates, visitors and locals (Acuto 2010, p. 280). In such projects, parascape is a landscape of privilege that insulates – for those who can afford it – the brutality of the surrounding hot, dry and congested city. In such exclusive communities, guards permit entry for large segments of Dubai's population only in a service capacity. Moreover, Dubai's exclusive communities deliberately minimize interaction with groups that differ in relation to religion, language and culture (Coles & Walsh 2010, p. 1330). In this respect, Dubai allows the wealthy to opt in or out of Dubai's multicultural demographic. As Sheikh Mohammed explains, 'Dubai is a city of options. Its residents can choose their own lifestyles and entertainment' (Al Maktoum 2012, p. 150).

Dubai's rulers and master developers aim to provide a high standard of living for wealthy expatriates in these exclusive communities for good reason. Urban economists explain the role of amenity in attracting wealthy visitors and residents to cities (Duranton & Puga 2013, p. 799) – a demographic that in turn helps to drive the economy. As Dubai's ruler, Sheikh Mohammed elaborates:

> Visitors are . . . smart enough to distinguish between the exclusive and the ordinary, and know from the first contact, that Dubai's reputation for excellence goes beyond its publicity.
>
> (Al Maktoum 2012, p. 143)

Through exclusive, gated communities, Dubai offers wealthy expatriates the ability to conduct business in The Gulf in a sumptuous, family-friendly, safe living environment, cocooning residents from both the trials of the city and its bewildering kaleidoscope of cultures.

Mohammed Bin Rashid Gardens (2008)

The zenith of parascaped exclusive communities in Dubai is the Mohammed Bin Rashid Gardens project. (See Figure 3.6.) This development has had two distinct iterations, the first launched just prior to the Global Financial Crisis (GFC) in 2008 and the second launched in 2018. Nonetheless, a verdant layer of parascape formed the backdrop to both.

The developers of the first iteration of the Mohammed Bin Rashid Gardens project proposed that a substantial 73 per cent of the 8,200-hectare site was to be green landscape (Commercial Outdoor Design 2008a, p. 37). Designed to house around a quarter of a million people, the project was to include substantial areas of housing for UAE citizens; four areas themed around wisdom, humanity, nature and commerce; a university campus and the largest 'civic park system created in the Middle East in over 10,000 years' (Howe 2008, p. 37). By positioning the project as part of a

Figure 3.6 The Mohammed Bin Rashid Gardens project.
Source: Image by CivicArts.

lineage of grand urban visions, its authors not only awarded the project an instant pedigree but also ensured that they had appropriately flattered their clients. The Mohammed Bin Rashid Gardens project was a socio-political as much as spatial gesture, the reasons for building it having as much to do with projecting a 'vision of a certain kind of state' as it did 'with the pragmatic concerns of civic life'[14] (Sudjic 1992, p. 16). A statement from the architect of the project, Eric Kuhne, reveals this dimension:

> Enlightened leadership has filled history with grand precedents for such grand designs. By ordering his Persian capital to be moved to Isfahan, Shah Abbas I realised a vision for his parks, gardens and libraries of Nisf-e-Jahan (Half the World) to reflect the heavens above. As Domenico Fontana was to Pope Sixtus V's Rome; Peter the Great to St Petersburg; L'Enfant to Washington DC; Hausmann to Napolean III's Paris; Frederick Law Olmstead to Manhattan; Edwin Lutyens to New Delhi; and Walter Burley Griffin to Canberra, so Sheikh Mohammed's vision for a new Dubai will redefine the quality of civic life for the citizens, residents and guests of the Arabian Gulf.
>
> (CivicArts 2008)

Kuhne further described how the urbanism was based on 'Arabian urban design principles, not European and North American principles' (Commercial Outdoor Design 2008a, p. 37). To achieve this, the design took on the plan form of the astrolabe, a navigational instrument 'perfected by Islamic scholars' (CivicArts 2008), which Sheikh Mohammed proudly claims preceded the development of the sextant (Al Maktoum 2012, p. 20). While the astrolabe formed a template for the project, the structure of the development was reminiscent of the City Beautiful movement in which planners placed civic monuments at the termination of grand radiating avenues. The City Beautiful movement reflects what Peter Hall describes as 'a total concentration . . . on architecture as a symbol of power . . . . This is planning for display, architecture as theatre, design intended to impress' (2002, p. 217). Also of significance is the City Beautiful movement's central tenet that the 'city itself could engender civic loyalty,' thus guaranteeing a harmonious moral and political order (Hall 2002, p. 46). Thus, while the form of Mohammed Bin Rashid Gardens Project mimics that of the astrolabe, it is also reminiscent of the geometries of the City Beautiful movement, which proponents aimed would impress the citizenry and inspire loyalty to the existing political order.

In its design language and marketing, the project also referenced the archetype of the oasis and traditional Islamic heritage in a bid to find a stable symbolic and poetic foothold in the cultural complexity of Dubai. In broad terms, the Sheikh Mohammed Gardens project reacted to a 'concern among more outspoken nationals that entire districts of the city and their emirate are effectively out of bounds; they have become exclusive enclaves for foreign rent seekers and tourists and were clearly never created with nationals in mind' (Davidson 2008, p. 6). Through the project, Sheikh Mohammed responded to such concerns both in pragmatic terms (through the provision of housing for nationals) but also on a symbolic level using icons such as the astrolabe.

Notwithstanding the tenuous links of the Sheikh Mohammed Gardens project to cultural heritage, the project completely denies the reality of its environmental context. The Gardens were depicted as both natural and 'purifying' (CivicArts 2008) when in fact the creation of such a vast artificial parascape would have required enormous amounts of water and energy. Additionally, a significant portion of the project was situated over a now degraded, remnant sabkha landscape, which continues to provide a natural filter for drainage to Ras Al Khor (Parsons Harland Bartholomew 1993, pp. 10–15). Branded as a garden when it is in fact a massive urban development, the Mohammed Bin Rashid Gardens project attempted rhetorically to reconcile the antithetical forces of modernity and tradition. The urban professions, through the creation of parascape and its related urban form, were crucial to this rhetorical positioning.

Mohammed Bin Rashid City (2012)

While Sheikh Mohammed put the Mohammed Bin Rashid Gardens project on hold during the GFC, it has resurfaced again, in the same site, as the Mohammed Bin Rashid City project. (See Figure 3.7.) This contemporary iteration is a joint project of the developers Sobha and Meydan – the latter of which is the 'visionary concept' of Sheikh Mohammed (Meydan 2018). Master-planned by multidisciplinary design firm AE7, this current iteration of the project dispenses with the astrolabe-inspired axial geometry in favour of more conventional curvilinear suburban patterns. Nonetheless, the project retains its extensive verdant parascape, containing over 240 hectares of greenery in the form of dedicated open spaces, community and play parks, lawns, green corridors and recreational spaces (Meydan & Sobha 2018b, p. 22). Proudly promoting this luxuriant landscape, the promotional material bills District One of the Mohammed Bin Rashid City as one of the 'lowest density villa developments in the heart of any international city' (Meydan & Sobha 2018a). As the developers opine:

> Just imagine an enchanted garden in the middle of Dubai as an ideal location for an exclusive villa community . . . a prime freehold development, home to expansive greens, verdant views, vibrant flora and sublime water features . . . star attractions like the stunning crystal lagoons, serene man-made beaches and a magnificent water park . . . a truly affluent lifestyle development set in the backdrop of nature . . . a lifestyle that blends luxury with natural beauty and nouvelle residential architecture to create one of the lowest density environments anywhere

Figure 3.7 Top photo: A model of District One of the Mohammed Bin Rashid City; bottom photo: the artificially constructed Crystal Lagoon.

Source: Photos by the author.

in the world . . . a community that has its way of slowing down time to a tranquil tempo and still be an integral part of vibrant Dubai.

(Meydan & Sobha 2018a)

The centrepiece of the project is to be the artificially constructed Crystal Lagoon that stretches over 700 hectares and yields over 14 linear kilometres of new shoreline (Meydan & Sobha 2018b, p. 36). Presumably, the desalinated seawater lagoon will make the project a significant consumer of both energy and water. Regardless, the developers of Mohammed Bin Rashid City bill it as being 'natural,' advertising literature inviting potential buyers to 'surrender to nature' (Meydan & Sobha 2018b, p. 32), notwithstanding that such a form of 'nature' is highly artificial in Dubai. Nonetheless, the project offers, to those who can afford it, an escape from the reality of an often scorching, dry and chaotic city. As the marketing material implores, 'Disconnect from the world and make room for peace. At ease, take a deep breath and feel your senses come to life with every step, every breath, as you leave the daily humdrum behind. Cleanse your mind, body, heart and soul. Make a connection that goes beyond words – with nature and yourself' (Meydan & Sobha 2018b, p. 26).

While the project's links to Emirati culture are less explicit than the previous iteration, it offers a fusion of traditional Arabic and modern architectural design. As the marketing material depicts:

Inspired by modern Arabic architectural form, these villas offer a perfect environment for people who are looking for exclusivity, pleasure and relaxation. A reflection of true Arabic culture and a delightful symphony of functionality and aesthetic splendour, the modern Arabic villas feature authentic nouveaux designs.

(Meydan & Sobha 2018a)

In the project, an upmarket Western suburban lifestyle is delivered in 'oriental settings, in which Emirati culture is equated with luxury' (Katodrytis & Syed 2016, p. 12). It is rumoured that Sheikh Mohammed personally owns a large central island in the Crystal Lagoon only accessible by boat, with a salesperson for the project suggesting that he might, in time, reside there. In this respect, the Mohammed Bin Rashid City development conforms to the age-old tribal structure of the region where the sheikh occupied the centre of the settlement and his sons and relatives surround him, with an outer ring formed of slaves and low-paid workers (Hamouche 2004, p. 524).

The project embodies the narrative of parascape in that it, in part, evokes the luxuriant landscapes of the Quranic paradise. The vast Crystal Lagoon is also particularly rich in symbolism. In traditional Arabic Islamic cities, water carried great symbolic meaning in that it both sustained the city and represented material economy and spiritual strength (Lehrman 1980, p. 34). 'Pure' water also has metaphorical cleansing properties. This symbolism is at the heart of baptisms and ritual ablutions (Fox & Wang 2016, p. 41). In Sheikh Mohammed Bin Rashid City, the symbolism of water as a morally purifying agent (Fox & Wang 2016, p. 41) is used to promote Dubai's richest members and rulers as being morally sanctified.

Pragmatically speaking, the project has also enabled Sheikh Mohammed to instil confidence in Dubai's economy and ruling family, as the emirate emerged out of the GFC and as the Arab Spring spread like wildfire across the region. As Sheikh Mohammed urged in 2012:

> Although we are a peaceful country, free from tension, should tension ever filter in from outside our borders, we will quickly reassure people and face the looming crisis head on. We will reassert our confidence in our country by launching new projects or expanding existing ones. We will also instruct everybody not to cancel any planned events under any circumstances.
>
> (Al Maktoum 2012, p. 167)

This gargantuan project has allowed Sheikh Mohammed to reassure nervous investors and stimulate economic development, as well as instil a sense of loyalty and pride in the local population and project a modern, clean and green image to the rest of the world (Moser, Swain & Alkhabbaz 2015, p. 71).

Freeway and road reserves

Such exclusive communities, in conjunction with Free Trade Zones and themed new 'city' developments (such as Dubai Festival City, Sports City and Internet City), result in a broader urban structure fragmented into a number of urban 'islands' operating as 'isolated enclaves' (Carbonell 2016, p. 238). Within this fractious urban environment parascape in freeway and road reserves is, in symbolic and aesthetic terms, the 'glue' that attempts to hold the city together. Often consisting of an understorey of turf or mass planting beneath a canopy of *Phoenix dactylifera* palm trees, the road reserve parascape has little ecological or programmatic value and requires significant amounts of irrigation.

Nonetheless, the Dubai Municipality proudly exhort the numerics of their freeway and road reserve planting:

> The Municipality has planted about 30 million flower seedlings in 132 hectares of area during the first nine months of 2013 with an increase of 25% comparing to the total flower planted area in 2012.
>
> (Awadi 2013, p. 4)

While parascape carries a rich semiotic load, its quantification into numeric sound bites is vital for the Municipality to display its allegiance to the Sheikh's vision for Dubai as a world-class 'green' city.

Symbolically, the landscaped road reserve also plays a key aesthetic role in concealing the divisions between Dubai's segregated urban 'islands.' (See Figure 3.8.) Beneath a verdant layer of parascape, the barriers of the city

Figure 3.8 Top photo: aerial view of Dubai's landscaped freeway reserves; bottom photo: migrant labourers inhabit a landscaped road reserve in Dubai under the watchful eye of the police.

Sources: Top photo by Prill/Shutterstock.com; bottom photo by the author.

disappear, except for those who may try to cross them. The landscape of the freeway and road reserve also ameliorates the brutality of the typically divisive and over-scaled road system, through cloaking it with a deceptive image of 'nature.'

Such landscapes represent the zenith of Dubai culture's predilection for stylistic landscapes, subsuming potential ecological or societal function in favour of creating a contrived image of nature. Mirroring the way eighteenth-century English designed landscapes, occluded evidence of work so as not to spoil 'the philosophical contemplation of natural beauty,' freeway and road reserves are rarely inhabited (Mitchell 1994, p. 15). In Dubai, the exception is the underclass of immigrant maintenance workers who maintain these landscapes or occasionally take refuge under the shade of roadside trees.

As with parascape more generally, landscaped freeway and road reserves lend legitimacy to Dubai's ruling elites, having likely begun as luxuriantly landscaped VIP roads emanating from the palaces of the Sheikh and extended ruling family (Doherty 2011, p. 189). The Municipality often place billboards with images of Dubai's rulers along parascape freeway and road reserves and roundabouts. There is a significant symbolic dimension to these roadside accoutrements. As Kim Dovey explains, manicured order along major streets 'works to legitimate the state, it signifies a strong state, while disorder on the streets tends to signify political disorder, signifying weakness' (Dovey 2016, p. 52).

Island super graphics

To relate large-scale urban design to a referential figure is common in Dubai. Eric Kuhne and his team, for example, based the design of the Sheikh Mohammed Bin Rashid Garden project upon the astrolabe. While its designers did not necessarily design it for legibility from the air, many other parts of Dubai are. The most famous projects are Palm Jumeirah, the World development and the now cancelled Universe development.[15] The most prominent of these projects, developers have 'written' into the shallow waters of The Gulf to achieve maximum legibility for their logo. As Sheikh Mohammed extolls:

> A few years ago, there were two structures in the world that could be seen from space. The first of these was the Great Wall of China, and the second the Hoover Dam, commissioned in the United States in 1936. If we told people in 1977 that we intended to join China and the US and build a structure that could be seen from space, the response might have been, 'Dream on!' But . . . this unique 'club' of structures visible from space has now been joined by The Palm Islands, the world's largest residential and tourism, man-made islands.
>
> (Al Maktoum 2012, p. 155)

Construction offshore for real estate and tourism purposes began during the 1990s with the Jumeirah beach extension and Burj Al Arab hotel. However, a significant increase in the pace and scale of reclamation took place in the early 2000s, with the construction of the Palm Jumeirah. Between 2003 and 2011, extensive changes in the coastline appeared as 6,800 hectares were added to the total land area of the Dubai Emirate by offshore reclamation projects (Nassar, Blackburn & Whyatt 2014, p. 56). The largest of the Palm developments was to be the vast Palm Deira – proposed to be bigger than Manhattan Island and to house over a million people. This project has not been completed, however, due to the GFC (Caton & Ardalan 2010, p. 46), and since 2011, many of these offshore projects have stalled.

In such projects that have been constructed, the requirements of branding take precedence over the daily lives of inhabitants (Al Sager, Al Rubaian & Khanafer 2007). On the ground, the figure (for instance a palm) does not lend itself to the basic principles of urban design, and, rather, its efficacy is that Google Earth users can instantly recognize its logo. Dubai's super graphic projects represent the ascendancy of branding in project conception aligned with a political system that can (almost) guarantee its construction. The proliferation of such developments in Dubai can even be attributed to the fact that Dubai's ruler (and chief designer) Sheikh Mohammed is an enthusiastic helicopter pilot (Basar 2007, p. 83). Further to his enjoyment of helicopter flight, Sheikh Mohammed is a keen poet. Designers tracing a poem of his in the form of houses over water, at the base of the Palm Jumeirah: 'Take wisdom from the wise. It takes a man of vision to write on water. Not everyone who rides a horse is a jockey. Great men rise to great challenges.'

While the recognition of these manufactured coastal landscapes as logos from Google Earth (and passing aircraft) is primary, the form of these coastal projects also aims to maximize exposure to water through convoluted 'coastal' edges, thereby maximizing marketability and land values. The original author of the palm motif, Sheikh Maktoum, sketched the shape of the palm and realized its fronds would provide more beach frontage than a traditional circular island (Caton & Ardalan 2010, p. 46). Sheikh Mohammed himself explains the attractiveness of this multiplied coastline:

> Whoever owns a home overlooking the sea is fortunate, but owning a home at sea, overlooking the beach, is out of the ordinary. Whoever lives on one of these islands will be living on one of the wonders of the New World.
>
> (Al Maktoum 2012, p. 161)

Such sentiments are in keeping with commentators who predict that in this century, urban living will be increasingly oriented towards lifestyle amenities, of which proximity to water will be the most prized. This is important because, as Alex Kreiger explains, the global elite, who help to drive economic growth, will decide where to work and where to live on the basis of the lifestyle amenities offered by a city (Kreiger 2004, p. 44). In this respect, Dubai's coastal multiplication programme and island super graphics serve the purposes of providing attractive water access, a moat to delineate the exclusivity of the development and a logo recognizable from Google Earth – all of which are powerful marketing tools.

The Palm Jumeirah development

In 2008, developers Nakheel delivered the first of the offshore projects, the Palm Jumeirah. (See Figure 3.9.) Since then, Nakheel has lined the Palm's trunk with apartment buildings, resorts, malls, restaurants and marinas, and its radiating fronds with luxurious villas – all in accordance with Helman Hurley Charvat Peacock's master plan (Helman Hurley Charvat Peacock 2018).

Beyond its impressive monumentality, the Jumeriah Palm's form is highly symbolic. The palm tree carries strong cultural associations in Emirati culture, Emiratis describing the palm tree as 'from our ancestors, it's our heritage' (Mitchell 2016, p. 196). The palm also symbolizes an oasis in the desert as well as representing its developer Nakheel; the translation of Nakheel in Arabic being palm (AMO, Reisz & Ota 2007, p. 262).

The diagram of a tree with its 'roots below the ground, its trunk on the earthy plane and its canopy in the heavens' also symbolizes three realms of existence (Cavendish 2004, p. 66), which are mirrored in the Palm Jumeirah development. On site, these realms are the trunk, the fronds and a 'privately gated crown' (Jensen 2007, p. 65), each becoming progressively more exclusive and privatized as the palm is 'ascended.' Such use of symbols is likely to have religious underpinnings, with anecdotal evidence suggesting that these 'inscriptions' may also be directed towards Allah, who as the omniscient creator of the universe, is said to be all seeing. Again, such projects legitimize Dubai's rulers, illustrating their strength and portraying them as performing the 'works of god' by deploying potent religious and cultural symbols at a massive scale.

The role of parascape in the Palm Jumeirah project has been to attempt to reconcile the branded super graphic with notions of both 'nature' and community – as such, parascape straddles the divide between the requirements of the 'dream city' and the 'real city' (Al Sager, Al Rubaian & Khanafer 2007). Maarten Venter of Cracknell landscape architects describes the landscape design philosophy for the Palm Jumeirah:

> The Palm Jumeirah is currently changing the shoreline of the Arabian Gulf and slowly becoming a world significant development. As it grows from the sea, we extend this growth into the design and draw from the shapes and forms of nature to develop the landscape elements to resemble this growing from the bottom of the sea, revealing captured

Figure 3.9 The first of the major offshore projects, the Palm Jumeirah.

Sources: Top photo by Basar/Shutterstock.com; bottom photo by Expeditionr/Shutterstock.com.

moments in time. . . . These changing events, these captured moments of the earth's evolution inspired the design. The textures and colour as earth revealed them to us as we find in conglomerates would become an inspiration for hard landscaped areas, the patterns left behind in fossils of shells and marine life would be finishes to architectural elements and site furniture . . . . Rooted in past events that shaped man and his environment the design evolves to embrace the vision of the development to be a contemporary island style living environment.

(Venter 2005)

In this instance, landscape designers employ parascape in a superficial attempt to naturalize a super graphic that belongs more to Google Earth than to the 'environment' (Venter 2005). However, this layer of parascape achieves little in this respect, projects such as the Palm Jumeirah have massive implications for the natural aquatic environment. Estimates predict that the construction of the Palm Jumeirah may have destroyed between 750 and 1,125 hectares of coral (Salahudin 2006, p. 59) with changes also occurring in the dynamics of currents, sediments, biogeochemical and ecosystem functions (Nassar, Blackburn & Whyatt 2014, p. 56).

Theme parks

While island super graphics brand the city at the scale of Google Earth, theme parks brand developments as interactive and experiential worlds. Indeed, most developments in Dubai strive to gain a recognizable thematic edge. This takes the form of themed 'old town' developments (which I discuss in the following chapter), themed shopping malls, residential communities such the Jumeirah Golf Course Estate, which designers themed according to the elements of 'earth, wind, fire and water' (Commercial Outdoor Design 2008b, p. 27), and, of course, theme parks, such as Meraas Holding's new Dubai Parks & Resorts theme park project in Jebel Ali and Tatweer's Dubailand.

Dubailand

Developers Tatweer took the idea of a theme park to a new level with the Dubailand project, originally planned to cover 27,800 hectares of land on the urban periphery of Dubai. (See Figure 3.10.) Announced in 2003, the developers put Dubailand on hold in 2008 (due to the GFC) but resumed construction in 2013. Regardless of such setbacks, in Dubailand the theme park is not a component of a larger tract of urbanism; it is the urbanism itself. In the pre-GFC iteration, it was to comprise seven theme parks and 45 themed mega projects, as well as to eventually accommodate 2.5 million people, including tourists, workers and residents when fully operational

Figure 3.10 A model of the pre-GFC iteration of Dubailand.
Source: Photo by the author.

(Dubailand 2007). Tatweer has divided Dubailand into several 'worlds,' which include the Attractions and Experience World (including Kids City theme park), the Retail and Entertainment World (including Dubai Outlet City), Themed Leisure and Vacation World (including Desert Kingdom theme park), Eco-Tourism World (including Al Sahra Desert Resort), Sports and Outdoor World (including Dubai Golf City) and Downtown (including the Mall of Arabia).

Whereas numerous urban professionals and branding consultants have produced the major attractions, landscape designers have provided a generic parascape backdrop for Dubailand. Tatweer has deployed this neutralized setting to evoke a sense of familiarity for the global tourist, as well as to maximize the revenue generation of the planned attractions. Where designers have allowed the desert to permeate Dubailand's verdant layer of parascape, it often emerges as a theme itself rather than a binding substratum. Dubailand, as the apotheosis of theme parks in Dubai, represents the wilful suppression of the local context in favour of a generic model of development for attracting global tourists and capital. Most of the theme parks of Dubailand are replicas of theme parks found elsewhere (such as the Universal Studios theme park). Designers have transplanted the landscape of the original theme parks to the Dubai desert context with a minimum of modification.

This is not surprising, given that developers build theme parks around the notion of escaping the local and regional context.

Moreover, landscape within the theme park becomes a device both to conceal the inner workings and segregations within the theme park and to neutralize, in aesthetic terms, the segregation of the theme park from its physical, societal and cultural context. As Wilson describes in such theme parks, 'economic and social inequalities remain as gross as ever,' yet design renders them 'curiously invisible.' 'Those without the passport of money are simply in absence,' invisibility being a critical feature of contemporary inequality (In Graham & Marvin 2001, p. 264). As urban and branding professions have implicitly disconnected Dubailand from reality, this has negated the usual references of the urban professions (and landscape design in particular) to environmental responsiveness and social progressiveness.

Special Economic Zones

Special Economic Zones (SEZs) have proliferated in Dubai, in part because they allow business immunity from taxes, labour regulation and environmental restrictions, as well as streamlining transhipment, materials handling and duty-free retail (Easterling 2008, p. 9). Established at a relatively modest scale in the 1970s, SEZs have become immense in size and are now a common feature of the Dubai landscape (Kanna 2010, p. 108).

Dubai Internet City

One of the first innovation hubs to be developed in Dubai was Dubai Internet City,[16] a 70-hectare SEZ that was the Middle East's first electronic SEZ, inaugurated in 2000 (Al Maktoum 2012, p. 23). (See Figure 3.11.) Today, it is a 'modern' business park for IT-based new technology companies such as Microsoft, Oracle, HP, IBM, Compaq and Sony (Jensen 2007, p. 138). The advantages for stakeholders who are investing in such SEZs include allowing foreign investors 100 per cent ownership rights of their assets, repatriation of capital and profits, tax and customs duties exemptions, amongst others (Al Maktoum 2012, p. 139).

The existence of SEZs such as Dubai Internet City nonetheless creates a significant internal conflict. As Boris Jensen describes: 'On one hand, the economy must be able to function without restrictions in order to ensure continued growth, while on the other hand the authority's control of the symbolic space is one of the issues that lies closest to the heart of the post political state' (2007, p. 138). Dubai's answer to this conundrum has been the introduction of SEZs, like Dubai Internet City, which, while being privileged zones of economic self-determination, exist on the proviso that companies operating within them continue to exercise political 'responsibility' (Jensen 2007, p. 138). Such 'smart' cities exemplify the spread of neo-liberal ideology that brings government into close collaboration with corporations (Moser 2015, p. 31).

Figure 3.11 Dubai Internet City.
Source: Photo by the author.

Unashamedly, the urbanism found in Dubai Internet City is a product and signifier of global forces. The mirrored facades of the box-like Dubai Internet City buildings 'repel the city outside' much as reflector sunglasses prevent the seer being seen (Harvey 1989, p. 88). Landscape architects Cracknell have set these buildings into a backdrop of pastoral, rolling green parascape containing a large artificial lake that would be equally at home in Google's Mountain View headquarters campus in California as in Dubai (Makhzoumi 2002, p. 225). In this way, the subversion of and separation from the local 'geography' required to become a SEZ finds expression in a completely generic global office park setting. As Sarah Moser explains, such developments 'reject indigenous knowledge, craftsmanship, morphology and commonly used local materials, resulting in the creation of a visual hierarchy that positions global corporate culture as the modern future and the local and indigenous as the "backwards" past' (Moser 2015, p. 33).

Conclusion

This chapter has investigated the cultural, societal, political and economic narratives that Dubai's rulers and related developers use parascape to promote. Parascape, rather than being merely a benign landscape, plays an active role in the socio-political, religious and economic status quo of Dubai. This is evident in the use of parascape in the legitimization of Dubai's socio-political hierarchy through the perceived religious righteousness of the 'greening' project (Ouis 2002, p. 338). Dubai's rulers and developers also deploy parascape as a symbolic and physical antidote to the often hubristic, neo-liberal excesses of Dubai. Finally, parascape plays a significant role in the construction of Dubai's global image, fuelling the creation of Al Sager's 'dream' city while simultaneously carrying associations of the 'real' city of everyday human interactions. The following chapter explores two designed landscape types that resist the dominance of parascape in Dubai.

Notes

1 I have based this chapter on a previous journal paper (Bolleter 2009).
2 Richard Weller and I coined the word 'parascape' in 2008.
3 I concede the difficulty in achieving a comprehensive understanding of the tropes operating in a culture, particularly as part of a cross-cultural exercise. Thus, I identify the trope of paradise in the Dubai landscape through statements of the UAE's and Dubai's rulers and developers and related passages from the Quran.
4 This connection between garden and Paradise can also be seen in the reference to Allah as 'The Gardener' (Cavendish 2004).
5 By 2001, the UAE boasted 41 million palm trees producing 40 million tons of dates (Mitchell 2016).
6 The United Nations Environmental Programme (UNEP) considered desertification to be one of the major environmental problems of the time, a situation that Sheikh Zayed was attempting to reverse (Anonymous landscape architect 2009a).
7 These include Sheikh Rashid bin Saeed Al Maktoum (Sheikh Rashid, 1958–1990), Sheikh Maktoum bin Rashid Al Maktoum (Sheik Maktoum, 1990–2006) and currently Sheikh Mohammed bin Rashid Al Maktoum (Sheikh Mohammed, 2006 till today).
8 The Bedouin are the Arabic-speaking nomadic peoples of the deserts of the Middle East.
9 The practice of land allocation to Emirati citizens has continued until recent times with national males and certain national females receiving a plot of land upon reaching 20 years of age (Parsons Harland Bartholomew 1993).
10 Tourism operations also romanticize and commodify the desert for tourists, as a site of authentic local culture.
11 The Emirate of Sharjah is the neighbouring emirate to Dubai.
12 Members of Dubai's lower socio-economic stratum are often denied entry into gated developments except in a service capacity (Davis 2007). Unskilled migrant labourers in the construction industry typically live in camps on Dubai's desert fringes.
13 Nonetheless, the exclusion of migrant labourers is not officially acknowledged by the municipality; instead, they refer to the fencing and entry fee as being required to pay for the upkeep of the park as well as to prevent people who enter the park from 'abusing' it (Ibid.).
14 Sudjic made this comment in general terms without specific reference to the Sheikh Mohammed Gardens development.

15 Developers Nakheel cancelled the The Universe development due to the difficulty selling and developing the comparatively more modest World development, in conjunction with the effects of the Global Financial Crisis.
16 This SEZ also includes Dubai Media City.

References

Abu-Gazzeh, T, 'Privacy as the Basis of Architectural Planning in the Islamic Culture of Saudi Arabia', *Architecture & Comportement*, vol. 11, no. 3, pp. 269–288.

Acuto, M 2010, 'High-Rise Dubai Urban Entrepreneurialism and the Technology of Symbolic Power', *Cities*, no. 27, pp. 272–284.

Al Maktoum, MBR 2012, *My Vision: Challenges in the Race for Excellence*, Motivate Publishing, Dubai.

Al Maktoum, MBR 2015, *Dubai Strategic Plan: Highlights*, Government of Dubai, Dubai.

Al Sager, A, Al Rubaian, A & Khanafer, S 2007, 'Neither Desperate nor Decadent', *Volume*, pp. 8–12.

AlSayyad, N & Guvenc, M 2015, 'Virtual Uprisings: On the Interaction of New Social Media, Traditional Media Coverage and Urban Space during the "Arab Spring"', *Urban Studies*, vol. 52, no. 11, pp. 2018–2034.

Al-Thaqafi, T 2017, 'Hajj Revenues Poised to Exceed $150bn by 2022: Experts', *Arab News*. Available from: www.arabnews.com/node/1151751/saudi-arabia.

Amirahmadi, H & Razavi, M 1993, 'Urban Development in the Muslim World: Encounter with Modernity and Implications for Planning', *Urban Development in the Muslim World*, pp. 1–36.

AMO, Reisz, T & Ota, K 2007, 'Gulf Survey', *Al Manakh*, vol. 12, no. 7, pp. 70–334.

Andraos, A 2007, 'Dubai's Island Urbanism: An Archipelago of Difference for the 21st Century?' in *Vision Plus Money Plus Historical Circumstance Equals 'Cities From Zero' Unapologetic Expressions of New-Found Economic and Therefore Political Prowess in the 21st Century*, pp. 47–56, Architectural Association Publishing, London.

Anonymous Dubai Municipality representative 2008, *Interview*, J Bolleter.

Anonymous landscape architect 2009a, *Email*, J Bolleter, Dubai.

Anonymous landscape architect 2009b, *Interview*, J Bolleter.

Anstey, T 2013, 'Dubai to Get $7.3m Quran Theme Park', *CLAD News*. Available from: www.cladglobal.com/architecture_design_news?codeid=305859. [29.08].

Awadi, MAR 2013, 'Dubai Plants 30 Million Flower Seedlings', *Landscape Middle East*, p. 4.

Bagader, A 1994, *Environmental Protection in Islam*, IUCN, Gland, Switzerland and Cambridge.

Bantey, P & Heintz, E 2007, 'The Architecture of Elsewhere: New Urban Contexts in Dubai and Shanghai', in *Regional Architecture and Identity in the Age of Globalization Conference*, pp. 1205–1218, Centre for the Study of Architecture in the Arab Region, Dubai.

Basar, S 2007, 'Twelve Ultimate Critical Steps to Sudden Urban Success', in *Vision Plus Money Plus Historical Circumstance Equals 'Cities From Zero' Unapologetic Expressions of New- Found Economic and Therefore Political- Prowess in the 21st Century*, pp. 73–95, Architectural Association Publishing, London.

Bolleter, J 2009, 'Para-Scape: Landscape Architecture in Dubai', *Journal of Landscape Architecture*, Spring, no. 4, pp. 28–55.

Bouman, O 2007, 'Desperate Decadence', *Volume*, pp. 4–7.

Brookes, J 1987, *Gardens of Paradise*, Weidenfeld and Nicolson, London.

Carbonell, A 2016, 'Dubai: The Political Project of a New Metropolis', in G Katodrytis & S Syed (eds), *Gulf Cities as Interfaces*, pp. 229–242, Gulf Research Centre Cambridge, Jeddah.

Caton, S & Ardalan, N 2010, *New Arab Urbanism, the Challenge to Sustainability and Culture in the Gulf*, Harvard Kennedy School, Cambridge, MA.

Cavendish, M 2004, *Paradise: A Cultural Guide*, Eastern Universities Press, Singapore.

Central Intelligence Agency 2008, *Central Intelligence Agency: The World Factbook*. Available from: https://www.cia.gov/library/publications/the-world-factbook/geos/ae.html. [24.01].

CivicArts 2008, *Mohammed Bin Rashid Gardens*. Available from: https://www.civicarts.com/mohammed-bin-rashid-gardens. [14.04].

Coles, A & Walsh, K 2010, 'From "Trucial State" to "Postcolonial" City? The Imaginative Geographies of British Expatriates in Dubai', *Journal of Ethnic and Migration Studies*, vol. 36, no. 8, pp. 1317–1333.

Commercial Outdoor Design 2008a, 'Dubai Government Unveils $54bn Gardens Project', *Commercial Outdoor Design*, vol. 1, no. 6, p. 07.

Commercial Outdoor Design 2008b, 'Four in One', *Commercial Outdoor Design*, vol. 1, no. 7, pp. 26–29.

Condon, P 1994, 'A Built Landscape Typology: The Language of the Land We Live In', in K Franck & L Schneekloth (eds), *Ordering Space: Types in Architecture and Design*, pp. 79–94, Van Nostrand Reinhold, New York.

Corner, J 1999, 'Eidetic Operations and New Landscapes', in *Recovering Landscape: Essays in Contemporary Landscape Architecture*, pp. 153–170, Princeton Architectural Press, New York.

Crewe, K & Forsyth, A 2003, 'Landscapes: A Typology of Approaches to Landscape Architecture', *Landscape Journal*, vol. 22, no. 1–3, pp. 37–53.

Davidson, C 2008, *Dubai: The Vulnerability of Success*, Columbia University Press, New York.

Davis, M 2007, 'Fear and Money in Dubai', *Topos*, pp. 62–70.

Doherty, G 2008, 'The Landscape of Dubai's Urbanism', in *Instant Cities; Emergent Trends in Architecture and Urbanism in the Arab World*, pp. 103–111, CSAAR, Amman.

Doherty, G 2011, 'Bahrain's Polyvocality and Landscape as a Medium', in S Egoz, J Makhzoumi & G Pungetti (eds), *The Right to Landscape: Contesting Landscape and Human Rights*, pp. 185–197, Ashgate, Burlington.

Doherty, G 2014, 'In the West You Have Landscape, Here We Have . . .', *Studies in the History of Gardens & Designed Landscapes*, vol. 34, no. 3, pp. 201–206.

Dovey, K 2016, *Urban Design Thinking*, Bloomsbury Academic, London.

Dubai Municipality 2001, *Dubai Parks*, Dubai Municipality Public Relations Section, Dubai.

Dubailand 2007, *Dubailand*. Available from: www.dubailand.ae/. [2008].

Duranton, G & Puga, D 2013, 'The Growth of Cities', CEPR Discussion Paper No. DP9590, pp. 751–853, Center for Economic and Policy Research, Washington, DC.

Easterling, K 2008, 'Extrastatecraft', *Perspecta 39 The Yale Architectural Journal: Re-Urbanism Transforming Capitals*, pp. 5–16.

Economist 2004, 'Sheikh Zayed', *Economist*. Available from: https://www.econo mist.com/obituary/2004/11/18/sheikh-zayed.

Egoz, S 2008, 'Deconstructing the Hegemony of Nationalist Narratives Through Landscape Architecture', *Landscape Research*, vol. 33, no. 1, pp. 29–50.

Forty, A 2000, *Words and Buildings*, Thames and Hudson, London.

Fox, M & Wang, A, 2016, *Symbols: A Handbook for Seeing*, Monacelli Press, New York.

Government of Dubai 2012, *Dubai 2020 Urban Masterplan*, Government of Dubai, Dubai.

Government of Dubai 2014, *2021 Dubai Plan*, Government of Dubai and Go Dubai, Dubai.

Graham, S & Marvin, S 2001, *Splintering Urbanism: Networked Infrastructures, Technological Mobilities and the Urban Condition*, Routledge, London.

Haines, C 2011, 'Cracks in the Façade: Landscapes of Hope and Desire in Dubai', in *Worlding Cities: Asian Experiments and the Art of Being Global*, pp. 160–181, Blackwell, Chichester.

Hall, P 2002, *Cities of Tomorrow: An Intellectual History of Urban Planning and Design in the 20th Century*, Third edn, Blackwell Publishing, Oxford.

Hamouche, M 2004, 'The Changing Morphology of the Gulf Cities in the Age of Globalisation: The Case of Bahrain', *Habitat International*, no. 28, pp. 521–540.

Harvey, D 1989, *The Condition of Post Modernity*, Basil Blackwell, Oxford.

Helman Hurley Charvat Peacock 2018, *Helman Hurley Charvat Peacock*, Helman Hurley Charvat Peacock. Available from: http://www.hhcp.com/the-palm-jumei rah-master-plan.html. [01.08].

Herrington, S 2013, 'An Ontology of Landscape Design', in P Howard, I Thompson & E Waterton (eds), *The Routledge Companion to Landscape Studies*, pp. 355–365, Routledge, Oxon.

Howe, M 2008, 'Green Credentials', *Commercial Outdoor Design*, vol. 1, no. 4, pp. 26–32.

Jensen, B 2007, *Dubai – Dynamics of Bingo Urbanism*, Architectural Publisher, Copenhagen.

Kanna, A 2010, 'Flexible Citizenship in Dubai: Neoliberal Subjectivity in the Emerging "City-Corporation"', *Cultural Anthropology*, vol. 25, no. 1, pp. 100–129.

Katodrytis, G & Syed, S 2016, 'Introduction', in G Katodrytis & S Syed (eds), *Gulf Cities as Interfaces*, pp. 11–22, Gulf Research Centre Cambridge, Jeddah.

Kennedy, T 2007, 'Place Telling at Dubai Creek: Encoded Visions', in *Regional Architecture and Identity in the Age of Globalization Conference*, pp. 407–416, Centre for the Study of Architecture in the Arab Region, Dubai.

Kreiger, A 2004, 'The Transformation of the Urban Waterfront', in Urban Land Institute (ed), *Remaking the Urban Waterfront*, pp. 22–47, Urban Land Institute, Washington, DC.

Landscape Middle East 2013, 'Grass Is Greener', *Landscape Middle East*, p. 8.

Landscape Middle East 2014, 'Dubai Holy Qur'an Park Project in Progress', *Landscape Middle East*, p. 4.

Landscape Middle East 2018, 'Dubai Municipality Intensifies Efforts on City Beautification and Spreading Green Areas', *Landscape Middle East*, p. 6.

Lehrman, J 1980, *Earthly Paradise: Garden and Courtyard in Islam*, Thames and Hudson, Glamorgan.

Levitt, T 1983, 'The Globalization of Markets', *Harvard Business Review*, no. May–June 1981, pp. 94–102.

Lindstrom, K, Palang, H & Kull, K 2013, 'Semiotics of Landscape', in P Howard, I Thompson & E Waterton (eds), *The Routledge Companion to Landscape Studies*, pp. 97–107, Routledge, Oxon.

Lockerbie, J 2008, *Catnaps*. Available from: http://catnaps.org/islamic/islaurb.html. [03.02].

Lootah, H 2014, 'DH 17mn for New Parks and Squares in Dubai', *Landscape Middle East*, p. 4.

Mahgoub, Y 2007, 'Impact of Globalisation on the Built Environment Identity in the Arabian Gulf Region', in *Regional Architecture and Identity in the Age of Globalisation Conference*, pp. 927–942, Centre for the Study of Architecture in the Arab Region, Dubai.

Makhzoumi, JM 2002, 'Landscape in the Middle East: An Inquiry', *Landscape Research*, vol. 27, no. 3, pp. 213–228.

Marcinkoski, C 2015, *The City That Never Was*, Princeton Architectural Press, New York.

McGlothlin, M 2007, 'National Chic: The Objectified Sensation of World Exposition', in *Regional Architecture and Identity in an Age of Globalisation Conference*, pp. 867–879, CSAAR, Tunis.

Meydan 2018, *Meydan*, Meydan. Available from: www.meydan.ae/about/. [08.01].

Meydan & Sobha 2018a, *Mohammed Bin Rashid City: District One*, Meydan. Available from: https://resources.lookup.ae/downloads/6585597321235058_375.pdf. [04.04].

Meydan & Sobha 2018b, *Mohammed Bin Rashid City: District One residences*, Meydan. Available from: https://resources.lookup.ae/downloads/6585597321235058_375.pdf. [04.04].

Mitchell, K 2007, 'Lamenting the Loss of a Past Constructed in the Present: The Case of Dubai', in *Regional Architecture in the Age of Globalization Conference Volume II*, pp. 645–653, Centre for the Study of Architecture in the Arab Region, Tunis.

Mitchell, K 2016, 'Beyond Greening: Approaches to the Contemporary Landscape in the United Arab Emirates', in M Gharipour (ed), *Contemporary Urban Landscapes of the Middle East*, pp. 191–206, Routledge, London.

Mitchell, WJT 1994, 'Imperial Landscape', in *Landscape and Power*, pp. 5–34, University of Chicago Press, Chicago and London.

Moosavi, S, Makhzoumi, J & Grose, M 2016, 'Landscape Practice in the Middle East Between Local and Global Aspirations', *Landscape Research*, vol. 41, no. 3, pp. 265–278.

Moser, S 2015, 'New Cities: Old Wine in New Bottles?' *Dialogues in Human Geography*, vol. 5, no. 1, pp. 31–35.

Moser, S, Swain, M & Alkhabbaz, M 2015, 'King Abdullah Economic City: Engineering Saudi Arabia's Post-Oil Future', *Cities*, no. 45, pp. 71–80.

Mumford, L 1961, *The City in History*, Harcourt, San Diego, New York and London.

Nassar, AK, Blackburn, GA & Whyatt, JD 2014, 'Developing the Desert: The Pace and Process of Urban Growth in Dubai', *Computers, Environment and Urban Systems*, vol. 45, pp. 50–62.

Orff, K 2001, 'Landscape', in *Great Leap Forward*, pp. 336–417, Harvard Design School, Cambridge.

Ouis, P 2002, 'Greening the Emirates: The Modern Construction of Nature in the United Arab Emirates', *Cultural Geographies*, no. 9, pp. 334–347.

Parsons Harland Bartholomew 1995, *Structure Plan for the Dubai Urban Area 1993–2012*, Dubai Municipality Planning & Survey Department, DMPS Department, Dubai. Ponte, A 1991, 'Public Parks in Great Britain and the United States: From a "Spirit of Place" to a "Spirit of Civilization"', in M Mosser & G Teyssot (eds), *The History of Garden Design*, Thames and Hudson, London.

Salahudin, B 2006, 'The Marine Environmental Impacts of Artificial Island Construction', Master's thesis, Duke University, Durham, NC, Nicholas School of the Environment and Earth Sciences.

Smith, B 2010, 'Scared by, of, in, and for Dubai', *Social & Cultural Geography*, vol. 11, no. 3, pp. 263–283.

Sorkin, M 1992, *Variations on a Theme Park*, Hill & Wang, New York.

Sudjic, D 1992, *The 100 Mile City*, Harper Collins, London.

Sudjic, D 2005, *The Edifice Complex*, Penguin Books, New York.

Swaffield, S & Deming, E 2011, 'Research Strategies in Landscape Architecture: Mapping the Terrain', *Journal of Landscape Architecture*, Spring, pp. 34–45.

Unitas Consultancy 2017, *Dubai: The Gate Keepers*, Reidin, Dubai.

Venter, M 2005, *The Palm Jumeirah*.

Weller, R 2007, 'Between Hermeneutics and Datascapes: A Critical Appreciation of Emergent Landscape Design Theory and Praxis Through the Writings of James Corner 1990–2000', *Landscape Review*, vol. 7, no. 1, pp. 3–44.

Wescoat Jr, JL 2013, 'The "Duties of Water" with Respect to Planting: Toward an Ethics of Irrigated Landscapes', *Journal of Landscape Architecture*, vol. 8, no. 2, pp. 6–13.

4 Urban and desert landscapes

Introduction

The grand narrative of parascape, as described in the previous chapter, irrigates a broad and varied range of projects in Dubai. Parascape reaches its zenith in Dubai in the verdant landscape of exclusive suburban communities as well as in the Municipality's park system. Nonetheless, two broad landscape types have emerged comparatively recently that provide various levels of resistance to the dominance of parascape. This includes designed landscapes that reference the desert, in the form of xerophytic landscapes (which I name 'xeriscape') or designed urban landscapes that are heavily themed and managed to create the appearance of an urbane and open society (urbscape).

This chapter explores these two landscape types both for the narratives they promote and for the urban developments that they furnish. My intention is that this approach will highlight that Dubai's designed landscapes are embedded in the 'discourses of power, race and nationality' (Lindstrom, Palang & Kull 2013, p. 99). The research questions structuring this enquiry are:

> *What cultural, societal and political narratives do designed urban spaces in Dubai promote?*

And similarly:

> *What cultural, societal and political narratives do designed xerophytic landscapes in Dubai promote?*

In answering these twin questions, I deploy an interpretive critique methodology (Swaffield & Deming 2011, p. 43) that seeks to provide insight into what the developers of such landscapes aim to attain at a symbolic level. As per the previous chapter, I derive such understandings (in part) from a review of Dubai's Strategic Plans (Al Maktoum 2015; Government of Dubai 2014; Government of Dubai 2012) and Sheikh Mohammed's book *My Vision: Challenges in the Race for Excellence* (Al Maktoum 2012).

Body

In the first decade of this century, the international community recognized Dubai for its engineering feats and architectural accomplishments (such as the Palm Jumeirah and Burj Khalifa respectively), its shopping mall culture and the luxuriant greenery of its exclusive residential estates and resorts (parascape). However, in recent years, the global community has increasingly come to know Dubai for its 'world-class' events and festivals (Newman 2016) and for a suite of heavily place-managed urban spaces such as Culture Village, Al Seef, Dubai Design District, The Opera District, City Walk, The Beach, Boxpark, Last Exit, The Outlet Village and Kite Beach (Meraas 2018c).

Urbscape narratives

I refer to these projects under the moniker 'urbscape.' It originates from the conjoining of the words 'urb' and 'scape.' 'Urb' (city) signifies Sheikh Mohammed's desire to brand Dubai as a 'real' city that is urbane, activated, creative, cultured and open – a process that is fundamental to his mission to transform Dubai into one of the 'cultural epicentres' of the world (Newman 2016). Such ambitions are also reflected in a government target of 20 million tourists visiting the city annually by 2020 (Newman 2016).

Facilitating the ambitious transformation of Dubai into a cultural epicentre has been an approach to urban development that puts experience at its core, with placemaking (or place management) playing a key role. As Hadley Newman, director of 'creative agency' Ombono, explains:

> [Visitors to Dubai] are seeking an experience. They want to take it home with them or look back on an event as something like a new adventure – one that they may never have a chance to do again. People expect a complete experience that is distinctive in each place.
>
> (Newman 2016)

While advocates for placemaking in the Western world articulate it as a bottom-up process, in Dubai, 'unelected ruler' Sheikh Mohammed (Davis 2007, p. 63) has to a significant degree driven the placemaking component of key urban projects. As he urged in 2014, 'Let us work as one team to transform our city into a cultural hub that attracts creative artists' (Nagraj 2014). Moreover, he explained that, 'We are giving you the opportunity to make your city into an open air museum – Dubai is your canvas' (Nagraj 2014). These aspirations are formalized in Dubai's Strategic Plan, which aims to enrich the urban environment by developing physical infrastructure to promote cultural activities (Al Maktoum 2015, p. 29).

The planned cultural activities are to occur in a suite of alternative forms of semi-public landscape types derived, in many cases, from European cities, such as piazzas, boulevards and waterfront promenades.[1] Delivering these urbscapes and their attendant 'experiences' are Dubai's master developers Nakheel, Meydan, Emaar, Dubai Holding and Meraas Holding (a majority of which Sheikh Mohammed and his ruling family own or control), who have many projects under way around the city. Working in conjunction with these developers is Brand Dubai, the creative arm of the Government of Dubai Media Office. As their marketing explains, Brand Dubai delivers street art and art installations aimed at 'enhancing the look and feel of Dubai to reflect its unique character as one of the world's most developed, fastest growing and culturally diverse cities' and to 'communicate positive messages about Dubai's unique culture, values and identity' – and by extension Dubai's leadership (Brand Dubai 2018). Rather than this constituting a bottom-up, organic process, the ruler of Dubai, Sheikh Mohammed (in part), dictates Brand Dubai's initiatives. This is not surprising because the Dubai Media Office (Brand Dubai's parent organization) is tasked with 'driving synergies between the Government and the Media' (The Media Office 2018).

The most significant of the urbane projects is the revitalization of the historic Dubai Creek districts, which Sheikh Mohammed describes as the 'very heart and soul of Dubai' and the source of Dubai's 'survival, distinction and growth over the years' (Al Maktoum 2012, p. 86). Other key projects driven – in part – by placemaking approaches are the Dubai Design District, which is expected to 'positively reflect on Dubai branding internationally, through designer fashion and interior design' (Newman 2016); Jumeriah Beach Walk, which offers up an image of a bustling yet exclusive coastal promenade; and City Walk, which showcases Dubai's emerging (yet largely faux) urbanity. The most heroic of these projects is the Mall of the World development, which the developers intend will be the world's largest mall, capable of hosting over 180 million visitors annually, in the form of a 'temperature-controlled pedestrian city' (Landscape Middle East 2015b, p. 10). Inside the mall, the Dubai Cultural District 'will be the hub for national and multinational cultural festivities and events in the UAE' (Landscape Middle East 2015b, p. 12). This dedicated theatre district will be commensurate in scale with London's West End and New York's Broadway. Celebration Walk, which designers have modelled on Las Ramblas in Barcelona, will connect the cultural district to the rest of the Mall (Landscape Middle East 2015b, p. 12).

In general, these projects tend to either assume a contemporary, minimal aesthetic or adopt a heritage look that (loosely) references the vernacular building traditions of The Gulf. Regardless, the primary agenda of these place-managed spaces is to trap global capital in the form of retail and tourist spending. Rather than the conventional shopping malls, which Dubai is synonymous with, many of these heavily place-managed 'urbane' spaces are – at their core – shopping malls with the roofs ripped off and their retail function distributed throughout urban districts and spaces. While this retail function is the dominant driver for such developments, they also further other agendas.

The 'open' city

Critics often label Dubai as superficial, fake and not a real city (*The Guardian* in Hyde 2010, p. 68), and the recent proliferation of heavily staged urbscapes in Dubai are, in part, an attempt to respond to these stinging criticisms. One of the key characteristics of a 'real' city is that it carries the potential for high-density random social encounters that occur within the 'crowd.' Richard Sennet, a professor of sociology, has long argued that such an encounter with difference is the key quality of urbanity – that the density and diversity of public space has a civilizing function that produces tolerance of difference and that enables the formation of new identities (Dovey 2005, p. 16). Sennett referred to this ideal as 'the open city' in that it frees people from the straitjacket of the 'fixed and the familiar' (McGuirk 2018), creating an urban landscape in which they can enrich and broaden their experience. In this respect, Middle Eastern societies generally celebrate contemporary public spaces as symbols of democracy, progress and openness (Gharipour 2016, p. 6).

While Dubai's heavily place-managed urban spaces tend to offer the image of an 'open city,' Dubai's unskilled migrant underclass of labourers, service and domestic workers is effectively denied entry by various 'soft' strategies (Acuto 2010, p. 278), a situation that conforms to Dubai's tendency to 'hide the majority population, the ones who Dubai is dependent on, from public view' (Haines 2011, p. 178). In Dubai's urbscape, this is often achieved through a sophisticated array of exclusion tactics such as distance from worker accommodations, parking prices, a lack of public transport and aesthetic codes. In relation to the latter, social exclusion in Dubai is (often) enacted by seduction and desire rather than by regulation and coercion – segregation in Dubai coming with glossy brochures and red-carpeted entrances that communicate who is and who isn't welcome (Acuto 2010, p. 281). Such urban projects are highly choreographed, and placemaking or destination branding consultants have carefully packaged the exclusive experiences they offer for the wealthy – in particular Dubai's rumoured 26,000 millionaires (Petch 2018).

As Kim Dovey explains, the consequence of this 'avoidance of risk' is the 'sanitisation' of urban experience (Dovey 2005, p. 15). As a result, urbscapes become 'protected playgrounds' – delivering experiences for wealthy tourists or locals – yet stripped of the uncertainty and interactions of authentic urban life (Dovey 2016, p. 48). This is unsurprising given that developers commission urbscapes to further profit, not to facilitate interaction and exchange between otherwise discrete socio-economic strata. While neo-liberal politics have been transforming the public domain of cities, all around the globe, into exclusive commercially driven landscapes (Gharipour 2016, p. 9), this process reaches its zenith in Dubai's urbscapes.

Defending identity

Many of the urbscape projects that Dubai's developers deliver re-imagine the historic built-form vernacular of the region as retail and leisure destinations for the mobile global leisure class and wealthy locals. Examples of this nostalgia-laced urbanism include the Old Town, Souq Al Bahar and Souq Madinat Jumeirah (Velegrinis & Katodrytis 2015, p. 77). Significant among these is the creation of 'historic' districts, along Dubai Creek, in what were recently undeveloped sites. These include the Al Seef and the Culture Village developments. These projects are complemented by the urban regeneration of existing historic neighbourhoods along Dubai Creek, such as the Bastakiya and Shindaga neighbourhoods (Velegrinis & Katodrytis 2015, p. 77).

Except for the regeneration of historic neighbourhoods, this nostalgic form of themed 'old town' development is superficial in that it is often historically inaccurate[2] and commodifies (and trivializes) local culture for the global tourist. Nonetheless, it is also a physical manifestation of Sheikh Mohammed's aim to protect 'national identity, culture and way of life' (Al Maktoum 2015, p. 12). The perceived need to protect Emirati culture has several causes. Firstly, as Mustapha Hamouche from the University of Bahrain explains, the comparatively recent shift from endogenous to exogenous systems in The Gulf and in Dubai in particular has been one of the 'deepest, sharpest and fastest in urban history.' There was no gradual transition between the two systems, as happened in the West (Hamouche 2004, p. 528). This rapid shift in Dubai has been a dislocating experience for many Emirati people who mourn the loss of a slower and quieter way of life. This in turn has triggered renewed critiques, especially from Dubai residents of ethnic Arab extraction, about the supposed cultural 'inauthenticity' of Dubai's modern path – a resentment that can, in informal conversations, morph into criticism of the regime (Kanna 2010, p. 105).

This reflects the Arab world more generally, where globalization is often viewed as 'another term for capitalism and imperialism' that is endangering a more traditional way of life (Mahgoub 2004, p. 507). In this respect, old town developments reflect an apparent reassertion of Emirati culture in the face of a numerically dominant expatriate community. Such projects align with measures to increase the awareness of the local culture by updating the content of the educational curriculum and developing the cultural literacy of the teaching faculty (Al Maktoum 2015, p. 27).

One challenge that designers confront in old town development is that vernacular built-form is the spatial product of many processes and is unique to the combination of those forces. As American anthropologist Lila Abu-Lughod explains, 'A city at one point in time is a still photograph of a complex system of building and destroying, of organizing and reorganizing' (Abu-Lughod 1987, p. 19). A modest list of the forces that created traditional Arabic Islamic urban form include terrain, climate; a technology of production, distribution and transportation; a system of social organization; and a legal, political system, amongst others (Abu-Lughod 1987, p. 19). By regurgitating a pastiche of historic Arabic, Islamic urbanism, designers are loosely recreating the shell of a historic city; however, the processes that would lend authenticity to this form have entirely changed – particularly in relation to the technology of production, transportation and social organization. The traditional crafts and activities, such as fishing, pearl diving and trading and sailmaking, long ago collapsed in favour of services and oil-related industries (Hamouche 2004, p. 529).

Political legitimization

The revival of traditional charades also has a political dimension that the urban professions do not acknowledge. Cities do not 'have' a memory – they 'make' one for themselves with the aid of symbols, images, rites, ceremonies, places and monuments (Bakshi 2014, p. 191). In these themed old town projects, Dubai's vernacular built-form is appropriated by Dubai's rulers to construct a narrative that the authority of Sheikh Mohammed sits in a 'natural line of progress' (Dovey 2016, p. 128) extending from Dubai's ancient history to the current day. The increasing propagation of such narratives in Dubai is, in part, a response to the Arab Spring, which has seen a harsher tone adopted by Dubai's rulers on issues of national identity and culture, with increasingly strident calls by locals for government intervention to defend against 'threats' allegedly posed by foreigners (Kanna 2010, p. 124).

One of the reasons the Arab Spring has not undermined the ruling dynasty in Dubai (and the UAE more generally) is that the rulers have been able to maintain the 'social contract' or 'ruling bargain' with the populace (Forstenlechner, Rutledge & Salem Alnuaimi 2017). This contract involves the provision of jobs, housing and urban amenities such as parks but also urban projects that reconstitute the local built-form vernacular (in part) to 'naturalise' the rule of Sheikh Mohammed and provide the appearance – but not the reality – of resisting the global (Bowring 2013, p. 270). As Australian urban critic Kim Dovey explains, 'vernacular architecture can be used to evoke the idea that authority is indigenous,' legitimated in the vernacular buildings that form the backdrop of day-to-day life (Dovey 2016, p. 128). Moreover, the fact that Sheikh Mohammed has taken such a keen interest in the nostalgic theming and related place management of urban spaces in

Dubai is not coincidental – given the mobilizations of the 'Spring' fomenting in urban spaces such as Tahrir Square in Cairo and Bahrain's Pearl Roundabout (Stadnicki, Pierre-Arnaud & Vignal 2014, p. 12). Sheikh Mohammed's programme to lace Dubai's urban spaces with nostalgic theming, I believe, is partly an attempt to claim these spaces as not being open for appropriation for protests – subtle or overt.

Urbscape projects

In this section, I identify several key urbscape projects in Dubai. Rather than explicitly focussing on the morphological (Condon 1994, p. 92) or programmatic dimension (Forty 2000, p. 304) of these projects, I concentrate on the relationship between the project and the larger context of the city in cultural, societal and political terms. Through this approach, I aim to position the projects in relation to the larger culture of Dubai and increase awareness of the symbolic roles their projects may be serving (Crewe & Forsyth 2003, p. 37).

Old towns

In an era of rapid flows across national borders, and as more cities compete for global city status, governments are fostering urban environments that are locally 'distinctive' and of interest to the global population (Teo 2014, p. 918). In this respect, Dean MacCannell, chair of Landscape Architecture at the University of California, argues that such government-led tourism strategies are merely constructing places as 'products' for consumption by a global leisure class (In Dovey 2016, p. 186). Readers can observe this process in the cleansing, rejuvenation and place management of old historical downtowns, particularly in Europe (Duranton & Puga 2013, p. 800), but also in Dubai, as I discuss in the following section.

Culture Village

Developed by Dubai Properties and master-planned by DSA Architects, Culture Village is a completely new, multistorey retail, residential and luxury hotel development conceived as an 'Arabesque' town along the banks of Dubai Creek. (See Figure 4.1.) The developers predict that the project will become the 'heart' of a destination known for 'embracing culture, heritage and art' through the architecture of its residences and the diversity of its retail offerings (Dubai Properties 2018). Bolstering this will be Culture Village's cultural, exhibition and art centres, which will form a 'tribute to the cultural diversity of Dubai' and 'rejuvenate the romance and mystique of a civilization that flourished by the creek' (Dubai Properties 2018).

The actual urbanism of Culture Village is reference to a mix of influences, including the Arabian and Persian built-form traditions (Carbonell 2016,

Figure 4.1 Culture Village on the banks of Dubai Creek.
Source: Photo by the author.

p. 236). The most iconic elements of the development are the faux wind catchers, which originally cooled traditional housing by allowing ventilation but today are often packed with air-conditioning equipment (Caton & Ardalan 2010, p. 49). The landscape designers have opted for typically hard-scape landscape treatments, with Arabesque paving patterns and the obligatory date palm plantings.

While the project is pleasant enough as a pedestrian experience, it is problematic from a heritage perspective. The project causes confusion between what is authentic and what is recreated 'heritage' and as such degrades the authenticity of the Dubai Creek area, which has been a haunt of fishermen, traders, smugglers and pirates over thousands of years. As Canadian social activist Naomi Klein argues in general terms, 'The terrible irony of these surrogates, of course is how destructive they are to the real thing' (Klein 2000, p. 176). Reflecting this, local expatriates have told me that the site of Culture Village was until recently where boatbuilders constructed traditional timber Arabic dhows, a tradition apparently erased to build Culture Village.

Al Seef

Located just up-creek of Culture Village is Al Seef, a similarly nostalgic urbscape project. (See Figure 4.2.) While entirely new, the cultural tourism

Figure 4.2 Top photo: A forlorn South Asian cleaner fastidiously sprays and polishes the (apparently) dusty surface of an Al Seef alleyway; bottom photo: the all but empty Al Seef public domain.

Source: Photos by the author.

project is billed as a 'living reminder of the city's past, present and future' (Cracknell 2018, p. 20). Delivered by Dubai developers Meraas and master-planned by Dubai architecture firm Godwin Austen Johnson, the project seeks to create a place of 'memories old and new that are layered in time, showing snapshots of Dubai's organic growth' (Cracknell 2018, p. 20).

The result is a series of (apparently) haphazardly placed low-rise buildings that reference vernacular building traditions and house restaurants and shops selling tourist novelties. Locals and tourists visit Al Seef (particularly in the evening) to promenade, dine al fresco, visit the boutique shops, and take in the view of Dubai Creek. In the spaces between the buildings, landscape architects Cracknell have carefully placed props such as traditional fishing nets. These evoke a simpler and slower time when 'daily activities included merchants with their carts and donkeys, the hustle and bustle of local markets, fishermen with their nets, pearl divers stepping off the docks onto handmade dhows, and community gatherings under handcrafted, makeshift shaded areas to escape the midday heat' (Cracknell 2018, p. 20). Finally, the project is complemented by a small open piazza designed to allow for the now obligatory community activities, gatherings, markets and festivities (Cracknell 2018, p. 22) required to sate the tourist's desire for authentic experiences and ensure that 'the traditions of a bygone era are kept alive for generations to come' (Meraas 2018a).

For the landscape architects, the challenge of the development lay in how to detail an entirely new project to appear authentic (Imanova 2018, p. 30). To this end, they drew inspiration from the historic photography of settlements along the Creek. As they explain:

> The design process was inspired by the elements and materials that made up daily life in Dubai. Against the backdrop of traditional architecture, such as barjeels [wind towers] and arish [palm-leaf architecture], Cracknell's choice of materials creates authentic moments at Al Seef.
>
> (Cracknell 2018, p. 20)

To achieve 'authenticity,' Cracknell used in-situ concrete to imitate the old, sandy alleyways and to achieve a 'less than perfect, authentic look – representing how it would have been laid over time' (Cracknell 2018, p. 22). Like Culture Village, the project confuses what is authentic historic urban form and what is simulation. The irony of such developments is that on a pleasant weekday afternoon, the Al Seef public domain is empty other than the ever-present security guards[3] (Figure 4.2, bottom photo) and a forlorn South Asian cleaner who fastidiously sprays and polishes the (apparently) dusty surface of the alleyway (Figure 4.2, top photo). While the project is pleasant and semi-successful in conjuring up the regional building traditions, any revival of the cultural milieu that generated these forms remains elusive.

Contemporary waterfronts

While the old town projects seek to revive the local built-form vernacular, other waterfront projects define a contemporary, urbane aesthetic for Dubai. (See Figure 4.3.) This form of contemporary urbscape reflects a desire of the regime to position Dubai globally as a leader (Moosavi, Makhzoumi & Grose 2016, p. 268). A generic expression, such urbscapes avoid regional design references, positing the project firmly within the global context. This generic landscape type is part of the regime's overarching programme to market the city as a 'safe' place to do business within the Middle East. Such urbscapes form part of 'the globe girdling cocoon' that Michael Sorkin identifies as enveloping the 'business traveller as he or she encounters the same airport, hotel' or waterfront 'from Denver to Dubai' (Sorkin 1992, xiv). Dubai's rulers achieve the perception of 'safety' (in part) through the creation of landscapes and urbanism that evoke a sense of familiarity for the business traveller and expatriate. The generic expression of such urbscape is also because its designers are (often) operating remotely and are not aware of or interested in local traditions and conditions. Without reference to the particularities of Dubai – extreme aridity and heat, amongst others – the resulting designs are completely generic (Moosavi, Makhzoumi & Grose 2016, p. 268).

Figure 4.3 The contemporary section of the Al Seef development along Dubai Creek.
Source: Photo by the author.

It is no coincidence that Dubai's rulers and master developers deliver such contemporary urban statements on Dubai's waterfronts. Waterfronts the world over are highly visible parts of their parent city and major sites for the production of contemporary design imagery. As Kim Dovey explains, 'the waterfront is an edge of the city and it has a certain edginess; it is a "front" or "frontier", a "face" or "mask" of the city that constructs urban character and identity' (Dovey 2005, p. 24). Through design, it can 'tell stories about who we are, where we have come from and where we are going; they establish what matters' (Dovey 2005, p. 18). This is particularly important for an aspirational global city, such as Dubai, because global city hierarchy can – to a large degree – be judged and modified through their waterfront images and realities (Oakley 2011, p. 223).

Presented as available for those who frequent Dubai's 'exclusive clubs and lobbies, gated seven-star hotels and jet-set malls,' these contemporary waterfronts prevent access by those who cannot afford the 'sophistication' – not by force but by price (Acuto 2010, p. 282). While in principle everybody is welcome, only well off tourists, expatriates and nationals can afford access, with low-income migrant workers in practice (generally) excluded (Acuto 2010, p. 282).

The Beach

An urbscape example that also aspires to global design language is The Beach development at Jumeriah Beach Residences. Designed by Cracknell, The Beach responded to the client Meras's brief to create a 'vibrant outdoor urban environment' (Landscape Middle East 2014, p. 18). Cracknell has sited this elegant project between the beach and a dense strip of tall residential and hotel towers on podiums. The project comprises an urban promenade dotted with beachside restaurants and bars, recreational amenities, retail outlets and food carts (Landscape Middle East 2014, p. 18). (See Figure 4.4.)

The promenade itself is paved with a mosaic cobble pattern using three grey tones to produce a pixelated wave pattern, which, according to Cracknell, 'represent the movement and eddies of the Arabian Sea washing onto the shore' (Landscape Middle East 2014, p. 21). The paving pattern also evokes other well-known urban projects such as Barcelona's Las Ramblas and Roberte Burle Marx's Copacabana promenade in Rio de Janeiro.

Where The Beach differs is in its array of high-end outdoor retail. Just a few metres off the promenade, a beach fashion outlet operates out of a shipping container and a luxury developer advertises their products in a shiny glass and steel pod. The project seamlessly mixes traditionally outdoor and indoor functions (Cracknell 2017, p. 19) and in many respects works like a shopping mall with its roof ripped off and dispersed along the beach. It is no surprise to see such emerging retail types inasmuch as Sheikh Mohammed

Figure 4.4 Top photo: the Beach's 'pixelated' wave pattern of the promenade; bottom photo: a beach fashion outlet operating out of a shipping container.

Source: Photos by the author.

has clearly advocated retail functions as being 'crucial' to Dubai's economic growth (Al Maktoum 2012, p. 144).

The Beach exudes an atmosphere reminiscent of California's Venice Beach or Sydney's Bondi Beach, providing a plethora of attractions, splashes of colour, sparkling water, palm trees and al fresco dining. However, developers and consultants have carefully contrived this atmosphere. Security guards constantly patrol, and one guard tells the mother of a young Western girl wearing a bikini that her daughter must cover her midriff. The hedonistic atmosphere that the project conjures up is an illusion.

Together with the exclusion of Dubai's underclass, this sanitization of experience results in a protected 'playground' for middle- and upper-class consumers. Techniques of exclusion here are more sophisticated than the walls and guarded entries of the gated communities. At The Beach, they include a lack of public transport from peripheral worker camps, aesthetic codes and the high pricing of parking, products, food and beverages. As Steve Velegrinis, head of master planning at Woods Bagot, explains, urban spaces such as The Beach are intended as 'places to see or be seen for those who can afford a $7 US coffee or bottle of Artesian Water' and that 'the number of shopping bags one carries matters in these places' (Velegrinis 2017, p. 40).

The Beach is inhabited by mostly Western expatriates and tourists (Velegrinis 2017, p. 40), who typically comprise the global leisure class. The irony of this situation is that Dubai's beaches were, prior to 2012, some of the only places in the city where you could find a truly representative mix of Dubai's multicultural population. Prior to the reconstitution of Dubai's beaches as retail destinations – such as Kite Beach and La Mer (Meraas 2018c) – beaches such as The Open Beach, on a Friday or Saturday, would be crammed with scantily clad Russian tourists basking in the sun, groups of unskilled migrant labourers, Western tourists and expatriates and, in the evening, Emiratis taking in the night air. Despite the 'improved high quality beach amenities' (Meraas 2018b), the reformulation of such spaces as retail destinations has erased some of the few truly unscripted and inclusive public spaces in Dubai.[4] (See Figure 4.5.)

Dubai Water Canal

Dubai's master developers have also created substantial new waterfront areas by excavating canals through previously landlocked sites – the inverse of the coastal super graphics (such as the Palm Jumeirah) that I discussed in the previous chapter. Nonetheless, the excavation of canals is part of the same coastal multiplication programme that aims to maximize water access, a powerful marketing tool for urban development. The most dramatic of these interior waterfronts is the Dubai Water Canal, a 6-kilometre-long waterway and promenade connecting The Gulf with the artificial extension of Dubai Creek into Business Bay, Dubai's effective Central Business

Figure 4.5 Top photo: The Open Beach in 2005, which Meraas has redeveloped as part of the La Mer project (bottom photo).

Sources: Top photo by the author; bottom photo by velirina/Shutterstock.com.

District. (See Figure 4.6.) The Canal terminates in a large 12-hectare lake at the base of the Burj Khalifa (currently the world's tallest tower), which contains the Dubai Fountain, designed to replicate and, needless to say, outdo Las Vegas's Bellagio Fountain (Acuto 2010, p. 278).

While developers are yet to deliver most of the urbanism that will eventually frame this canal, in time gourmet restaurants, boutiques, first-class hotels, a shopping mall, private marinas and a trade centre will line the canal. More than a device for luring global investment and tourists, developers project that the 'canal's green walkways and cycle paths will inspire a healthier and happier lifestyle' for Dubai's residents (Meydan & Sobha 2018). Landscape architectural firm Cracknell has been a 'key player' in the design for this promenade itself (Cracknell 2015, p. 22).

Dubai Water Canal is a transformative project for the city. While Dubai's urban grain runs parallel to the coast, the canal cuts across this structure and forges important pedestrian connections between the natural coastline and Business Bay. The canal has required the resumption and demolition of swaths of established housing, the truncation of both major and minor roads and the partial deletion of Al Safa Park, which was once one of the cities predominate green spaces (a trade-off that reflects the growing ascendency of urbscape over parascape). Clearly, such a dramatic vision required an autocratic and strong leader to wrestle it into reality.

Figure 4.6 Dubai Water Canal, a transformative project for the city.

Source: Photo by Jag_CZ/Shutterstock.com.

A cool night-time cycle journey along the length of the yet mostly undeveloped Dubai Water Canal reveals a plethora of Indian and Pakistani labourers and Filipino maids promenading in the relative darkness, lounging on benches and talking on the phone to perhaps partners, friends and family in their home countries. The test for Dubai is, when developers install the urban frame of the promenade, with its gourmet restaurants, boutiques, first-class hotels and exclusive malls, whether such a wide diversity of Dubai's cultural mix will feel 'at home' in appropriating this space.

Creativity hubs

Sheikh Mohammed aims to transform Dubai into one of the 'cultural epicentres of the world' (Newman 2016), an ambition supported by Dubai's Strategic Plan, which sets out to 'enrich the cultural environment by developing physical infrastructure to promote cultural activities' (Al Maktoum 2015, p. 29). These aims find expression in a series of planned 'creativity districts' – otherwise known as 'knowledge precincts,' 'knowledge locations' and 'innovation clusters' or 'districts' (Pancholi, Yigitcanlar & Guaralda 2017, p. 1). The government focus on fostering creativity stems from the need to establish a diversified base of economic activity to help the Emirate 'withstand future disruptive shocks to its economy' (Government of Dubai 2014, p. 17). Sheikh Mohammed declared in 2012 that 'we want Dubai to become a global centre for excellence and creativity' (Al Maktoum 2012, p. 130). While Sheikh Mohammed doesn't explain exactly what constitutes creativity, public intellectual Richard Florida defines creative occupations generally as including science and engineering, architecture and design, arts, music and entertainment, where the principle economic function is to create new ideas, new technology or new creative content (Florida 2002, p. 8).

The creative precincts that aim to deliver Sheikh Mohammed's ambitions are Dubai Design District and the Opera District. These precincts are clustered to manifest the theory of the 'agglomeration economy' implying that larger clusters of complementary businesses are effectively able to produce better outputs with the same inputs (Duranton & Puga 2013, p. 815). This is due to the advantages of clusters, which include a critical mass of workers and infrastructure and dense networks of suppliers and collaborators that collectively enable firms and workers to learn from one another (Nathan & Overman 2013, p. 386).

The creative precincts require Sheikh Mohammed to maintain a precarious balance between providing the freedom in which creativity thrives and not allowing subversion of the ruling dynasty. As Richard Florida reminds us, 'Creativity flourishes best in a unique kind of social environment: one that is stable enough to allow continuity of effort, yet diverse and broadminded enough to nourish creativity in all its subversive forms' (Florida 2002, p. 35). The creative class that Sheikh Mohammed aims to lure to Dubai has historically gravitated towards certain kinds of communities, such as the Left Bank in Paris or New York's Greenwich Village. Such places provide the stimulation, diversity and a richness of experiences that are the wellsprings of creativity (Florida 2002, p. 15) and are characterized by being tolerant, diverse and open to creativity (Florida 2002, p. x). As with the SEZs this requires a tricky balancing act by Dubai's rulers who simultaneously apply 'strict controls over creative processes' that undermine the ruling elite (Haines 2011, p. 166), while nourishing the creativity that is crucial to Dubai's economic prosperity.

An example of the regime's tendency to stamp out subversive creativity was the 2013 jailing of eight Dubai residents (including two Emiratis). Dubai authorities charged these residents with harming the image of UAE by producing a 'silly' spoof documentary and handed out prison sentences ranging from eight months to one year and fines up to $2,700 US (Al Ameri 2013). This example indicates that the regime believes there are right and wrong forms of creativity, as well as limits to the degree of creative subversion that they will tolerate.

Dubai Design District

Contemporary aspirations for Dubai to become a global centre for creativity (Al Maktoum 2012, p. 130) and assume a prominent position on the global design map (Landscape Middle East 2015a, p. 14) find expression in the Dubai Design District known as 'D3.' Developed by a subsidiary of Dubai Holding – of which Sheikh Mohammed is the current major shareholder – the yet unfinished project is located on the Dubai Water Canal adjacent to Business Bay. Designed by Wood Bagot, its developers, Tecom Group, intend it to function as an 'ecosystem for global design and creative minds . . . offering a full lifestyle experience; alive day and night offering a vibrant atmosphere and cutting-edge creative events more often found in London, New York, Paris and Milan' (Landscape Middle East 2015a, p. 16). The district seeks to capitalize on Dubai's status as highest per-capita consumers of luxury and designer goods (Velegrinis & Katodrytis 2015, p. 79). While still unfinished, D3 contains a plethora of high-end fashion boutiques to satisfy such consumers, as well as gourmet restaurants, cafes, bars and office spaces for design-related companies.

More than being a 'home to the region's community of creative thinkers,' d3 has recently introduced a set of 21 'smart initiatives' in an effort to contribute towards Dubai being one of the world's 'smartest' cities (Rogers 2017). So far, these include the obligatory electric vehicle–charging stations, smart working spaces, smart bus shelters and smart self-driving cars (Rogers 2017), as well as Wi-Fi for the whole development and facial recognition access control (Sutton 2017). The latter of these allow centralized monitoring of the district in relation to occupancy and the movement of people (Sutton 2017). These smart city initiatives have been developed in conjunction with Smart Dubai, a group 'whose mission is to create happiness through embracing technological innovation' (Rogers 2017). However, they allow the administrators of the creativity district (who are responsible to the major shareholder Sheikh Mohammed) the ability to closely monitor the districts workers for signs of subversion – or in the case of unskilled migrant workers, 'their performance, the bathroom breaks they take, who and for how long they talk with someone, and if they are ever out of position' (Haines 2011, p. 175).

The public domain of D3, designed by Cracknell, comprises minimalistic outdoor spaces, which seamlessly connect various buildings and merge exterior and interior spaces. The intention of the designers was to create a flexible, predominantly hard-scape solution suitable for hosting 'pop-up' design, art, music and fashion events, outdoor films and a plethora of urban art projects (Landscape Middle East 2015a, p. 15). Eschewing local references, these generic landscapes evoke the central city malls and streetscapes of global fashion hubs such as 'London, New York, Paris and Milan' (Landscape Middle East 2015a, p. 16) but could be (almost) anywhere. The minimalistic design extends to a relative lack of tree planting, glazed and reflective building facades and swaths of grey paving, which make D3 a furnace in Dubai's summer months.

The recreational facility for D3 is the funky Block Park, designed by landscape architecture firm desert INK. This award-winning project seeks to promote an image of creativity, hedonism and openness. However, in some areas, placemakers and destination branders have heavily stage-managed this ambience. (See Figure 4.7.) The stylish and contemporary aesthetic of Block Park derives from projects like Barcelona's San Sebastia Beach promenade with its urbane use of paving and gravel, precast concrete,[5] scatterings of date palms and splashes of colour. The clients and designers have directed the park towards the desires of a youthful creative class, and it includes a basketball and a volleyball court, climbing walls, equipment for table tennis, badminton and callisthenics, an urban beach, entertainment areas and a setting for food festivals.

The presence of a hip skatepark within the park is emblematic of the way Dubai's rulers and developers use urbscapes to promote certain images to a global audience. While skate parks in the West are (sometimes) associated with an anarchic teenage culture of antagonism towards society, in D3 and in other urbscapes such as La Mer, the skatepark functions as a transplanted symbol of subversion rather than a genuine site of resistance to authority. This is not to say that the skatepark is poorly designed or would not be fun for kids to skate; rather that such an offering embodies both a pragmatic purpose (i.e. skating) and a symbolic function in which it promotes an image of Dubai as an open society that is tolerant of subversion.

Figure 4.7 Urbscapes in D3 such as the funky Block Park promote an image of creativity, hedonism and openness. However, in some areas placemakers/ destination branders have heavily stage-managed this ambience – in this case, for the Miami Vibes Dubai Food Festival.

Source: Photo by the author.

The Opera District

While D3 comprises a creative hub that Dubai's rulers employ to attract a youthful creative class, Sheikh Mohammed is also intent on establishing Dubai as a centre for high culture through a new Opera District master-planned by multidisciplinary design firm HOK. The Opera District seeks to compete with Frank Gehry's Louvre Gallery in Abu Dhabi – amongst others – as the marketing exemplifies:

> In the Opera District, Dubai will find its new cultural soul. Located in the thriving precinct of Downtown Dubai, this new centre for the very best in global culture will set out to capture the hearts and minds of every visitor. With Dubai Opera, a multi-format, performing arts centre at its core, it will attract performers from around the world to a thronging audience in Dubai. From searching all nations for their

greatest talents, to showcasing the best of the UAE, Dubai Opera will highlight an unprecedented artistic exchange and change the face of local culture forever.

(Emaar 2018b)

The Opera District – which the developers Emaar humbly promote as 'the most prestigious square kilometre in the world' – will in time house a dedicated modern art museum, two new 'art hotels,' design studios and galleries (Emaar 2018a), as well as an assortment of commercial and residential developments. The centrepiece of the district is the recently opened Dubai Opera building. Dubai Opera is considered by its proponents a 'masterpiece of contemporary design' (Landscape Middle East 2017, p. 12). Since opening in 2016, Dubai Opera has entertained thousands of visitors from all around the world with theatre productions, ballets, operas, orchestras, fashion shows, conferences, galleries and art exhibitions (Landscape Middle East 2017, p. 12).

Structuring the Opera District is the 3.5-kilometre long Mohammed Bin Rashid Boulevard, which its proponents intend will serve as the dining, entertainment, culture and arts nucleus of Downtown Dubai (Emaar 2018a) – and perhaps flatter the ego of Sheikh Mohammed. The landscape of this extended urbscape is grand, with polished stone finishes, extravagant lighting displays, Parisian-style al fresco outdoor dining and regular plantings of Dubai's ubiquitous date palms.

The symbolism of such a project is no doubt partly a reaction to the stinging criticisms of Dubai, by detractors, that Dubai is superficial and lacking in culture. Through the high-culture associations of opera, Sheikh Mohammed is attempting to recast Dubai not as a mindless consumer of luxury but as an active participant in, and creator of high culture. While this campaign seeks to bolster national pride and identity, it also embodies an economic imperative in that such projects are crucial to Dubai's capacity to lure global investment and tourism, which in turn ensure its continued economic prosperity.

In conclusion to this section, Dubai's urbscapes represent a comparatively new form of designed landscape for the city. The projects I have reviewed herald an emerging yet sophisticated design culture in Dubai. Nonetheless, despite their (apparently) benign qualities, the urbscapes I have discussed encapsulate cultural and political agendas that are generally not recognized by the professions or that (understandably) have been subsumed by commercial concerns. It is this slippage between what the urban professions presume such landscape types to signify, such as societal 'openness' and the reinforcing of local culture, and the realities of their implicit cultural and political agendas, which I have attempted to tease out in this section.

Xeriscape narratives

While urbscape in Dubai provides an alternative to parascape, another designed landscape type, xeriscape, challenges parascape. This takes the form of xerophytic landscapes that designers have conceived to minimize water and fertilizer consumption and to resonate with the local 'sense of place.'

Dubai's Government is (to some degree) driving this transition, and certainly government documents pay lip service to the sustainable use of resources. The '2021 Dubai Plan' and 'Dubai 2020 Urban Masterplan' both aim for a city that 'uses its resources sustainably over the long-term' (Government of Dubai 2014, p. 15) and that achieves a 'balance between urban development and conservation of natural environments' (Government of Dubai 2012, p. 1). The Dubai Municipality is also attempting to reduce Dubai's profligate water usage, which amounts to 550 litres per day per capita – a figure that is one of the highest in the world (Dubai Municipality 2016). The Municipality are tackling this through putting a 'strict' limit on the usage of treated wastewater for irrigating private land (Dubai Municipality 2016).

It is unclear to what degree such Municipality initiatives reflect Sheikh Mohammed's motivations. His book *My Vision* refers only to sustainability in an economic sense of the word, and his pet projects (such as The Sheikh Mohammed Bin Rashid Gardens project) require vast inputs of water, fertilizer and energy. Perhaps Sheikh Mohammed's ambivalence towards xeriscape is that, with exhausted oil reserves and ever uncertain economic conditions, Dubai may not always have the required water and energy supplies to maintain the huge swaths of parascape created to date. The fear for Dubai's ruler is that if the green of parascape were to 'wither' and die, so too could the political legitimization it provides.

As a result, landscape design firms (in particular) are driving a timely shift to xerophytic landscapes. In this respect, Duncan Denley, managing director of landscape design firm desert INK, explains they been developing local material and plant pallets 'to create something that looks like it belongs here' that 'will be inherently more sustainable' not needing the 'huge investment of an extensive irrigation system to survive' (Denley 2015, p. 23). The UAE Government, through the Estidama[6] programme, has also established regulations for landscape and urban design. As a result, some landscape architectural firms in Dubai have adapted their 'specifications, water demand strategies, plant lists and material selections' to support Estidama as 'much as is feasible' (Cracknell 2012, p. 14)

More than a technical exercise in minimizing water usage, quasi arid landscapes referencing the local reality often arise to assuage the nagging doubt that an expatriate designer can experience concerning cultural authenticity while working in a 'foreign' context. This is also the case for designers of Middle Eastern background, 'many of whom are deeply concerned with the imposition of designs which ultimately change or conceal locally distinctive characteristics, and create a break between communities, their past and their land' (Moosavi, Makhzoumi & Grose 2016, p. 276). In response to such concerns, the indigenous landscape and culture of the Arabian Peninsula become a source of inspiration to generate contemporary landscape design.

The archetypal landscapes and urban forms designers reference are most commonly those of the desert, the *wadi*[7] and its 'braided systems of dry and occasional deluges' (Moosavi, Makhzoumi & Grose 2016, p. 272), traditional agricultural landscapes with intricate irrigation channels (*faluj*[8]) and traditional Arabic Islamic urban forms, all of which have been shaped by the dictates of aridity (Makhzoumi 2002, p. 219). However, such references to these landscape and urban morphologies are often form driven rather than replicating or engaging with the 'underlying processes and ecological and cultural dynamics within these landscapes' (Moosavi, Makhzoumi & Grose 2016, p. 276). Such projects include the dune forms at the Dubai Convention Centre and Dubai Autodrome (both of which are now demolished) and the *wadi*-style landscapes in the Festival City streetscapes and public realm (Cracknell 2012, p. 16) and in the entry landscaping of the Dubai Hills development. (See Figure 4.8.)

Ironically, the recreation of these archetypal landscapes in design projects can sometimes occur in parallel with the destruction of the original landscapes. For instance, the Dubai Government prohibited construction firms from removing cobbles from authentic *wadis*, in part to build replicas, because the original *wadis* were becoming severely depleted of stones.

Figure 4.8 A *wadi*-inspired landscape design at Dubai Hills.

Source: Photo by the author.

Similarly, landscape designers deploy dune motifs in urban projects at the same time as Dubai sprawls further into the Rub al Khali desert, which has a detrimental effect on desert ecology.

Xeriscape developments also, to some degree, carry their own cultural and political agendas. As with the urbscape old town developments I discussed earlier, xeriscape – through reference to the archetypal natural and cultural landscapes of the region – resonates with Sheikh Mohammed's aim to protect 'national identity, culture and way of life' (Al Maktoum 2015, p. 12). In this respect, xeriscape reasserts Emirati culture in the face of a numerically dominant expatriate community, as well as aligning with measures to increase awareness of the local culture (Al Maktoum 2015, p. 27). In Dubai, developers also deploy xeriscape to promote, typically deceptive, image of Dubai as sustainable and environmentally responsible to a local, regional and global audience.

Xeriscape projects

Xeriscape projects assume different forms in Dubai; nonetheless, the over-arching narrative of minimizing resource use and connecting with the local sense of place remain. The projects I set out in this section include a proposal for an approximately 340-hectare new park (Project 'P'), a 45-hectare new urban district (Xeritown) and a new 5-hectare sports hub (Green Sports Hub).

Project 'P'

An example of a key xeriscape in Dubai was a proposal for a 4-kilometre long park, called project 'P,'[9] designed by multidisciplinary Australian design firm Urbis, sited near the base of the Jebel Ali Palm. This project is now defunct, probably because the adjacent Jebel Ali Palm development remains 'on-hold' and possibly because of the proposed park's significant size. Its developers predictably succumbed to the 'lure of the large' and proposed that it should be commensurate in scale with Manhattan's Central Park.

Regardless, the project is instructive in relation to the design processes of xeriscape. Facing the challenge of providing a convincing narrative for a vast and largely undifferentiated expanse, Urbis structured the proposed park in four sections, each roughly a kilometre long, which would 'tell the story of the Arabs coming out of the desert' (Anonymous landscape architect 2009). The first section was to represent a formal interpretation of the desert landscape, the landscape from which the Arabs 'had emerged.'[10] The second section was to consist of an interpretation of traditional Emirati agricultural landscapes, including plantings of dates and pistachios and traditional *faluj* irrigation systems (Anonymous landscape architect 2009). The third was a tribute to Islamic culture, which was 'actually based on Islamic values and attitudes' (Anonymous landscape architect 2009) and was to consist of a series of for-mal interpretations of Islamic gardens (none of which existed historically in Dubai). The fourth, somewhat ambiguous section of the park was to comprise contemporary Islamic gardens or at least 'our interpretation of what they might look like' (Anonymous landscape architect 2009). Clearly, the designer's remote location and lack of in-depth knowledge of Emirati culture forced them to take a few liberties with how the theme manifests in form.

While the design was superficial, constructed around a series of generalizations about Emirati culture, it emerged from a genuine desire of outside designers to avoid foisting Western design on a 'regional' culture and an unfamiliar desert landscape. As one of the designers explains in relation to Emirati culture, 'I would prefer to see them have strength of character to take possession of their own country and we can work around them. It's a much more honourable thing' (Anonymous landscape architect 2009). Further to this, its designers regard the park as a tool with which to address cultural relations through landscape design:

> [The park] brings back some of the social awareness and recognition of the values that Arab culture has made to agriculture and horticulture . . . .[T]he paradise garden is the iconic element in the foundation of western landscape architecture . . . to actually have that expressed in the landscaping and give that back to the Arabs to say; 'look you guys really did this and we've been trading off you ever since.'
> (Anonymous landscape architect 2009)

The contradiction inherent in such projects, however, is that, given the lack of Emirati landscape designers, clients task designers from elsewhere to interpret this connection to place and culture. Further, whereas regionalist design 'incorporates regional elements in order to represent aspirations of liberation from a power perceived as alien and illegitimate' (Lefaivre 2003, p. 13), this is contradicted when the resistance comes from within the 'alien power' itself (Lefaivre 2003, p. 13). Instead of resisting the global homogeneity that parascape exemplifies, the project risks producing a nostalgic theme park that commodifies (and trivializes) Arabic culture for global consumption.

While constructed arid landscapes, designed to reference to the local 'sense of place,' can embody a sincere engagement with 'place' and culture, they can also be a means to gain approval of a scheme by clients or regulatory bodies. As P. Johnson and Kathryn Moore conclude, the tendency of landscape designers to engage with the 'genius loci' is often to 'justify the correctness of what they design, mostly without external verification' (Johnson 1994). The recourse to the genius loci in such xeriscape projects in Dubai becomes a potent method to garner approval from clients by superficially ameliorating concerns about the marginalization of traditional Emirati culture.

Xeritown

Planning for xeriscape in Dubai found its purest expression in the 45-hectare Xeritown urban development for 7,000 people proposed to be part of the Dubailand mega project. The project was to be a 'test site' for sustain-ability, through both minimizing the use of water and maximizing the recy cling of water. Despite its worthy intent, Dubai Properties, the developers of Xeritown, cancelled the project as Dubailand struggled due to the severe impacts of the Global Financial Crisis and Dubai's fiscal crisis.

Master-planned by X-Architects from Dubai, the design philosophy of Xeritown was significant in that it was one of the few urban projects in Dubai that rejected the tabula rasa of conceptualization of the desert, which is typical of parascape. (See Figure 4.9.) To this end, in the project's design process, humid zones were mapped out from satellite imagery of exist-ing vegetation, as areas to be protected from development[11] (Al Manakh 2007, p. 52). The proposed landscape was to remain (predominantly) arid with more verdant green areas concentrated in humid zones mapped out from satellite imagery of existing vegetation. This sensitive and site-specific approach rarely occurs in Dubai and particularly not within the Dubailand context, which was a giant, parascape infused theme park.

The urbanism of Xeritown was a contemporary interpretation of tradi-tional Arabic Islamic urbanism (Al Manakh 2007, p. 52) which, like desert landscapes, has been shaped by the dictates of aridity (Makhzoumi 2002, p. 219). Replete with shaded souqs, verdant courtyards protected by low-rise built-form and wind towers, designers set out the urban form in a linear manner to facilitate 'breathability' and to funnel cooling breezes through the development.

Green Sports Hub

A current xeriscape project in Dubai, which (the aptly named) SAND is developing, is the Green Sports Hub. Its developers intend that when it opens in 2020, the project will be the 'premiere destination for sports training, sports leisure and sports tourism in Dubai' (SLA 2018, p. 17). To achieve this ambition, the 5-hectare project will consist of sports academies, indoor and outdoor sports facilities, shops, restaurants, a gym and a sports hotel (SLA 2018, p. 17).

Designers of the project SLA have based their landscape strategy on 'local landscape typologies' – in particular the Middle East's *wadi* systems that channel both water and greenery (SLA 2018, p. 17). SLA's use of a *wadi* as the conceptual model serves two main purposes.

Firstly, it creates an ordering logic for vegetation, the '*wadi*' acting as a central green corridor that connects the various functions of the hub and that, through passive cooling, creates 'refreshing shade, gentle breezes and a natural lowering of the temperature' (SLA 2018, p. 18). The planting of the *wadi* was based on SLA's (apparently) comprehensive research on all the native plants in the UAE (SLA 2018, p. 18). (See Figure 4.10.)

Figure 4.9 Xeritown.

Source: Images by SMAQ, X-Architects.

Figure 4.10 The Green Sports Hub.
Source: Images by SLA, Cedra.

Secondly, through referencing a uniquely Middle Eastern landscape phenomenon, the designers SLA, who are from Denmark, flatter Emirati clients by 'celebrating and expressing the unique nature and culture of the UAE' (SLA 2018, p. 18). Again, landscape designers in Dubai sometimes use this form of flattery to elicit approvals from Emirati clients for project design strategies. Moreover, by positioning the landscape strategy in relation to an endemic landscape type, landscape designers feel reassured they are delivering a landscape design that resonates with the spirit of place, even though they may be designing the project from a remote location, as in this case. Nonetheless, Green Sports Hub displays an unusual affinity with its desert context and should help to further expertise in xerophytic, endemic plant species.

Conclusion

In this chapter, I have discussed the cultural and political narratives that urbscapes and xeriscapes promote. Despite their apparently benign qualities, the urbscapes the urban professions are producing in Dubai encapsulate cultural, societal and political agendas that the professions do not tend to recognize or that commercial concerns have subsumed.[12] I have identified that Dubai's rulers directly or indirectly use urbscape to project the image of an open society to the global community and, in the case of nostalgic urbscape, to evoke the idea that their authority is indigenous. I have explained that expatriate landscape designers, ironically, design xeriscape to evoke the local 'sense of place,' an aim which resonates with Sheikh Mohammed's goal to protect 'national identity, culture and way of life.' However the formal recreation of these archetypal landscapes (E.g. 'the desert') in design projects can occur in parallel with the destruction of the original landscapes elsewhere. The slippage between the presumptions of what Dubai designed landscape types signify, such as societal openness, historical continuity, or environmental sensitivity and the realities of their implicit agendas has been the focus of this chapter. In the next chapter, I use the now well-defined landscape types of parascape, urbscape and xeriscape to assess the current practice of the urban disciplines in Dubai in relation to global aspirations for environmental sustainability, societal inclusiveness and cultural sensitivity.

Notes

1 Of course, an increasing focus on well designed, activated urban spaces is not just happening in Dubai – many global cities are attempting to lure the investment and tourism that such spaces can attract. Indeed, the evolution of Las Vegas's Strip, in some respects, mirrors that of Dubai (Al 2015). Where the Las Vegas experience differs from Dubai is the degree to which a single autocratic ruler controls this cultivation of urbanity.

2 Dubai has always been a land of trade and migration, and as such it does not have a specific architectural typology or urban morphology but rather a mix of various influences, mainly based on Arabian and Persian vernacular heritages (Carbonell 2016). ' As a result, many of the recreated forms have been influenced, whether wittingly or not, by a body of literature produced by Western Orientalists purporting to describe the essence of the Islamic city (Abu-Lughod 1987).

3 The presence of security guards in Dubai's urbscapes also reflects an ever present threat of terrorism that has the potential to damage Dubai's reputation as a 'safe place' for Westerners to live and conduct business in the Gulf region.

4 This tendency for development to erase areas that have a genuine cultural mix occurs elsewhere. Threatening historic neighbourhoods such as Satwa, which provided a 'real mix' of Dubai's multicultural population, are large-scale redevelopments such as Jumeirah Gardens (Reisz 2010).

5 The project recycled 27 tons of concrete block forms, which the contractors had left over after building the Dubai Water Canal.

6 The word *Estidama* refers to 'sustainability' in Arabic (Estidama 2008).

7 *Wadi* is the Arabic word for a dry land river.

8 A *faluj* is a narrow channel of water used for irrigation in traditional Emirati agriculture.

9 I have not revealed the project's real name due to a secrecy clause, and thus I will refer to the project as Project 'P.'

10 The difficulty of replicating the desert landscape exactly was described by the designers: '[Y]ou can't just build a desert landscape because when the Shamal comes it will blow all over the joint (Anonymous landscape architect 2009). Thus, the designers abstracted the desert landscape to be stabilized and as such suitable for urban conditions.

11 I do wonder whether this approach would be somewhat self-defeating in that the urbanism and constructed landscape, regardless of its location, would be likely to significantly change existing patterns of humidity anyway.
12 While this assertion is difficult to prove, I have arrived at this opinion through reviewing the UAE and Middle Eastern landscape architectural magazines *Commercial Outdoor Design* and *Landscape Middle East*, in which landscape design's relevance to Dubai culture in a wider sense is not largely referenced, as well as from my experience engaging with the urban professions in Dubai.

References

Abu-Lughod, JL 1987, 'The Islamic City – Historic Myth, Islamic Essence, and Contemporary Relevance', in H Amirahmadi & S El-Shakhs (eds), *Urban Development in the Muslim World*, pp. 11–36, Transaction Publishers, London.

Acuto, M 2010, 'High-Rise Dubai Urban Entrepreneurialism and the Technology of Symbolic Power', *Cities*, no. 27, pp. 272–284.

Al Ameri, K 2013, 'Spoof Video Case Shines Light on How We Are as a Society', *The National*. Available from: www.thenational.ae/spoof-video-case-shines-light-on-how-we-are-as-a-society-1.299212. [07.06].

Al Maktoum, MBR 2012, *My Vision: Challenges in the Race for Excellence*, Motivate Publishing, Dubai.

Al Maktoum, MBR 2015, *Dubai Strategic Plan: Highlights*, Dubai Government, Dubai.

Al Manakh 2007, 'Project with the Secret Name', *Al Manakh*, vol. 12, no. 7, pp. 52–55.

Al, S 2015, 'The Evolving Architecture of Pleasure', *LA+*, no. Pleasure, pp. 46–53.

Anonymous landscape architect 2009, *Interview*, J Bolleter.

Bakshi, A 2014, 'Urban Form and Memory Discourses: Spatial Practices in Contested Cities', *Journal of Urban Design*, vol. 19, no. 2, pp. 189–210.

Bowring, J 2013, 'Navigating the Global, the Regional and the Local: Researching Globalization and Landscape', in P Howard, I Thompson & E Waterton (eds), *The Routledge Companion to Landscape Studies*, pp. 263–271, Routledge, Oxon.

Brand Dubai 2018, *Brand Dubai*, Dubai Media Office. Available from: www.brand-dubai.com/indexen.php/. [18.08].

Carbonell, A 2016, 'Dubai: The Political Project of a New Metropolis', in G Katodrytis & S Syed (eds), *Gulf Cities as Interfaces*, pp. 229–242, Gulf Research Centre Cambridge, Jeddah.

Caton, S & Ardalan, N 2010, *New Arab Urbanism: The Challenge to Sustainability and Culture in the Gulf*, Harvard Kennedy School, Cambridge, MA.

Condon, P 1994, 'A Built Landscape Typology: The Language of the Land We Live In', in K Franck & L Schneekloth (eds), *Ordering Space: Types in Architecture and Design*, pp. 79–94, Van Nostrand Reinhold, New York.

Cracknell 2012, 'Interview: Cracknell Have Responded to the Challenge of the Changing World Economic Situation', *Landscape Middle East*, 1, no. 6, pp. 10–16.

Cracknell 2015, 'Connecting Destinations', *Landscape Middle East*, pp. 20–22.

Cracknell 2017, 'Transformers of the Public Realm', *Landscape Middle East*, pp. 18–19.

Cracknell 2018, 'Al Seef, Dubai', *Landscape Middle East*, pp. 20–23.

Crewe, K & Forsyth, A 2003, 'Landscapes: A Typology of Approaches to Landscape Architecture', *Landscape Journal*, vol. 22, no. 1–3, pp. 37–53.

Davis, M 2007, 'Fear and Money in Dubai', *Topos*, pp. 62–70.

Denley, D 2015, 'Interview', *Landscape Middle East*, pp. 22–28.

Dovey, K 2005, *Fluid City: Transforming Melbourne's Urban Waterfront*, Routledge, London and New York.

Dovey, K 2016, *Urban Design Thinking*, Bloomsbury Academic, London.

Dubai Municipality 2016, *A Sustainable Dubai*, Government of Dubai and Go Dubai, Dubai.

Dubai Properties 2018, *Dubai Wharf*, Dubai Properties. Available from: https://richlanddubai.com/wp-content/uploads/2017/07/Dubai-Wharf-Brochure.pdf. [04.04].

Duranton, G & Puga, D 2013, 'The Growth of Cities', CEPR Discussion Paper No. DP9590, pp. 751–853, Center for Economic and Policy Research, Washington, DC.

Emaar 2018a, 'BLVD Heights', *Emaar*. Available from: www.emaar.com/en/Images/FINAL_BLVD_HEIGHTS.white_tcm223-66054.pdf [04.04].

Emaar 2018b, 'Forte: The Opera District', *Emaar*. Available from: www.emaar.com/en/Images/Forte%20Brochure%20V5_tcm223-79963.pdf. [04.04].

Estidama 2008, 'Who Are We?' *Estidama*. Available from: www.estidama.org/aboutestidama/default_en_gb.aspx. [06.09].

Florida, R 2002, *Rise of the Creative Class*, Basic Books, New York.

Forstenlechner, I, Rutledge, E & Salem Alnuaimi, R 2017, *The UAE, the "Arab Spring" and Different Types of Dissent*, The Middle East Policy Council, Washington. [07.04].

Forty, A 2000, *Words and Buildings*, Thames and Hudson, London.

Gharipour, M 2016, *Contemporary Urban Landscapes of the Middle East*, Routledge, London.

Government of Dubai 2012, *Dubai 2020 Urban Masterplan*, Government of Dubai, Dubai.

Government of Dubai 2014, *2021 Dubai Plan*, Government of Dubai and Go Dubai, Dubai.

Haines, C 2011, 'Cracks in the Façade: Landscapes of Hope and Desire in Dubai', in *Worlding Cities: Asian Experiments and the Art of Being Global*, pp. 160–181, Blackwell, Chichester.

Hamouche, M 2004, 'The Changing Morphology of the Gulf Cities in the Age of Globalisation: The Case of Bahrain', *Habitat International*, no. 28, pp. 521–540.

Hyde, R 2010, 'Dubai Bashing', *Al Manakh- Gulf Cont'd*, vol. 25, no. 2, p. 68.

Johnson, P 1994, *The Theory of Architecture Concepts, Themes and Practices*, Van Nostrand Reinhold, New York.

Kanna, A 2010, 'Flexible Citizenship in DUBAI: Neoliberal Subjectivity in the Emerging "City-Corporation"', *Cultural Anthropology*, vol. 25, no. 1, pp. 100–129.

Klein, N 2000, *No Logo*, Flamingo, London.

Landscape Middle East 2014, 'The Beach', *Landscape Middle East*, pp. 18–21.

Landscape Middle East 2015a, 'Cracknell Is the Landscape Architect for Dubai's New Design District', *Landscape Middle East*, pp. 14–16.

Landscape Middle East 2015b, 'Mall of the World', *Landscape Middle East*, pp. 10–14.

Landscape Middle East 2017, 'Flowpoint Is the Star of the Show in Dubai', *Landscape Middle East*, p. 12.

Lefaivre, L 2003, 'Critical Regionalism: A Facet of Modern Architecture Since 1945', in L Lefaivre & A Tzonis (eds), *Critical Regionalism, Architecture and Identity in a Globalized World*, pp. 24–56, Prestel Publishing, London.

Lindstrom, K, Palang, H & Kull, K 2013, 'Semiotics of Landscape', in P Howard, I Thompson & E Waterton (eds), *The Routledge Companion to Landscape Studies*, pp. 97–107, Routledge, Oxon.

Lmanova, A 2018, 'Al Seef', *Middle East Architect*, vol. 12, no. 3, pp. 30–32.

Mahgoub, Y 2004, 'Globalization and the Built Environment in Kuwait', *Habitat International*, no. 28, pp. 505–519.

Makhzoumi, JM 2002, 'Landscape in the Middle East: An Inquiry', *Landscape Research*, vol. 27, no. 3, pp. 213–228.

McGuirk, J 2018, 'Can Cities Make Us Better Citizens?' *The New Yorker*. Available from: www.newyorker.com/books/page-turner/can-cities-make-us-better-citizens. [26.04].

The Media Office 2018, *Mission, Vision, Values*, Government of Dubai. Available from: www.mediaoffice.ae/en/the-media-office/mission-vision-values.aspx. [18.08].

Meraas 2018a, 'Al Seef', *Meraas*. Available from: www.meraas.com/en/destinations/al-seef/. [09.10].

Meraas 2018b, 'La Mer', *Meraas*. Available from: www.meraas.com/en/destinations/la-mer/. [09.10].

Meraas 2018c, *Meraas*, Meraas. Available from: www.meraas.com/en/. [09.10].

Meydan & Sobha 2018, *Cassia at the Fields*, Meydan. Available from: http://gco-properties.com/wp-content/uploads/2017/05/cassia_main_brochure_on.pdf. [04.04].

Moosavi, S, Makhzoumi, J & Grose, M 2016, 'Landscape Practice in the Middle East Between Local and Global Aspirations', *Landscape Research*, vol. 41, no. 3, pp. 265–278.

Nagraj, A 2014, 'Dubai's Ruler Approves Dhs2bn Creek Front Project', *Gulf Business*. Available from: http://gulfbusiness.com/dubais-ruler-approves-dhs2bn-creek-front-project/. [09.05].

Nathan, M & Overman, H 2013, 'Agglomeration, Clusters, and Industrial Policy', *Oxford Review of Economic Policy*, vol. 29, no. 2, pp. 383–404.

Newman, H 2016, 'How Creative Placemaking Is Helping Put Dubai on the Cultural Map', *In Business.ae*. Available from: http://www.mediavataarme.com/index.php/industry-news/advertising/item/5200-brand-dubai-how-creative-placemaking-is-helping-put-dubai-on-the-cultural-map. [09.05].

Oakley, S 2011, 'Re-Imagining City Waterfronts: A Comparative Analysis of Governing Renewal in Adelaide, Darwin and Melbourne', *Urban Policy and Research*, vol. 29, no. 3, pp. 221–238.

Orff, K 2001, 'Landscape', in *Great Leap Forward*, pp. 336–417, Harvard Design School, Cambridge.

Pancholi, S, Yigitcanlar, T & Guaralda, M 2017, 'Place Making for Innovation and Knowledge-Intensive Activities: The Australian Experience', *Technological Forecasting and Social Change*. Available from: https://www.researchgate.net/publication/319993085_Place_making_for_innovation_and_knowledge-inten-sive_activities_The_Australian_experience.

Petch, N 2018, *The Amazing Pull of 'Brand Dubai'*. Virtuzone Business Intelligence. Available from: https://vz.ae/the-amazing-pull-of-brand-dubai/. [18.08].

Reisz, T 2010, 'Jumeirah Gardens and the Urban Checklist', *Al Manakh- Gulf Cont'd*, vol. 25, no. 2, pp. 55–57.

Rogers, J 2017, *21 Smart New Initiatives at Dubai Design District*. Emirates Woman. Available from: http://emirateswoman.com/21-smart-new-initiatives-dubai-design-district/. [29.10].

SLA 2018, 'Green Sports Hub Is a True Sports Community Hub', *Landscape Middle East*, pp. 16–20.

Sorkin, M 1992, *Variations on a Theme Park*, Hill and Wang, New York.

Stadnicki, R, Pierre-Arnaud, B & Vignal, L 2014, 'Assessing Urban Development After the Arab Spring: Illusions and Evidences of Change', *Built Environment*, vol. 40, no. 1, pp. 5–13.

Sutton, M 2017, *Dubai Design District Unveils Smart Plans*, Arabian Industry, Abu Dhabi. [29.10].

Swaffield, S & Deming, E 2011, 'Research Strategies in Landscape Architecture: Mapping the Terrain', *Journal of Landscape Architecture*, Spring, pp. 34–45.

Teo, S 2014, 'Political Tool or Quality Experience? Urban Livability and the Singaporean State's Global City Aspirations', *Urban Geography*, vol. 35, no. 6, pp. 916–937.

Velegrinis, S 2017, 'Night Time: Ecology and Nocturnal Urbanism in the Gulf', *Landscape Middle East*, pp. 38–44.

Velegrinis, S & Katodrytis, G 2015, 'Drawing on Sand: Cities in the Making', *Architectural Design*, vol. 85, no. 1, pp. 72–79.

5 Challenges in practice

Introduction

The survey of Dubai's designed landscapes in the previous chapters led to the identification of three principal types that the urban professions produce: firstly, the paradisiacal image of greening the desert (parascape); secondly, heavily themed and managed urban spaces (urbscape); and finally, xerophytic designed landscapes that reference the Rub al Khali desert (xeriscape). The major hypothesis of this chapter is that the urban professions in Dubai, as 'handmaidens' of global capital, struggle to reconcile practice with pressing environmental, societal and cultural issues (Bolleter 2009). In establishing this claim, I compare the designed landscapes of the urban professions with the 'shared ideals' for cities ventured by the United Nations and others to identify a major discrepancy between theory and practice. To structure this enquiry, I pose twin research questions, firstly:

> What environmental, societal and cultural goals should the urban professions aspire to in landscape design practice in Dubai?

And secondly:

> Do the landscape designs produced by the urban professions in Dubai conform to prevailing environmental, societal and cultural goals for practice?

In answering the first question, I conduct a literature review on existing normative frameworks for assessing design practice. This review includes the charters of the United Nations and its Sustainable Development Goals and the charters of the International Federation of Landscape Architects (IFLA), of the International Union of Architects and the International Society of City and Regional Planners. These charters, in part, reflect aspirations for sustainability, social equity and inclusiveness, and cultural sensitivity and enrichment.

In answering the second question, I employ an evaluative research strategy (Swaffield & Deming 2011) to assess the landscape design practice of the urban professions against the normative framework established in the first section of this chapter. This exploration identifies slippages between theory and practice, which I focus on reconciling in latter chapters.

A brief note to readers regarding terminology: as in earlier chapters, I use the term 'landscape designers' as inclusive of planners, urban designers, landscape architects, architects and placemakers – all of whom have an influence on the design of constructed landscapes in Dubai. I refer to these disciplines collectively as the 'urban professions.'

Body

In this section, I analyze the goals for urban development, planning and design set out by the United Nations (UN) (United Nations 2017; United Nations Development Programme 2014; United Nations General Assembly 2016), the International Federation of Landscape Architects (IFLA) (International Federation of Landscape Architects Asia Pacific 2015), the International Union of Architects (IUA) and the International Society of City and Regional Planners (ISOCARP).

A normative framework for evaluating practice

The UN is an intergovernmental organization whose objectives include promoting human rights, fostering social and economic development and protecting the environment. The UN is the largest, most familiar, internationally represented and powerful intergovernmental organization in the world (United Nations 2018). In understanding the UN's goals for urban development, I refer to the UN Sustainable Development Goals (United Nations 2017) and the draft Outcome Document of the United Nations Conference on Housing and Sustainable Urban Development (Habitat III) (United Nations General Assembly 2016).

IFLA is the global governing body for all national landscape architectural associations (International Federation of Landscape Architects 2003). For the purposes of this chapter, I reference the IFLA Asia–Pacific Region Landscape Charter, as no charter informing the practice of landscape architecture currently exists for the Africa–Middle East region. Nonetheless, the Asia Pacific Region Landscape Charter extends to nearby Iran, and I therefore believe the same key principles are broadly relevant to Dubai. The IFLA explain that this charter serves as a set of guiding principles for landscape architects (International Federation of Landscape Architects Asia Pacific 2015, p. 4).

The International Society of City and Regional Planners (ISOCARP) brings together individual and institutional members from more than 80 countries globally. Members are planners and other stakeholders involved in the development of the built environment. Recognized by the UN and the United Nations Human Settlements Programme (UNHCS/UN-HABITAT) in particular as a non-governmental organization, ISOCARP also has a formal consultative status with the United Nations Education, Scientific and Cultural Organisation (UNESCO) (International Society of City and Regional Planners 2017). Given these connections, I treat ISOCARPS goals for practice as aligned with those of the UN.

Similarly, the International Union of Architects (IUA) responds directly to the UN Sustainable Development Goals. In doing so, the IUA aims to ensure that 'architects are not just responsive to the new agenda for Sustainable Development, but prescriptive in its implementation and evolution' (International Union of Architects 2017). Given this situation, I treat IUA's goals for practice as aligned with those of the UN.

In the following section I discuss the shared goals for city planning and design – as defined by the UN, IFLA, ISOCARP and IUA – in relation to environmental, societal and cultural aspirations.

Environmental goals

The UN advocates for cities and urban centres that protect, conserve and restore their ecosystems, water, natural habitats and biodiversity, minimize their environmental impact, and embody sustainable consumption and production patterns (United Nations General Assembly 2016, p. 4). This is proposed to be achieved by integrating ecosystem and biodiversity values into national and local planning and development processes (United Nations 2015, p. 29).

These sentiments are also present in the IFLA Asia Pacific Region Landscape Charter that sets out that landscape architects should aspire to sustainable management of landscapes through considering and integrating ecological health, economic viability, social vitality and cultural expression (International Federation of Landscape Architects Asia Pacific 2015, p. 4). This chapter focusses specifically on Principle 3.3 Stewardship:

> We all have a responsibility to nurture the continued health and diversity of landscapes, and ensure the sustainable integration of protection, production, recreation, and habitation values for all living things.
> (International Federation of Landscape
> Architects Asia Pacific 2015, p. 5)

Societal goals

The UN advocates for cities and human settlements that promote inclusivity and ensure that all inhabitants, without discrimination of any kind, are able to inhabit just, safe, healthy, accessible, affordable, resilient and sustainable urban areas to foster prosperity and 'quality of life for all' (United Nations General Assembly 2016, p. 4). In more detail, such areas are to promote civic engagement; engender a sense of belonging and ownership among all their inhabitants; prioritize safe, inclusive, accessible, green and quality public spaces that are family friendly; enhance social and intergenerational interactions, cultural expressions and political participation; and foster social cohesion, inclusion and safety in peaceful and pluralistic settings, where the needs of all inhabitants are met (United Nations General Assembly 2016, p. 4).

These aspirations resonate with the IFLA's definition of the societal responsibilities of landscape architects, set out in Principle 3.7 Inclusivity. This principle intends that landscape designers should facilitate the active participation of communities in the 'sustainable planning, design and management of their landscapes' (International Federation of Landscape Architects Asia Pacific 2015, p. 5). The importance of inclusive design, which allows all communities to benefit from natural, cultural or designed landscapes, is set out in Principle 3.5, which explains 'physical, emotional, spiritual and cultural wellbeing are aspects of human health and vitality that can be sustained, enhanced and revitalized by landscapes' (International Federation of Landscape Architects Asia Pacific 2015, p. 5).

Cultural goals

The UN is committed to the 'sustainable leveraging of natural and cultural heritage, both tangible and intangible, through integrated urban and territorial policies and adequate investment . . . to safeguard and promote cultural infrastructures and sites, museums, indigenous cultures and languages, as well as traditional knowledge and the arts' (United Nations General Assembly 2016, p. 8). Moreover, the UN promotes 'innovative and sustainable use of architectural monuments and sites with the intention of value creation, through respectful restoration and adaptation' (United Nations General Assembly 2016, p. 17). This relates to IFLA Principle 3.4 Identity in the IFLA Asia Pacific charter:

> People may be grounded in place by tradition, forebears, or identification with 'home'. This can occur at both a local and regional scale, as well as at a national scale, and is powerfully expressed through the palimpsest of landscapes and the ways in which landscapes shape their communities.
>
> (International Federation of Landscape
> Architects Asia Pacific 2015, p. 5)

As such, the charter states that landscape architects have a 'duty of care to ensure that the distinctive characteristics, and potential, of their landscapes are not compromised through insensitive or inappropriate change,' and that their communities are not 'diminished' by 'inappropriate development' (International Federation of Landscape Architects Asia Pacific 2015, p. 2).

The following sections set out the challenges the urban professions face in delivering these environmental, societal and cultural aspirations in landscape design practice in Dubai.

Environmental aspirations and practice

The challenges faced by landscape designers in Dubai in achieving environmental goals are twofold. First is the consumption of massive amounts of resources to sustain verdant parascape, a designed landscape that clients often demand. Second is the widespread destruction of natural ecosystems that (almost) inevitably occurs in Dubai's urban development process – a process that Dubai's developers, as opposed to environmental regulators or the urban professions, tend to direct.

Resource consumption

Dubai is one of the least sustainable cities in the world. In terms of carbon emissions, the UAE is globally the fifth largest emitter of carbon dioxide per capita, and Dubai's figure probably exceeds this national average due to its relative opulence (International Energy Agency 2017). Moreover, the UAE has the highest water usage per capita in the world, and Dubai also probably exceeds this (Water Footprint Calculator 2017). While the exact contribution of Dubai's parascape to this figure is difficult to quantify, irrigation demands and a sprawling city form are significant factors.

As I discussed earlier, the luxuriance of parascape requires significant amounts of 'energy, water and chemicals' to survive Dubai's hot and arid climate (Nassar, Blackburn & Whyatt 2014, p. 54). Parascape is undoubtedly a contributor to UAE residents, on average, using a 550 litres of water per day per capita – or the equivalent of a suburban swimming pool per year (Dubai Municipality 2016). The water used for the irrigation of parascape in Dubai comes from several sources. The water that the Dubai Municipality uses for irrigation is generally treated sewage effluent (Anonymous Dubai Municipality representative 2008). While this use of recycled water makes sense, the priority placed on irrigating parascape precludes the opportunity to direct this water towards more productive agricultural ends.

Some urban developers irrigate with desalinated seawater, which requires extremely energy-intensive treatment. The desalination process also raises salinity levels in The Gulf (Waugh 2011, p. 247). Reports from the UAE Ministry of the Environment and Water reveal that the increasing discharge of brine has caused salinity levels to increase by 25 per cent in the last decade. This situation runs the risk of pushing The Gulf to a point of Peak Salt where it becomes so salty that relying on it for freshwater becomes untenable, not to mention devastating for aquatic biodiversity (Hanahan 2010, p. 286). Desalination is also an expensive process. Indeed in 2010, experts calculated that it cost more money to produce a litre of water than it did to produce a litre of oil (Hanahan 2010, p. 286).

Some urban developers also use groundwater for irrigation. As a result, and in combination with other uses, the UAE's total groundwater depletion amounts to over 1,500 million cubic meters per year. This level of over-extraction has lowered the UAE's water table, on average, by more than one metre since the late 1980s (The Encyclopedia of Earth 2008).

The predilection of developers for parascape not only consumes significant amounts of water for irrigation; it also contributes to excessive resource consumption by encouraging a sprawling city form. In 1972, Dubai had 85 hectares of green space, a figure that increased to 4,131 hectares by 2011, a compound annual growth rate of over 10 per cent (Nassar, Blackburn & Whyatt 2014, p. 54). In roughly the same period, the total built-up area of Dubai ballooned from 5,400 hectares to 97,700 hectares (Zaatari 2017). Clearly, parascape is unsustainable not only in terms of its requirements for irrigation water but also in terms of the sprawling city it shapes. This city form is environmentally destructive, reduces opportunities for effective public transport and means that freedom of mobility is predicated on having access to a car (Farr 2008, p. 44).

Regardless, parascape is a marketing ploy that attracts consumers who automatically regard more green landscape as positive. This is exemplified in the marketing of the Sheikh Mohammed Gardens project, which proudly claimed that 73 per cent of its site area was to be green space (Michele Howe 2008a, p. 40). In Dubai, developers (and sometimes designers) promote a correlation between the area of green space and the degree of sustainability. By way of example, the designers of the Sheikh Mohammed Gardens project, CivicArts, referred to the project's system of linear parks as 'the lungs of the city . . . carbon sinks which purify the surrounding air' (Michele Howe 2008b, p. 40). While this is technically true, each resident of the project would require a veritable forest of a much larger scale to sequester their annual carbon emissions.

In a similar manner, the 380-hectare Al Barari urban development, part of Dubailand, advertised its status as 'the lowest density development in the region' so as to 'give people a space to breathe' (Commercial Outdoor Design 2008b). As Mohammed Bin Zaal, chief operating officer, argued:

> Others may talk about sustainability, greenery, the environment, culture and societal values, but we are actually delivering it through billions of dirhams of investment. We have devoted $381 million US towards our themed gardens, woodlands, waterways, streams and water bodies and as part of the process we will be planting 4.6 million trees, shrubs and groundcovers.
>
> (Commercial Outdoor Design 2008b, p. 28)

The degree to which the urban professions believe in the connection between vast swaths of manufactured green space and sustainability is difficult to gauge. However, it appears that the urban professions are often willing to perpetuate such misrepresentations in the pursuit of commercial gain.

One of the major conundrums for the urban professions is summed up by a straight-speaking landscape architect in Dubai: '[Y]ou can question the whole fundamental of allowing a city like Dubai to be built in an environment which is essentially not very sustainable for human life' (Anonymous landscape architect 2009b). Given, however, that Dubai's population is projected to more than double to 5 million by 2027 (Zaatari 2017), landscape designers in Dubai need to engage with xerophytic landscape strategies adapted to this climatically hostile context rather than through deploying parascape and effectively denying that the context exists.

Assisting the transition towards xeriphytic landscape design are several comparatively recent government programs. In late 2007, Sheikh Mohammed directed that the urban professions design all developments in relation to the Leadership in Energy and Environmental Design (LEED) rating system. This system provides a broad framework for environmental design by awarding credits for efficient water and energy usage and the use of 'sustainable sites' (Michelle Howe 2008b, p. 29). However, as one landscape architect describes the problem with the LEEDs rating system within the Dubai context, 'LEEDs is designed for building sustainability; it is not about open space. It's all about how to make buildings sustainable and what's worse is it's designed for North America . . . it's not at all applicable to Dubai; totally ridiculous.'

Responding (in part) to the lack of relevance of the LEEDs system for landscape design, the UAE Government, through the Estidama[1] programme, has recently established regulations for landscape and urban design. As a result, some landscape specialists in Dubai have adapted their 'specifications, water demand strategies, plant lists and material selections' to support Estidama 'as much as possible' (Cracknell 2012, p. 14). Despite this gradual regulatory shift towards greater sustainability, Dubai landscape design practice (generally) continues to be at odds with the IFLA charter that predisposes practitioners to 'nurture the continued health and diversity of landscapes' (International Federation of Landscape Architects Asia Pacific 2015, p. 5). In contrast, Dubai's parascapes continue to threaten the environment, locally and globally, through excessive resource consumption.

Ecological destruction

In the frenetic application of parascape, the urban professions in Dubai often have relegated the concerns of the earth and its non-human creatures to below those of marketable landscape imagery. In addition to their excessive irrigation demands, much parascape has minimal ecological value (Doherty 2008, p. 106). They are largely driven by image, have little substantive ecological merit, and conflict directly with indigenous, desert ecosystems (Doherty 2008, p. 106). Evidence of the artificiality of most designed land-scapes in Dubai is that 91 per cent of what the Dubai Municipality catego-rize as 'cultivated green areas' is lawn (Dubai Statistics Centre 2016), an imported and ecologically sterile plant material. This is indicative of the lack of an ecological agenda or basic levels of environmental responsiveness in many designed landscapes. As Jensen explains in relation to the Municipal-ity parks:

> Dubai's parks have no references whatsoever to the geographical con-text, and understood as landscapes, they are often stranger than an equivalent portion of the moon would be in relation to the natural surroundings.
>
> (2007, p. 119)

This use of exotic plant species represents an issue because they can over take the existing desert flora as these introduced species often do not have natural enemies (Abella 2017, p. 16). This is an issue because endemic tree and plant species are the ecological basis upon which life depends in the desert – without this habitat, the fauna that coevolved with endemic flora cannot survive (Abella 2017, p. 16). The local Ghaf tree (*Prosopis cineraria*) is one such example. Evolutionary processes have adapted it to browsing by animals, such as camels and goats, and other desert wildlife eat the seed pods of the Ghaf tree (Abella 2017, p. 16). Many birds build nests on the Ghaf, including the desert eagle owl, brown-necked raven, yellow-throated sparrow and long-legged buzzard. Still others nest in holes in the trunks and branches, and many more use the trees as roosts. Flowers, fruits, leaves, bark, branches and roots of the Ghaf tree all provide resources and habitat for a variety of native fauna and flora, making the tree a keystone species, one that plays an integral part in the food chain of the desert ecosystem (Abella 2017, p. 16).

Many members of the urban professions in Dubai are undoubtedly supportive of the preservation of such keystone species; however, one of the challenges is that landscape designers often rely on scant data on local plants, and there is poor availability of endemic plants species in the quantities needed for commercial landscape projects. These issues are very challenging and create hurdles to ecological design in Dubai and in the region more broadly (Moosavi, Makhzoumi & Grose 2016, p. 274).

One of the conceptual problems the urban professions have faced in pre-serving desert ecosystems has been the reading of this desert landscape as a tabula rasa. As an anonymous Dubai landscape architect attests:

> [P]eople tend to treat the place like a sandbox; they can just level it out and re-sculpt it in any way they choose. I think that is part of the

problem; people perceive that there is nothing intrinsically about the place which is unique and therefore they can do whatever they want.

(Anonymous landscape architect 2009b)

Thus, clients and the urban professions often consider the desert landscape as something that development needs to defeat in order to establish 'real' landscape, i.e. parascape.

Evidence of the urban profession's complicity in the destruction of indigenous ecology can be witnessed in the substantial erasure of Dubai's 'sabkha and important biological areas' (Parsons Harland Bartholomew 1993, pp. 10–8) by urban developments – all of which have engaged the services of the professions. (See Figure 5.1.) The urban professions are also complicit in the destruction of the aquatic environment. Offshore developments such as the Palm Jumeirah have had massive implications for the dynamics of currents, sediments and biogeochemical and ecosystem functions (Nassar, Blackburn & Whyatt 2014, p. 56). Moreover, researchers predict that the construction of the Palm Jumeirah alone may have destroyed between 750 and 1,125 hectares of coral (Salahudin 2006, p. 59).

Nonetheless, readers should consider this culpability from a broader perspective. Ecological destruction in Dubai results (in part) from urban development being both unregulated and market driven, as opposed to conforming to government-led planning that seeks to protect areas of ecological significance. For example, real estate developers Emaar oversaw their own planning and approval processes in its substantial Emirate Hills project (Ramos 2010, p. 53), which undoubtedly has had major implications for desert ecology and resource use. In such examples, development rights are brokered through a favour economy with the Sheikh rather than through formal approval processes (Ramos 2010, p. 53). By way of other examples, a plan for Dubai's urban area was prepared in 1993 using McHargian environmental planning principles (Parsons Harland Bartholomew); however, it appears to have had minimal impact in the structuring of subsequent urban expansion – a fate (to some degree) shared with the succeeding Dubai 2020 Plan (Government of Dubai 2012, p. 2).

As a result of the ecological destruction inherent in rampant urban development (in both aquatic and terrestrial environments), amongst other issues (Gallacher 2007), the UAE has a significant number of threatened animal species. The International Union for Conservation of Nature estimate that the UAE has 60 species that are threatened, in particular fish and bird species (International Union for Conservation of Nature 2018). This is a disproportionately high figure given the relative sparseness of species in the Rub al Khali desert and sabkha regions. While it is difficult to assess how responsible Dubai's urban development is for the destruction of ecological diversity, the tabula rasa approach to 'natural' sites (terrestrial or aquatic) and their replacement with ecologically sterile landscapes certainly

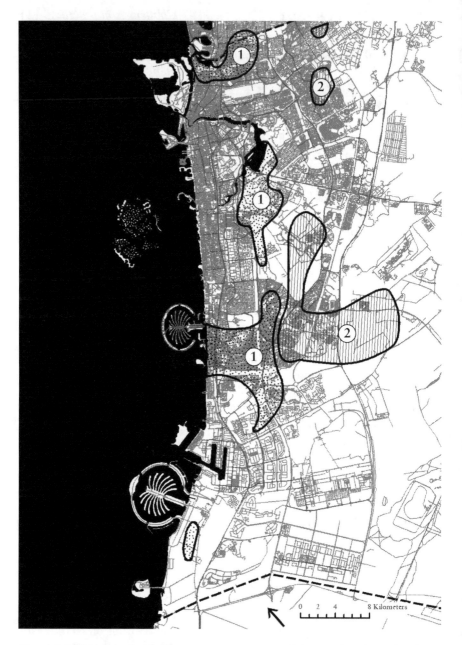

Figure 5.1 This map shows the approximate extent of destruction, through urbanisation, of 'sabkha and important biological areas' identified by Parsons
Harland Bartholomew in 1993. The 'important biological areas' comprised open desert woodland.

Key:
1 Sabkha
2 Important biological areas

Source: Base GIS data courtesy of Trimble Maps.

contribute to the UAE's high number of threatened species. It is yet to be seen whether Dubai's Green City programme – the recent dedication, by law, of 25 per cent of Dubai's land for wildlife conservation – will fare better than previous planning efforts and help to address this worrying situation (Kolo 2016, p. 172).

The commoditization of nature

Excessive resource consumption and widespread ecological destruction in Dubai have emerged, in part, out of confusion about what constitutes 'nature.' For example, citizens often incorrectly equate 'nature' with manufactured parascape. The urban professions in Dubai commit a sleight of hand when they, along with branding consultants and developers, suggest that new developments are somehow reconciled with nature (Sama Dubai 2007; Meydan & Sobha 2018; Landscape Middle East 2014). The degree to which parascape is associated with nature in Dubai often goes unquestioned by the urban professions themselves, perhaps because many of the people employed in the urban professions in Dubai are expatriates who have imported their own culture's conflation of 'green' landscapes with nature. While understandable (to some degree), such conflation poses a real issue in that it negates the value of desert landscapes in both conceptual and actual terms.

Such commoditization of nature can be witnessed in The Lagoons[2] development, a 650-hectare project adjacent to the Ramsar-listed[3] Ras al Khor Wildlife Sanctuary. This wetland and sabkha ecosystem is home to migratory flamingos and 265 other aquatic and terrestrial fauna (Dubai Municipality 2003). Marketing for The Lagoons invokes a harmony with nature despite its siting in an area that the Dubai Urban Area Structure Plan 2003 listed as being a sabkha conservation area that provided an important drainage filter to Ras al Khor (Dubai Creek) (Parsons Harland Bartholomew 1993, pp. 10–15). As The Lagoons developers averred:

> This is the vision behind The Lagoons. To create a space where nature may flourish, while also providing all the requirements for elite modern living. World class commercial office space, business and retail properties, residences, hotels and leisure venues – all in a beautiful waterfront landscape that is alive with many different species of plants, birds and other wildlife. Our modern world interwoven with natural splendour, right in the heart of Dubai.
>
> (Sama Dubai 2007)

The Lagoons project recently morphed into the Dubai Creek Harbour project, which Emaar are developing. (See Figure 5.2.) Despite comprising a forest of 50-storey towers (Emaar 2018b), the narrative of 'ecological responsibility' remains (Emaar 2018a).

Figure 5.2 The Dubai Creek Harbour project adjacent to sensitive sabkha/wetland ecology.

Source: Photos by the author.

Suggesting that developers can build a massive urban development immediately adjacent to a sensitive sabkha/wetland ecology without environmental degradation is dubious. The role of landscape designers is to minimize and to compensate for this degradation. In this respect, the landscape design professionals are essential enablers of the marketing of the development. The commodified 'nature' that landscape designers typically produce to compensate, however, is highly artificial and constructed. Through such a compensatory role, the urban professions often minimize the development of collective 'guilt' for and awareness of ecological destruction, reducing the potential for a genuine environmental movement to gather strength in Dubai. This tendency, in environmental or societal or cultural terms, becomes a repeating theme of this chapter.

In conclusion to this section, the urban professions in Dubai struggle to reconcile aspirations of the UN and IFLA to protect ecosystems and minimize environmental impact (United Nations General Assembly 2016, p. 4) with landscape design practice. Evidence of this is the substantial destruction of 'important biological areas' (Parsons Harland Bartholomew 1993, pp. 10–18) by urban developments that have employed the services of the urban professions and by the ubiquity of parascape, which requires vast quantities of freshwater and fertilizer. The primary reason for this is that the urban professions are a service industry that must respond to needs of clients who regard parascape as necessary from a marketing perspective. Compounding this situation is the prevailing view of the desert as a tabula rasa, which developers and some designers must defeat in a bid to instal 'real landscape.'

Societal aspirations and practice

The UN advocates for cities that 'promote inclusivity' and that are 'just, safe, healthy, accessible, affordable, resilient and sustainable' (United Nations General Assembly 2016, p. 4). The IFLA summarize their ethos concerning societal inclusivity in the Asia Pacific Charter Principle 3.7 Inclusivity. This principle dictates that landscape architects should facilitate the active participation of all communities in the 'sustainable planning, design and management of their landscapes' (International Federation of Landscape Architects Asia Pacific 2015, p. 5). Understandably, the urban professions (generally) struggle to reconcile such lofty societal goals with everyday practice in Dubai.

Privatized communities and a dearth of truly public space

A significant stratum of Dubai's population consists of unskilled migrant labourers and domestic workers, who perform often exhausting tasks for minimal pay. This population contrasts with an Emirati and professional expatriate population who live a life of comparative ease and affluence. For

Dubai's unskilled migrant underclass, much of the highly privatized city is not available, including (in some cases) the gated and ticketed 'public' park system. (See Figure 5.3.)

In Dubai's proliferating exclusive communities, surveillance systems and fortifications deny access. Typically, the underclass in Dubai do not consume the parascape of exclusive communities; they maintain it. Dubai's migrant underclass is also typically denied access to urbscapes (such as urban waterfronts like The Beach or La Mer) not through overt regulation or coercion (Acuto 2010, p. 281) but through various 'soft' strategies. These include distance, a lack of public transport from some areas, parking prices, the prices of commodities and attractions, and aesthetic codes (Dovey 2005, p. 15), which signify to the unskilled migrant underclass that they are both out of place and unwelcome. As urban politics expert, Michele Acuto explains: '[S]ymbolic power has substituted for brute force . . . oppression in Dubai comes with glossy brochures and red-carpeted entrances' (Acuto 2010, p. 281). (See Figure 5.4.)

Of course, the translation of democratic ideals regarding public space to Dubai are problematic. Significantly, Dubai has no real history of secular public space in the form of major park systems, such as in London or New York. Another fundamental obstacle for the creation of democratic public space in Dubai is the restrictive political context. The actual establishment of truly 'public' space is, in conceptual terms, difficult to achieve due to Dubai's having ultimately 'one landlord,' Sheikh Mohammed (Davis 2007).

We cannot hold the urban professions accountable for the prevailing socio-political context that denies opportunities for genuinely democratic space. However, its failure to articulate a response to this context represents a regression into merely facilitating the societal, cultural and economic agendas of Dubai's ruling elite. As British writer Deyan Sudjic describes, in such situations the urban professions find themselves being defined not by their own logic but 'by the impulses that have driven the rich and the powerful to employ architects, and to seek to shape the world' (Sudjic 2005, p. 327). The urban profession's failure to define itself against the dominant socio-political context represents a regression to a historical model of practice that merely provides 'an entertaining demonstration of political power by the privileged' (Balfour 1999, p. 275) and limits the urban profession's broader societal relevance.

The commoditization of community

In Dubai's stratified society, clients often reduce the urban professions to creating the appearance rather than the function of a genuinely integrated and inclusive community. Readers can see this exemplified both in fenced municipal parks and in the fabricated image of 'community' inside rapidly proliferating gated real estate developments; currently a major component

Figure 5.3 A highly privatised city. This map shows (with hatching) Dubai's rapidly proliferating gated communities, gated parks and secured Special Economic Zones, amongst others. This map is indicative only.

Source: Base GIS data courtesy of Trimble Maps.

Figure 5.4 The Dubai City Walk project. Urban projects in Dubai are often highly choreographed, and the exclusive experiences they offer have been carefully packaged by designers and branding consultants for the wealthy 'visitor class.' Graffiti is used, in part, to promote the image but not typically the reality of creativity and subversion.

Source: Photos by the author.

of the urban profession's quotidian fabric. Marketing for the exclusive Al Furjan development deploys a traditional Arabic notion of community:

> Al Furjan symbolises a collection of homes or a small village. A fareej [village] represented a way of life to its residents, one that created a community of extended family and friends, rather than merely neighbours. It fostered lifelong bonds, a shared sense of responsibility and reliance on each other. Today, Al Furjan builds on this tradition.
>
> (Nakheel 2008)

Despite such nostalgia-laced marketing, contemporary Dubai residents would (likely) consider as highly burdensome the level of communal responsibility found in a traditional *fareej*. As Acuto explains, Dubai society increasingly reflects Ferdinand Tönnies' description of '*gesellschaft*' – a society that merely operates to sate its members' individual interests, where neither community spirit nor social bond has much meaning (Acuto 2010, p. 282).

Moreover, the notion of community promoted in Dubai's gated developments is reliant more on the exclusion of low socio-economic strata rather than on inclusion. (See Figure 5.5.) David Harvey refers to this tendency:

Figure 5.5 Beneath a verdant layer of parascape, the barriers of a gated community disappear, except for those who may try to cross them.

Source: Photo by the author.

> The darker side of this communitarianism remains unstated . . . . Well-founded communities often exclude, define themselves against others, erect all sorts of keep out signs (if not tangible walls), internalise surveillance, societal controls and repression.
>
> (2002, p. 170)

In this respect, the role of landscape design in gated communities is to deliver the private community parks and attendant pedestrian interconnections as well to integrate the security system of walls, gates and cameras into a benign layer of parascape, neutralizing the disengagement of the development from its societal context and fabricating an often deceptive image of community Urbscapes also tend to fabricate the image of an inclusive community, through the relative invisibility of barriers to entry by Dubai's low socio-economic strata.

In both parascape and urbscape, the urban professions typically fabricate and commodify the symbols of community as the surrounding city becomes increasingly fractured into islands of discrete socio-economic strata. The overarching problem is that the tendency of Dubai landscape design to conceal certain societal realities inhibits Dubai culture's ability to confront these realities and develop a more organic and authentic urban culture, entailing greater risk, more diversity and higher inclusivity.

In conclusion to this section, the urban professions in Dubai struggle to produce landscapes that promote societal inclusivity as advocated by the UN (United Nations General Assembly 2016, p. 4) and the IFLA (International Federation of Landscape Architects Asia Pacific 2015, p. 5). The primary reason for this is that many Dubai urban developers actively market their projects as both luxurious and exclusive – and as such societal inclusivity is completely at odds with their marketing strategy. This occurs at both the project and city scales – Sheikh Mohammed promoting an image of Dubai to the global audience that highlights the 'exclusive' over the 'ordinary' (Al Maktoum 2012, p. 143).

Cultural aspirations and practice

The UN states that cities should 'safeguard and promote cultural infrastructure and sites . . . and traditional knowledge' (United Nations General Assembly 2016, p. 8). This resonates with the IFLA Asia Pacific region charter that sets out that landscape architects have a 'duty of care to ensure that the distinctive characteristics and potential of landscapes are not compromised through insensitive or inappropriate change' (International Federation of Landscape Architects Asia Pacific 2015, p. 2). This reflects one of the landscape architecture profession's key concerns, that with the homogenization and universalization of landscape, humanity loses its crucial sources of identity as individuals and societies (Bowring, Egoz & Ignatieva 2009, p. 6).

Orientalism

An expatriate member of the urban professions in Dubai aiming to provide a 'duty of care to ensure that the distinctive characteristics' of landscapes are 'not compromised' and that existing communities are 'not diminished' (International Federation of Landscape Architects Asia Pacific 2015, p. 2) faces a fundamental challenge. As cultural outsiders, they are unlikely to know enough about the local culture or landscape to identify and then subsequently protect them from being 'diminished.' This conundrum is in large part because the expatriate designer in Dubai is (generally) a product of a Western society and education. As town planner Anthony Minoprio, who prepared the 1951 master plan for the modernization (and to a large degree destruction) of Kuwait City's historic core, explains, 'All we could give them was what we knew' (Gardiner 1983, p. 35). Public intellectual Edward Said describes this conundrum faced by the expatriate:

> No one has ever devised a method for detaching the scholar from the circumstances of life, from the fact of his involvement (conscious or unconscious) with a class, a set of beliefs, a societal position, or from the mere activity of being a member of a society. These continue to bear on what he does professionally.
>
> (1991, p. 10)

While ignorance has (sometimes) hampered attempts by design professionals to bridge the cross-cultural gulf between expatriate and Emirati culture, compounding this in some instances has been arrogance. Bianca Stefano describes how Western professionals have often presumed pre-eminence in the region:

> The unshakeable conviction of their own superiority led certain western thinkers to believe that they had invalidated other, much richer and more meaningful cultural systems, while what really happened was simply a shift in interests and perspective, enforced by the power of an aggressive technological civilization.
>
> (Bianca 2000, p. 186)

Moreover, the problem Western expatriate designers experience in Dubai, in terms of escaping their own cultural 'baggage,' is the lack of a parallel discipline in Emirati culture. The lack of this counterpart leaves the 'oriental,' in landscape design terms, without a professional voice. Said described the tendency of the Occident (Westerner) to 'speak' for the Orient: 'The exteriority of the representation is always governed by some version of the truism that if the Orient could represent itself, it would; since it cannot, the representation does the job' (1991). The difficulty for the Occidental landscape designer in Dubai is that they are employed to 'speak' for the Dubai landscape and culture because no Emirati alternative yet exists. This is a reflection of only one accredited degree programme in landscape architecture being available in the UAE (Mitchell 2016, p. 190).[4]

As a reflection on Said's comment, it is intriguing to imagine Emirati landscape designers practicing in a Western country to the exclusion of any Western landscape designers. What would an Emirati version of a landscape that attempts to divine the genius loci constitute in the Australian or American context? Said refers to the implausibility of reversing the dynamics of Orientalism:

> To speak of scholarly specialization as a geographical 'field' is, in the case of Orientalism, fairly revealing since no one is likely to imagine a field symmetrical to it called Occidentalism.
>
> (1991, p. 50)

This reflects the fundamental cultural conundrum that the Western expatriate designer in Dubai faces in providing a 'duty of care to ensure that the distinctive characteristics and potential of landscapes are not compromised and that their communities are not diminished' (International Federation of Landscape Architects Asia Pacific 2015, p. 2). The questions such goals elicit are, 'What are the distinctive characteristics?' and 'According to whom?' Both are difficult to answer, particularly for the outsider. Compounding this situation is the presence of many cultural groups in Dubai, which extends the cross-cultural conundrum faced by the Western expatriate designer to include Indian, Pakistani and other Arab cultures.

Language obstacles

An inability to speak Arabic also creates a significant obstacle for expatriate designers in Dubai endeavouring to protect a community or landscape from 'inappropriate development.' American landscape architect Anne Whiston Spirn refers to the importance of language in that 'language has consequences. It structures how one thinks and what kinds of things one is able to express' (Spirn 2002, p. 42).

Tim Kennedy describes how 'the people of the UAE are from a culture of the spoken word' (Kennedy 2007). An exploration of place names, particularly in the historic neighbourhoods around Dubai Creek, 'indicate[s] a past intimacy' between landscape and culture (Kennedy 2007, p. 408) that is invisible to most expatriate design practitioners. As Kennedy explains, these ancient areas reveal via their place names a historic narrative between landscape and culture: 'Al Rigga district – refers to a landscape pattern where a shallow water table precipitates the ease of digging a water well . . . . Al Barsha district is named after the planting of trees in groups, which looked like a decorated landscape' (2007, p. 411).

Such place names denote an intimacy between traditional Emirati culture and the endemic landscape that, in some cases, predicated survival. Through a reading of traditional place names, the city is revealed as a palimpsest in which 'traces of diverse layers apparent beneath the surface of the built environment' can be read (Kennedy 2007, p. 411), something that eludes most expatriate design practitioners in Dubai. A survey of contemporary place names reveals the erosion of this palimpsest as in Dubai Silicon Oasis, the Greens, The Palm, The World, Emirates Hills, The Lakes and so on. While such place names reference contemporary typologies, they are generic and imported, offering nothing by way of an in-depth reading of the land.

Language also poses an issue in terms of how a Western expatriate designer and an Emirati may understand the word *landscape*. As Jala Makhzoumi explains, '[T]here is as yet no word for "landscape" in Arabic' (Makhzoumi 2002, p. 218). The Arabic translation of landscape is therefore ambiguous and can include natural scenery, land scenery and view of the countryside (Makhzoumi 2002, p. 218). Moreover, Emirati's sometimes conflate landscape design with garden design and horticulture, its potential narrowed down to the 'beautification' of places through the use of ornamental plants (Makhzoumi 2002, p. 223). Such interpretations of landscape design account (to some degree) for the prevalence of parascape – the 'beautification' of previously 'barren' areas using decorative and highly artificial planting.

Divergent beliefs

While the presence of different languages can cause complexities in terms of how different cultures perceive landscape, divergent spiritual beliefs compound this situation. British explorer Wilfred Thesiger described the reaction of Dubai's residents to him in 1950:

> [E]veryone else was fanatical and unpleasant. The elders spat on the ground whenever we passed, and the children followed me round chanting derisively, 'Al Nasrani, al nasrani,' the name by which these Arabs know a Christian.
>
> (Thesiger 1991, p. 238)[5]

While the role of spirituality in Emirati life was comparatively stable in the period between the first recorded mention of Dubai in 1095 and the first major oil boom of the 1960s, Occidental culture had been through a prolonged process of secularization, beginning with the Renaissance and subsequently the Enlightenment. This process in Western history saw the increasing separation of human existence, in spiritual terms, from what Stephano Bianca describes as its 'divine origins and the corresponding deeper reality' (Bianca 2000, p. 162).

The split between the enduring spirituality of contemporary Emirati culture (Central Intelligence Agency 2008) and the (generally) secular nature of the urban professions[6] also contributes to the cross-cultural conundrum.

This split is of particular significance when Western science, technology and politics operate in the context of a 'regional culture,' and claim to provide superior, value-free tools for development using rational and secular means (Bianca 2000, p. 186). Architectural historian Stefano Bianca argues that perceived superiority and efficiency derived from the secular, Occidental viewpoint belie the fact that 'values are divorced from deeper existential realities and therefore are unable to provide meaningful directions' (2000, p. 186). As such, the Occidental design professional is in a difficult conceptual position. Unable to enter the Islamic spiritual domain, he or she is destined to produce either merely technical solutions or superficial references to 'authentic' culture and spirituality or unwittingly produce landscapes that are spiritually symbolic – which can perpetuate socio-political agendas – an example being parascape.

In part because of this situation, a schism has formed between the physical city of Dubai and its Islamic spiritual core. Bianca describes the coexistence of a conjoined city and spirit in traditional Arabic Islamic urbanism, in which, 'The city was conceived as a closed universe, and man was 'enveloped by multiple architectural shells embodying and reflecting his cultural and spiritual values' (2000). Given the strong linkages between the containing urbanism and the human life within, she argues, architecture functioned as a 'second body' in which the division perceived by the Occident between 'an independent observer and a neutral architectural object' did not apply; 'man was always within his comprehensive universe, in both ontological and physical terms' (2000, p. 186). The loss of this matrix of urbanism that supports culture, identity and spirit in Dubai's modernization and development has manifested as nostalgia for this lost urbanism and its culture within contemporary Emirati society.

The commoditization of traditional culture

The Dubai Strategic Plan 2015 reflects this prevailing sense of loss. It refers to the development of 'physical infrastructure to promote cultural activities,' as well as to immigration policies revised to maintain a demographic 'balance.' This sense of cultural loss results in Emirati culture being vulnerable to superficial, neo-traditional design exercises (often by expatriate urban professionals) offering to reconcile contemporary Emirati society with nostalgic notions of community, culture and spirituality. The firms delivering such projects are often those who are concurrently associated with modernization, as exemplified in the Sheikh Mohammed Gardens Project designed by CivicArts/Eric Kuhne and Associates. The promotional text for this project attempts to reconcile modernity and development with a superficial interpretation of traditional Islamic culture:

> The Mohammed Bin Rashid Gardens offer a culturally resonant alternative to the sterile Western-style street grids that currently dominate

the Middle East. They replace those rigid, rectilinear lines with the sweeping arcs and circles of the planispheric astrolabe; an instrument perfected by Islamic scholars, artisans and astronomers . . . . Dubai is likewise a product of great imagination . . . . A royal vision for a modern city that has risen from an ancient land. To base a new city plan upon an object embodying 2000 years of human invention is to build upon the bedrock of civilisation itself.

(Commercial Outdoor Design 2008a)

Through mimicking the form of the astrolabe, the designers capitalize on – what I perceive to be – a sense of cultural loss in the Emirati, in a bid to secure project approvals and sell real estate. Yet, with nothing more in cultural terms than sound bites for promotion, such concepts distance contemporary Emirati culture even further from its roots by commodifying cultural references. The urban professions are complicit in this process: while they often regard themselves as defining cultural continuity and resisting global forces, they are (in many cases) a fundamental part of a development process that endangers the very thing that should be protected. This is because the labour, technology and capital required to deliver such projects in Dubai are all inherently global in nature. Given this, it is a formidable task for design professionals to marshal the global forces needed to build projects, while at the same time ensuring the protection of the 'distinctive characteristics' of local landscapes and culture.

It is within this complex cross-cultural context that the urban professions in Dubai find the realization of IFLA's avocation of 'landscape that is valued and expressive of local culture' (International Federation of Landscape Architects 2005) so difficult to realize, creating a schism between the goals set out by IFLA and the UN and reality of practice in Dubai.

Conclusion

In this chapter, I have set out the environmental, societal and cultural aspirations of the UN and IFLA as a normative framework. Subsequently, I have assessed the practice of the urban professions in Dubai in relation to this framework and concluded that they struggle to reconcile practice with the environmental, societal or cultural goals of the UN or of IFLA. This situation is not unique to Dubai. Landscape design practice achieves these goals in just a few areas globally because it requires substantial amounts of time, resources and skills and a detailed knowledge of the endemic landscape.

While the urban profession's (general) inability to rise to these challenges in Dubai has detrimental implications for the environment, societal equity and local culture, further compounding this situation is that the professions often commodify the things they are attempting to 'save.' As James Corner reminds us:

> Landscape is not necessarily for the benefit of all in society . . . its apparent innocence and idealism can often mask hidden agendas and conceal societal inequities and ongoing ecological destruction.
>
> (1999, p. 11)

This situation sees landscape design sometimes create the mere appearance of 'nature,' societal inclusiveness and/or local culture rather than embodying a progressive environmental, societal or cultural agenda that could yield genuine societal progression.

Nonetheless, readers should consider the schism between principles and practice in Dubai within the context of a socio-political system that is at odds with the aspirations of these organizations. For the urban professions to straddle the gulf between the ethos of the UN and IFLA and the demands of clients is a formidable challenge. In this respect, the discrepancy between principles and practice highlights the need for a critical analysis of the UN and IFLA advocated ethos itself within a context such as Dubai. The requirement for designed landscapes to 'educate, enlighten, edify, redeem' presents a challenge anywhere, let alone in Dubai (Oles & Lickwar 2015, p. 83).

It is also important for readers to note that many of the issues raised in this chapter, such as extreme socio-economic stratification, while having a spatial dimension, are not exclusively spatial. For instance, the differences in pay between skilled and unskilled professions in Dubai also results in socio-economic stratification, in conjunction with the desire of socio-economic groups to live with their own 'kind.' As such, there are obvious limits to what spatial design, directed by the urban professions, can achieve in such areas.

It is within the context of this predicament and a region undergoing a process of accelerated urbanization that the subsequent chapter explores how emerging theory could reframe the way in which the urban professions grapple with these thorny issues.

Notes

1 The word *Estidama* refers to sustainability in Arabic (Estidama 2008).
2 Sama Dubai were the original developers of The Lagoons project, a company established by the government of Dubai. Emaar are now developing the same site.
3 Ramsar refers to an international treaty for the conservation of wetland environments.
4 In the Gulf region, there are also landscape architecture programs in Jedda and Dammam in Saudi Arabia.
5 It should be noted that Thesiger is 'widely criticized by older Bedouin people' for his sometimes 'patronizing and arrogant description of the Arabs' (Anonymous landscape architect 2009a).
6 This is not to say that all members of the urban professions in Dubai are non-spiritual but that the ethos of the professions is secular in nature.

References

Abella, TA 2017, 'Top 5 Reasons to Plant Indigenous Trees', *Landscape Middle East*, p. 16.

Acuto, M 2010, 'High-Rise Dubai Urban Entrepreneurialism and the Technology of Symbolic Power', *Cities*, no. 27, pp. 272–284.

Al Maktoum, MbR 2012, *My Vision: Challenges in the Race for Excellence*, Motivate Publishing, Dubai.

Anonymous Dubai Municipality representative 2008, *Interview*, J Bolleter.

Anonymous landscape architect 2009a, *Email*, J Bolleter, Dubai.

Anonymous landscape architect 2009b, *Interview*, J Bolleter.

Balfour, A 1999, 'What Is Public in Landscape?' in *Recovering Landscape: Essays in Contemporary Landscape Architecture*, pp. 275–284, Princeton Architectural Press, New York City.

Bianca, S 2000, *Urban Form in the Arab World: Past and Present*, Thames and Hudson, London.

Bolleter, J 2009, 'Para-Scape: Landscape Architecture in Dubai', *Journal of Landscape Architecture*, Spring, no. 4, pp. 28–55.

Bowring, J, Egoz, S & Ignatieva, M 2009, ' "As good as the West": Two Paradoxes of Globalisation and Landscape Architecture in St. Petersburg', *Journal of Landscape Architecture*, vol. 4, no. 1, pp. 6–15.

Central Intelligence Agency 2008, *Central Intelligence Agency: The World Factbook*. Available from: www.cia.gov/library/publications/the-world-factbook/geos/ae.html. [24.01].

Commercial Outdoor Design 2008a, 'Dubai Government Unveils $54bn Gardens Project', *Commercial Outdoor Design*, vol. 1, no. 6, p. 07.

Commercial Outdoor Design 2008b, 'Paradise Found?' *Commercial Outdoor Design*, vol. 1, no. 11, pp. 24–28.

Corner, J 1999, 'Recovering Landscape as a Critical Cultural Practice', in *Recovering Landscape: Essays in Contemporary Landscape Architecture*, pp. 1–26, Princeton Architectural Press, New York.

Cracknell 2012, 'Interview: Cracknell Have Responded to the Challenge of the Changing World Economic Situation', *Landscape Middle East*, 1, no. 6, pp. 10–16.

Davis, M 2007, 'Fear and Money in Dubai', *Topos*, pp. 62–70.

Doherty, G 2008, 'The Landscape of Dubai's Urbanism', in *Instant Cities: Emergent Trends in Architecture and Urbanism in the Arab World*, pp. 103–111, CSAAR, Amman.

Dovey, K 2005, *Fluid City: Transforming Melbourne's Urban Waterfront*, Routledge, London and New York.

Dubai Municipality 2003, *Ras Al Khor Wildlife Sanctuary*, Brochure, Dubai Municipality. Available from: www.panda.org/who_we_are/wwf_offices/united_arab_emirates/news/?20230/Ras-Al-Khor-Wildlife-Sanctuary.

Dubai Municipality 2016, *A sustainable Dubai*, Government of Dubai and Go Dubai, Dubai.

Dubai Statistics Centre 2016, *Chapter 15: Climate and environment*, Dubai Statistics Centre. Available from: www.dsc.gov.ae/en-us/Themes/Pages/Climate-and-Environment.aspx?Theme=35#DSC_Tab2. [07.06].

Emaar 2018a, 'Dubai Creek Harbour', *Emaar*. Available from: www.emaar.com/en/Images/Creek%20Horizon%20Brochure%20no%20floorplans_tcm223-98191.pdf. [04.04].

Emaar 2018b, 'Harbour Views: Dubai Creek Harbour', *Emaar*. Available from: www.emaar.com/en/images/Harbour-Views-Brochure.pdf. [04.04].

The Encyclopedia of Earth 2008, *Water Profile of United Arab Emirates*, Encyclopedia of Earth. Available from: www.eoearth.org/article/Water_profile_of_United_Arab_Emirates. [14.08].

Estidama 2008, 'Who Are We?' *Estidama*. Available from: www.estidama.org/aboutestidama/default_en_gb.aspx. [06.09].

Farr, D 2008, *Sustainable Urbanism: Urban Design with Nature*, John Wiley & Sons, Hoboken, NJ.

Gallacher, D 2007, 'Overgrazing Their Welcome', *Zawaya*, pp. 30–33.

Gardiner, S 1983, *Kuwait the Making of a City*, Longman, Aylesbury.

Government of Dubai 2012, *Dubai 2020 Urban Masterplan*, Government of Dubai, Dubai.

Hanahan, J 2010, 'A Demand for Water', *Al Manakh- Gulf Cont'd*, vol. 25, no. 2, pp. 286–289.

Harvey, D 2002, *Spaces of Hope*, Cromwell Press, Edinburgh.

Howe, M 2008a, 'Garden Extraordinaire', *Commercial Outdoor Design*, vol. 1, no. 8, pp. 37–40.

Howe, M 2008b, 'Green Credentials', *Commercial Outdoor Design*, vol. 1, no. 4, pp. 26–32.

International Energy Agency 2017, *Global Energy & CO_2 Status Report*, International Energy Agency. Available from: www.iea.org/geco/emissions/. [07.09].

International Federation of Landscape Architects 2003, *Proposed IFLA Strategic Plan*, International Federation of Landscape Architects.

International Federation of Landscape Architects 2005, *IFLA/UNESCO Charter for Landscape Architectural Education*.

International Federation of Landscape Architects Asia Pacific 2015, *IFLA Asia-Pacific Region Landscape Charter*, International Federation of Landscape Architects Asia Pacific, IFoL Architects Asia Pacific Region.

International Society of City and Regional Planners 2017, *International Society of City and Regional Planners*. Available from: https://isocarp.org. [22.07].

International Union of Architects 2017, *Sustainable Development Goals Commission*, International Union of Architects. Available from: www.uia-architectes.org/webApi/en/working-bodies/sdg. [22.07].

International Union for Conservation of Nature 2018, *The IUCN Red List of Threatened Species*, International Union for Conservation of Nature. Available from: https://www.iucn.org/resources/conservation-tools/iucn-red-list-threatened-species. [07.09].

Jensen, B 2007, *Dubai – Dynamics of Bingo Urbanism*, Architectural Publisher, Copenhagen.

Kennedy, T 2007, 'Place Telling at Dubai Creek: Encoded Visions', in *Regional Architecture and Identity in the Age of Globalization Conference*, pp. 407–416, Centre for the Study of Architecture in the Arab Region, Dubai.

Kolo, J 2016, 'Accidental or Envisioned Cities: A Comparative Analysis of Abu Dhabi and Dubai', in G Katodrytis & S Syed (eds), *Gulf Cities as Interfaces*, pp. 161–180, Gulf Research Centre Cambridge, Jeddah.

Landscape Middle East 2014, 'Damac properties introduce "Akoya Oxygen"', *Landscape Middle East*, p. 4.

Makhzoumi, JM 2002, 'Landscape in the Middle East: An Inquiry', *Landscape Research*, vol. 27, no. 3, pp. 213–228.

Meydan & Sobha 2018, *Mohammed Bin Rashid City: District One*, Meydan. Available from: https://resources.lookup.ae/downloads/6585597321235058_375.pdf. [04.04].

Mitchell, K 2016, 'Beyond Greening: Approaches to the Contemporary Landscape in the United Arab Emirates', in M Gharipour (ed), *Contemporary Urban Landscapes of the Middle East*, pp. 191–206, Routledge, London.

Moosavi, S, Makhzoumi, J & Grose, M 2016, 'Landscape Practice in the Middle East Between Local and Global Aspirations', *Landscape Research*, vol. 41, no. 3, pp. 265–278.

Nakheel 2018, 'Al Furjan', *Nakheel*. Available from: https://www.nakheel.com/en/communities/al-furjan. [10.1].

Nassar, AK, Blackburn, GA & Whyatt, JD 2014, 'Developing the Desert: The Pace and Process of Urban Growth in Dubai', *Computers, Environment and Urban Systems*, vol. 45, pp. 50–62.

Oles, T & Lickwar, P 2015, 'The Evolving Architecture of Pleasure', *LA+*, no. Pleasure, pp. 82–83.

Parsons Harland Bartholomew 1995, *Structure Plan for the Dubai Urban Area 1993–2012*, Dubai Municipality Planning & Survey Department, DMPS Department, Dubai.

Ramos, S 2010, 'Diversification, Clustering, and Risk in Dubai', *Al Manakh- Gulf Cont'd*, vol. 25, no. 2, pp. 51–54.

Said, E 1991, *Orientalism*, Penguin Books, London.

Salahudin, B 2006, 'The Marine Environmental Impacts of Artificial Island Construction', Master's thesis, Duke University, Durham, NC, Nicholas School of the Environment and Earth Sciences.

Sama Dubai 2007, *The Lagoons*, Sama Dubai. Available from: www.lagoons.ae/. [10.02.09].

Spirn, AW 2002, 'The Authority of Nature: Conflict, Confusion and Renewal in Design Planning, and Ecology', in *Ecology and Design; Frameworks for Learning*, pp. 29–50, Island Press, Washington, DC.

Sudjic, D 2005, *The Edifice Complex*, Penguin Books, New York.

Swaffield, S & Deming, E 2011, 'Research Strategies in Landscape Architecture: Mapping the Terrain', *Journal of Landscape Architecture*, Spring, pp. 34–45.

Thesiger, W 1991, *Arabian Sands*, Penguin Books, London.

United Nations 2015, *Transforming Our World: The 2030 Agenda for Sustainable Development*, Resolution adopted by the General Assembly.

United Nations 2017, *The Sustainable Development Goals Report 2017*, United Nations, New York.

United Nations 2018, *United Nations*, United Nations. Available from: www.un.org/en/index.html. [06.08].

United Nations Development Programme 2014, *Human Development Report 2014: Sustaining Human Progress: Reducing Vulnerabilities and Building Resilience*, United Nations Development Programme, New York.

United Nations General Assembly 2016, 'Draft Outcome Document of the United Nations Conference on Housing and Sustainable Urban Development (Habitat III)', in, Document A/CONF.

Water Footprint Calculator 2017, *Water Footprint Comparisons by Country*, Water Footprint Calculator. Available from: www.watercalculator.org/footprints/water-footprints-by-country/. [07.09].

Waugh, E 2011, *Recycling Spaces: Curating the Urban Evolution*, ORO Editions, New York.

Zaatari, S 2017, 'Dubai Population to Double by 2027?' *Gulf News*. Available from: https://gulfnews.com/going-out/society/dubai-population-to-double-by-2027-1.2249245. [14.05].

6 The potential of Landscape Urbanism in Dubai

Introduction

Landscape Urbanism is a theory that has emerged from the United States and to a lesser degree Europe and Australia. Most of the key authors associated with the conversation regarding Landscape Urbanism hail from the nexus of the University of Pennsylvania and Harvard, which some consider the 'intellectual twin peaks of landscape architecture' (Thompson 2011, p. 8). Given it is some years since Landscape Urbanism entered its 'middle age' (Waldheim 2010), it is timely to ask how it may be applied in regions outside of North America (Thompson 2011, p. 8), regions that differ markedly in environmental, societal and cultural terms. For example, the conditions from which Landscape Urbanism first arose, deindustrialization and the depopulation of the city core (Thompson 2011, p. 23), are in stark contrast to Dubai's modest but growing industrial base and rapid increase in urban population.

The application of Landscape Urbanism outside of North America has been initiated via Kelly Shannon's research (2008), which focusses attention on urbanization in the watery landscapes of Vietnam, and the praxis of Landscape Urbanism theoretician James Corner via his commercial office Field Operations in Qianhai, China (Bull, Weller & Bolleter 2013, p. 62), amongst others. I endeavour to further this process by exploring the potential of Landscape Urbanism to bolster the practice of landscape architecture in Dubai.

Dubai is an appropriate case study because proponents of Landscape Urbanism have yet to apply it in either theoretical or practical terms in the Middle East. Also, as I discussed previously, Dubai is the reference point by which the development of other Middle Eastern cities, particularly in the Gulf region, are charted – elements of its development either being copied or used as an example of what is to be avoided (Abaza 2011). As such, the application of Landscape Urbanism theory in Dubai has the potential to inform practice over a much broader region.

I have argued in the previous chapter that the urban professions in Dubai have diverged from the UN's and IFLA's various charters concerning environmental stewardship, social equity and responsiveness to local culture (Bolleter 2009, p. 28). Proponent James Corner claims that Landscape Urbanism offers some of the most compelling future directions for the 'advancement of a more socially just, politically emancipating and ecologically sane mix of spatio-temporal production processes' in a world gone awry (Corner 2003, p. 62). In the light of this claim, this chapter will consider whether Landscape Urbanism theory can assist in dealing with the various environmental, societal and cultural challenges designers of the urban landscape in Dubai face. The related research question is:

> *What aspects of Landscape Urbanism theory could the urban professions in Dubai employ in the design of environmentally, societally and culturally enriching landscapes?*

In answering this question, I briefly summarize the shortfalls in current practice and 'evaluate' (Swaffield & Deming 2011, p. 42) what Landscape Urbanism theory could contribute in these areas. I carry out this evaluation in relation to several key tenets:

- Landscape Urbanism rejects a binary construction of nature and culture and directly engages the city as a hybrid ecology (Weller 2006b; Thompson 2011). I discuss this assertion in relation to its ability to bolster landscape architectural practice to support biodiversity in Dubai.
- Landscape Urbanism is less concerned with what things look like and more with what they do (Thompson 2011, p. 12). I discuss this assertion in relation to its ability to bolster landscape architectural practice to support social equity and integration in Dubai.
- Landscape Urbanism privileges an objective understanding of site forces, not the designer's subjectivity (Weller 2006b, p. 67). I discuss this assertion in relation to its ability to bolster landscape architectural practice to be more responsive to local culture.

While Landscape Urbanism embodies other tenets, these relate less directly to the environmental, societal and cultural issues that were the focus of the previous chapters. For the sake of brevity, I have omitted these from this discussion.

In this chapter, I refer to several terms that require clarification. 'Orthodox' landscape design practice refers to practice broadly in alignment with the environmental, societal and cultural goals set out by the UN and IFLA. While in previous chapters I used the term 'landscape designers' – as inclusive of planners, urban designers, landscape architects, architects and placemakers – in this chapter, I refer explicitly to landscape architects. This is because Landscape Urbanism is an 'ism' of landscape architecture specifically. A hypothetical designer in Dubai aspiring to apply Landscape

Urbanism theory to practice I refer to as a Dubai Landscape Urbanist. To focus this chapter, I consider principally what Landscape Urbanism can offer in the landscape design of the public realm in Dubai, as opposed to private podium decks or resort landscapes, for instance. This is because the public realm is most likely to be able to contribute to the environmental, societal and cultural issues I raised in the previous chapter.

Body

The following sections discuss the potential of Landscape Urbanism theory to bolster the practice of landscape architecture in relation to prevailing environmental, societal and cultural issues.

Environmental issues

As stated in chapter 2, Dubai sits at the northern tip of the Rub al Khali desert. The city has been built over a coastal sabkha (salt marsh) in the intertidal areas (Kurschner 1998, p. 64) and the edges of the Rub al Khali desert itself. Conceptions of what constitutes nature and culture, in Dubai's hyper-arid environment, tend to be confused. The highly artificial landscape, parascape, that typically swaths Dubai's developments and forms the backdrop of the Municipality park system, often is equated with nature despite its having almost no real ecological value (Doherty 2008). The situation whereby green verdure becomes associated with paradise and henceforth is naturalized tends to cast the desert and sabkha, Dubai's endemic landscapes, as a tabula rasa.

This conceptualization appears to have been instrumental in the relative failure of McHargian ecological planning methods in Dubai. The *Structure Plan for the Dubai Urban Area 1993–2012* was organized by an, albeit superficial, McHargian mapping of 'important biological areas' requiring conservation (Parsons Harland Bartholomew 1995). Despite this, rampant urban development in Dubai since 1993 has seen these areas degraded and in some cases destroyed. These important biological areas included terrestrial habitat in the form of 'open desert woodland' that extends east of Dubai's urbanized area. This landscape contains species such as the desert hare, gazelles, oryx, foxes and falcons (Gallacher 2007). Other important biological areas identified included sabkha areas on Dubai Creek and along the coast (Dubai Municipality 2003).

The partial destruction of these important biological areas has occurred, in part, because these landscapes have not been assigned any value as natural systems due to their hyper-arid and sparsely vegetated nature (Bolleter 2009, p. 37), which has provided little resistance to development. Aesthetically, the vast, hyper-arid Rub al Khali desert and the desiccated salt-encrusted sands of sabkha do not align with a construction of forest wilderness as nature. Indeed, desert landscapes of the Arabian Peninsula have been associated historically with savagery, hardships and deprivations, and the ecological value of these landscapes is not immediately apparent to the untrained eye.

Landscape Urbanism and conserving and incubating biodiversity

The characterization of city as landscape (Office for Metropolitan Architecture, Koolhaas & Mau 1995, p. 835), which underpins Landscape Urbanism's claims for an expanded sphere of urban influence, reflects the emergence of cities in the late twentieth and early twenty-first centuries in which the 'traditional notion of the city . . . has been largely replaced by a more polycentric and web-like sprawl' (Wall 1999, p. 234). In such cities, proponents argue, the traditional binary notions of a defined, compact city and fringing landscape can be reconceptualized as a form of 'hybridised chaotic ecology' (Weller 2008, p. 248). While Landscape Urbanism theory identifies a blurring of the traditional binary coupling of a city and its landscape, it also entails a collapse of the grand, polarized narratives of nature and culture implied by McHarg's environmental planning methods (Waldheim 2002, p. 12; Thompson 2011, p. 9) and modernity in general.

The problem that Landscape Urbanism proponents identify with a binary coupling of nature and culture is that landscape architecture tends to be relegated to being the passive, subjugated part (Weller 2006b, p. 67). Further to this is the notion of clearly delineated boundaries between 'natural' wilderness areas and 'cultural' urban areas that Landscape Urbanists regard to be detrimental in ecological terms. Contemporary ecological science relies on a more complex understanding of a given site as part of an expanded system that receives and provides matter, energy and organisms (Pulliam & Johnson 2002, p. 54).

The potential of a hybridized ecology model in Dubai

The model of a 'hybridised ecology' (Weller 2008, p. 248) has implications for both the conservation of remnant biodiversity and the potential creation of new 'hybridised' ecological systems. As Richard Weller suggests, 'In a model where nature and culture are hybridised, and nature is not an absolute to be protected, landscape architecture is potentially able to develop a more creative relationship with ecology' (Weller 2007). This shift from conservation to creative proposition has significance for Dubai given that many of its important biological areas have already been significantly degraded by development (Bolleter 2009, p. 37). These areas need not just reservation but also (to some degree) reconstruction.

A Landscape Urbanist in Dubai keen to pursue a model of 'hybridised ecology' may struggle, however, because Landscape Urbanism does not provide much in the way of direct guidance as to what this means. The hybridizing of natural and cultural systems has, in some Landscape Urbanist projects, amounted to the structuring of urban areas around their hydrological systems. This is exemplified by James Corner Field Operations' Quinhai Water City project (Bull, Weller & Bolleter 2013) and Richard Weller's Wungong Urban Water project (2008). Both these projects reflect what critics of Landscape Urbanism refer to as the 'hydrological privilege' (Duany & Talen 2013, p. 7) because urban form is laid out in relation to hydrological networks.

Due to its extremely arid climate, Dubai does not have the hydrological systems that could directly structure urban districts. While Dubai does experience flooding, this is due to drains filling up with sand in the extended periods between significant rainfall events. Contrasting with the temperate regions from which Landscape Urbanism theory emerged, the systems of vegetation in the desert to Dubai's south are also relatively sparse and so would be difficult to interweave with urban development (Gallacher & Hill 2007, p. 856) or deploy as a template for an urban setting. In addition, ecological science is a poorly developed field in Dubai, which leaves the urban professions practicing in a vacuum in relation to ecological matters.

Landscape Urbanism proponents such as Richard Weller concede the difficulty of this process of hybridization:

> In practice it is hard to reconcile the land's ecological systems with suburban (or urban) systems. The reason for this is fundamental; ecological systems are organic and boundless whereas suburban systems are mechanistic; ecological systems are radically site specific whereas suburban systems are standardised and generic.
>
> (Weller 2008, p. 254)

This challenge, which is tricky in temperate climes, becomes particularly difficult in Dubai where the natural systems are not heavily vegetated or are not 'wet' or 'dense' enough to structure urban form.

A 'negotiated' landscape that synthesizes the hyper-arid desert and the verdant artificiality of parascape could entwine with Dubai's urban form as a model of 'hybrid ecology.' However, this negotiated landscape is unlikely to be a habitat to support local biodiversity, reflecting the difficulty of organisms trading one habitat for another (Marsh 2005, p. 380). Unlike humans, who have a wide range of habitat versatility, most organisms displaced from one habitat cannot simply take up life in another (Marsh 2005, p. 380). In Dubai, many verdant green spaces have little biodiversity value because they actively conflict with indigenous ecosystems, disrupting the native desert habitats with foreign and ecologically sterile species (Doherty 2008, p. 106).

The model of 'hybridised ecology' in urbanizing areas is also potentially problematic as the basis for protecting existing biodiversity. As Weller worries, 'by forsaking pure nature as a site of resistance,' Landscape Urbanism is in turn prone to 'complicity' in the destruction of natural areas (Weller 2006b, p. 67). The 'naturalisation of the contemporary city confers a certain inevitability upon its growth, which in turn can seem to justify its rampant and destructive spread' (Weller 2008, p. 249).

Employing the notion of a 'hybridised ecology' as a means of protecting remnant ecologies in the Dubai context – where massive amounts of capital are turned instantly into high-value property (Basar 2007b) – seems risky. If the clear spatial delineation of McHargian planning was historically not able to protect 'important biological areas' from Dubai's unregulated development, then it is doubtful that a blurry conception of nature and culture will prevent further transgressions. While Landscape Urbanism proponents might identify that a clearly delineated edge between Dubai's 'nature' and 'culture' does not represent the true complexity of ecological relationships, it at least provides designers a (potentially) persuasive tool to lobby Dubai's developers and rulers.

In conclusion, the model of the city as 'hybridised ecology' (Weller 2008, p. 248) offers little by way of practical assistance to the landscape architect in Dubai working towards fulfilling the UN's or IFLA's ethos of environmental 'stewardship' and 'nurturing the continued health and diversity of landscapes' (International Federation of Landscape Architects Asia Pacific 2015, p. 5). It appears difficult to adapt to the sparse and fragile desert and sabkha ecologies. Neither is it suited to Dubai's typically unregulated development industry that would be quick to exploit or dismiss its spatial and conceptual ambiguities.

Societal issues

The dominant economic ideology in Dubai is one of neo-liberalism. Social geographer David Harvey describes the aspiration of the neo-liberal state as to manufacture a 'good business climate' and thus to 'optimize conditions for capital accumulation no matter what the consequences' for the environment or social well-being (Harvey 2005, p. 25). In this respect, Dubai has achieved what 'neo liberal reactionaries only dream of; a paradise of free enterprise without income taxes, trade unions or opposition parties' (Davis 2007, p. 67).

As discussed in earlier chapters, while Dubai is extremely multicultural, there is significant socio-economic stratification, and little interaction tends to occur between the various strata. In this respect, Dubai has been successful in creating spaces for diverging cultural groups without requiring significant assimilation (Kirchner & Rab 2007, p. 18). While the separation of cultural groups along economic lines has allowed for a 'functioning' multicultural society, it has also created conditions by which some socio-economic strata become 'othered.' In Dubai, the 'other,' is associated with the unskilled South Asian labourers whom construction companies house in camps in peri-urban areas and who typically earn a fraction of the wage of most Dubai residents. That labourer is male and becomes a symbolic threat to women, encouraging further separation from the city. Much of the highly privatized city remains unavailable to Dubai's unskilled migrant labourers and domestic workers (Davis 2007). Even in the 'public' park system, the Dubai Municipality fences parks and charges an entry fee and, as such, the park system is semi-public, at best.

For much of the public landscape outside of the park system, landscape architects have designed as scenography without an obvious use and not in support of any specific programmatic function. As discussed previously, parascape is employed to legitimize the power of the ruling dynasty (Ouis 2002). Despite significant efforts towards modernization in some arenas, Dubai remains an autocracy in which any evidence of meaningful democracy proves difficult to find, a situation maintained by Dubai's rulers through what Christopher Davidson refers to as the 'ruling bargain' (2008, p. 138). This ruling bargain exists between Dubai's rulers and the city's population and involves the 'careful exploitation of a range of ideological, religious, and cultural resources' and the buying of loyalty with distributed revenue (Davidson 2008, p. 138).

With its symbolic paradisiacal associations, Dubai's rulers have used parascape effectively as a tool to reinforce this 'ruling bargain.' As Jonathon Smith attests, the seductive appeal of 'judiciously styled' visual landscape 'may forestall reflection on the failure of society to furnish its members with the means to consume landscapes in more practical [and equitable] ways' (In Corner 1999, p. 157). In relation to this deception, Dubai landscape architecture often becomes an unwitting tool of the prevailing political and economic power brokers (Ouis 2002).

Landscape Urbanism and social equity and inclusiveness

The charters of the Congress for the New Urbanism (2007) advocate urban form as a mechanism through which designers can engage society for positive ends. In contrast, Landscape Urbanist James Corner refers to geographer David Harvey's proposition that what is required is a 'utopia of process,' not a 'utopia of form' (Harvey 2005, p. 25). This shift from 'form' to 'economic, socio-political, and ecological process' (Thompson 2011, p. 6) underpins Landscape Urbanism's claims to actively engage societal structures to achieve its socio-ecologically enriching ends (Lootsma 1999, p. 273).

Discussion around process in Landscape Urbanism literature has two dimensions: firstly, that Landscape Urbanists should focus attention on process within the larger societal, political and economic context; secondly, that designed spaces should become more infrastructural and process orientated and less driven by aesthetic concerns (Corner 1999, p. 160). This section discusses the potential of these two approaches to support landscape architects in promoting social equity and integration in Dubai's designed landscapes.

The potential of a 'utopia of process' in Dubai

Through a focus on process, Landscape Urbanism seeks to engage with 'uncontrolled capital accumulation' and 'gross inequalities of political and economic power' (Harvey in Corner 2006, p. 28), underlying forces that to a large degree have generated the physical form of Dubai. It is this utopia of process, 'how things work in space and time' (Corner 2006, p. 29), that Landscape Urbanism uses to distinguish itself from competing disciplines such as New Urbanism. Both Landscape Urbanism, and a number of urban design and planning theorists (Fishman 2003; Fainstein 2003), criticize New Urbanism for its 'easy elision of physical form with social condition' and little theoretical thoroughness (Fainstein 2003, p. 182). New Urbanism is criticized for its tendency to create 'utopias of spatial form' (Harvey 2002, p. 156) rather than delineating the process of achieving them. Social geographer David Harvey is often quoted in Landscape Urbanism literature (Corner 2003, p. 62; Waldheim & Berger 2008) as identifying the task as to bring together a 'spatio-temporal utopianism,' a 'utopia of process' (Harvey 2002, p. 196).

Such processes, in which a Landscape Urbanist in Dubai should engage, remain, however, ambiguous in Landscape Urbanism literature. Harvey's argument, cited by Corner, is that deregulation, globalization, environmental protection, codes and regulations, market trends and so on are much more significant for the shaping of urban relationships than are spatial forms per se (Corner 2003, p. 61). By extension, what Corner seems to be saying is that Landscape Urbanists in Dubai could combat social inequity more effectively if they directly engaged the development industry or government to have greater influence over the economic and regulatory settings that influence the resultant form and urban relationships of the city.

In this respect, the hypothetical Landscape Urbanist in Dubai would be a lobbyist for social equity and integration with Dubai's power brokers. While the urban professions have, to date, passively relied on Dubai's rulers to legislate for public open space with disappointing results, potentially a Landscape Urbanist could engage with clients to find models for public areas that are potentially both profitable and socially inclusive. While Landscape Urbanism literature cites no particular examples in this respect, perhaps Olmsted's meticulous justification of the costs of Manhattan's Central Park in relation to the capitalization of the park's value to proximate homeowners provides one such example (Crompton 2005, p. 218).

The challenges of attempting such an engagement with the Dubai's political and economic power brokers would be significant. The ruling tribal family who control both government regulation and the development industry believe the minds of a select few should map national visions for the rest (Basar 2007a, p. 92). So, the ability of a Dubai Landscape Urbanist to carry sway within this extremely closed and hierarchical socio-political structure is difficult to imagine. In this respect, it is of paramount importance that landscape architects and others form institutes that can lobby for broader societal outcomes.

Beyond lobbying for public space, social equity and inclusivity in Dubai encapsulate many other issues such as housing affordability, access to public transport and schools, to name a few. Landscape Urbanists in Dubai seeking to broaden their sphere of influence to include 'all that is in the landscape – infrastructure and buildings' (Weller 2006b, p. 67) would find that Landscape Urbanism theory has very little to say about pragmatic issues of social equity, including 'housing segregation . . . pollution, concentrated poverty, traffic congestion, bad schools, affordability, safety, accessibility,' the 'issues [that] form-based urban designers . . . have been toiling with' (Talen 2013, p. 112). Certainly critics of Landscape Urbanism see its predilections for indeterminacy and process, as well as its overt ecological focus as a way of 'forestalling the need to deal with such clichéd social concerns' (Talen 2013, p. 112). While a Landscape Urbanist in Dubai may be able to navigate this complex terrain, the body of Landscape Urbanism literature certainly does not provide much direct practical assistance.

The potential of Landschaft *in Dubai*

Landscape Urbanism calls for a focus on process also in the design of landscapes themselves. Here, the emphasis shifts from what things look like to how they work and what they do (Corner 2003, p. 61). As Alex Wall describes, 'the goal of designing the urban surface is to increase its capacity to support and diversify activities in time' (Wall 1999, p. 233). A precursor to Landscape Urbanism's conceptual shift between scenography and programmatic landscape is OMA's second-place entry for the Parc De La Villette competition in Paris, France, in 1982, a scheme that appears frequently in Landscape Urbanist literature (Wall 1999; Waldheim 2002; Waldheim 2006; Weller 2006a). The project's designers, Rem Koolhaas and Bruce Mau, describe the conventional park as a 'replica of nature serviced by a minimal number of facilities that ensure its enjoyment' (1995, p. 921). The alternative to this approach, which their Parc de la Villette design encapsulates, is the orchestration of the

> most dynamic coexistence of activities x, y, and z and to generate through their mutual interference a chain reaction of new, unprecedented events . . . a social condenser, based on horizontal congestion, the size of a park.
>
> (Office for Metropolitan Architecture,
> Koolhaas & Mau 1995, p. 921)

Central to the notion of the 'social condenser' to which Koolhaas and Mau refer is the idea that design can affect social behaviour, the purpose of social condensers being to break down societal hierarchies. This concept, derived from Russian constructivist theory, found expression in OMA's La Villette proposition in the creation of intersections between varied constituencies. In literal terms, this manifests itself as a series of physical striations, each containing different park functions – the idea being that social friction and exchange will occur on the edges between these bands. The rejection of stylized nature in favour of programmed landscape, as in OMA's La Villette, becomes a central theme in Landscape Urbanism literature (Corner 1999; Wall 1999).[1]

If parascape can be employed to promote particular socio-political agendas to a populace (Bolleter 2009), then presumably alternatively designed public landscapes could communicate more enriching and inclusive narratives to Dubai's society. In this respect, Corner identifies the potential of '*Landschaft.*' In Corner's writing, *Landschaft* is a German word that refers not to scenery but to the environment of a working community (Corner 1999, p. 154).[2] In the contemporary context, Corner considers *Landschaft* to constitute a landscape that is occupied and programmed, not preoccupied with the creation of a fixed scene with a correspondingly fixed agenda (Corner 1999). Following on from Corner's logic, the deployment of highly programmed, interactive and inclusive landscape in Dubai has the potential to counter the symbolic fixity offered by Dubai's scenographic landscapes. As Wall explains about the work of landscape architect Adrian Geuze, which he aligns with *Landschaft*, 'it is about making things and places that are indeterminate in their functions and thereby allow their users to invent and claim space for themselves' (Wall 1999, p. 245). The shift from stylistic, unprogrammed landscapes to *Landschaft* is regarded by proponents as one mechanism by which Landscape Urbanism can transform landscape from being 'a product of culture to landscape as an agent producing and enriching culture' (Corner 1999, p. 4).

Landscape Urbanism's predilection for highly programmed, indeterminate and inclusive landscapes sits in complete opposition to Dubai's existing parks that are highly scenographic, pastoral, (relatively) unprogrammed and semi-private. While the Dubai Municipality describe their parks as being for 'everyone,' the Municipality intend them as family areas for locals and wealthy expatriates. Landscape Urbanism's model of *Landschaft* and its attendant aim to erode social hierarchies raise issues when applied to Dubai's restrictive social context.

While in the West the privatization of public space amounts to a reduction in civil liberties and freedom of expression, privatization in Dubai often brings forth an expanded area of relative freedom for female Emiratis, for example. Within the confines of spaces owned by respectable Emirati families and corporations where gates, guards and camera surveillance are seen, the permissible space where a woman can move unveiled is extended (Andraos 2007, p. 53). The fact that Islamic women in semi-private, as opposed to public, space often enjoy greater freedoms is an irony that a Landscape Urbanist could overlook in a quest for public space that erodes social hierarchies. A similar situation occurs at a larger scale in which cultural groups in Dubai 'maintain strict segregatory measures, by having their own set of institutions which enable them to maintain their cultural values' (Elsheshtawy 2004, p. 172).

It is within this context that Landscape Urbanism's model of *Landschaft*, as a social condenser aiming to break down societal hierarchies, has issues. While such a segregated society requires more spaces that allow for the interaction of various cultural groups, a Landscape Urbanist would need to handle this interaction with care and respect complex cultural sensitivities. Landscape Urbanism's discussion of *Landschaft*, reflecting the various authors' origins, provides little guidance as to its more nuanced application in this cross-cultural context.

A further issue that arises in the deployment of *Landschaft* in Dubai and indeed in OMA's unbuilt scheme for La Villette, which Alex Wall aligns with *Landschaft*, is the question of just what this programmed *Landschaft* is. While Koolhaas and Mau refer to La Villette as a 'landscape of social instruments,' the actual programme proposed for the park is ambiguous. In the accompanying text for their competition entry, Koolhaas and Mau specifically identified only a limited number of what are actually traditional park functions: kiosks, playgrounds, refreshment bars, picnic areas, amphitheatres, chess tables, puppet theatres, and roller-skating surfaces, amongst others (1995, pp. 925, 927). The question remains, in relation to both OMA's La Villette and *Landschaft* in Dubai today, as to whether this limited amount of programming could really constitute the 'engine of the project' that Wall argues it is (Wall 1999, p. 237). A study of recreational activities in Dubai reveals that recreation is often driven indoors by exceedingly hot temperatures and a restrictive culture (Dubai Municipality 2001). Taken as a guide, it appears there would be precious few outdoor recreational activities to deploy to activate *Landschaft* in Dubai, at least in the summer months.

Despite its attendant problems and challenges, Landscape Urbanism's 'utopia of process' whether applied to the conceptualization of a Landscape Urbanist's role in a project or to the design of public landscapes in Dubai seem to have some potential. For landscape architects to be more involved in the process behind the eventual formal resolution of urban landscapes is timely, as is a greater level of functionality in Dubai's overtly stylistic landscapes, which invites usage and interaction, with more malleable symbolism. Whether these strategies could enable Dubai Landscape Urbanists to achieve Harvey's 'advancement of a more socially just, politically emancipating and ecologically sane mix of spatio-temporal production processes' (Corner 2003, p. 63) is, however, questionable – particularly when viewed within the context of a society where 'no real effort is made to resolve social problems, address concerns of the lower class, or try to make the urban environment more liveable' (Elsheshtawy 2004, p. 172).

Cultural issues

The numeric dominance of expatriates in Dubai is a result of the waves of immigration that the city has absorbed since the discovery of oil in the 1960s. The accelerated rate of urban development that has accompanied this extreme population growth has, in recent decades, been a response to diminishing oil reserves. A relative lack of industry, agriculture or naturally occurring attractions means the city relies on global investment and tourism to survive. Dubai constantly craves attention, concerned that fading from global view will herald its demise. One expression of this fear is The Palm and The World developments that brand whole areas for the city from the perspective of Google Earth.

In this section, I question what Landscape Urbanism could offer landscape architects in terms of establishing a deeper resonance with the local culture and landscape in the face of Dubai's global ambitions. Certainly, the theory of Landscape Urbanism offers little guidance as to how to conduct a cross-cultural design exercise or more generally to reconcile development with 'a sense of place.' The tone of Landscape Urbanism literature characterizes landscape as typically an 'accelerant,' 'matrix' and 'continuous surface,' something available for anything, anytime, thus relieving 'landscape of its traditional burden as culture's anchor in a world adrift' (Wall in Weller 2008, p. 254). Alex Wall's rationale for this conception of urban landscape is based on the 'new urban conditions of placelessness and the mobility of capital, goods and people,' conditions seemingly at odds with landscape architecture's traditional desire for 'groundedness, orientation and emplacement' (Weller 2007, p. 29). Other Dutch Landscape Urbanists such as Bart Lootsma do, however, propose the method of datascaping, which they believe could begin to articulate differences between regional locations. While this tool does not provide a guide for a cross-cultural design or for reconciling development with 'place,' it is the aspect of Landscape Urbanism theory that is most relevant to the complexities of practice in regional locations.

Landscape Urbanism and engaging regional culture

Landscape Urbanism theory claims to privilege an objective understanding of site forces rather than the designer's own subjective artistic intuitions (Weller 2006b, p. 67). Proponents propose to drive this, in part, through the analysis and design methodology of datascaping. As Lootsma explains:

> Datascapes are visual representations of all the measurable forces that may influence the work of the architect or even steer or regulate it. These influences may be planning and building regulations, technical and economic constraints, natural conditions such as wind and sun, or legislative measures such as minimum working conditions.
>
> (Lootsma 1999, p. 270)

Datascaping is a methodology that features strongly in the design process of a number of Dutch landscape architects and architects including OMA, West 8 and MVRDV (Lootsma 1999, p. 265) and can be seen as part of a larger focus on the understanding of site forces as generating design.

Datascapes promise to remove subjectivity from the design process, a premise that has polarized reactions to it. Winy Maas, principal of the design firm MVRDV, describes how, through datascaping, artistic intuition is replaced by 'research' (Maas 1998, p. 49). If enough data is 'plugged in' and extrapolated, then a form will 'materialise' that is beyond artistic intuition (Maas 1998, p. 49).

Lootsma proposes that datascaping will, in time, produce forms of 'synthetic regionalisation' in response to data 'gravity fields' that are specific to particular places and states that datascaping is concerned with 'critical pragmatism' not 'critical regionalism' (Lootsma 1999, p. 270). Critical regionalism aspires to the 'grand narrative of reconciling modernity to place' (Weller 2007, p. 40) and relies on creative interpretations of the local topography, climate, culture, materials and light to achieve this reconciliation. In contrast, 'critical pragmatism' – which derives from datascaping – employs detailed and utilitarian site data in order to articulate a site's identity in the design process.

In the critique of globalization as inimical to difference, as found in the writings of Lootsma (1999), Zaera Polo (1994) and Maas (1998), it is proposed that, through attention to the abstract data of globalization, the enhancement of diversification that globalization causes will necessarily follow. In short, Landscape Urbanists suggest that globalization can actually enhance difference. For Maas, places are manifestly different, and this difference is quite simply because of the basic data that lies behind their formal properties (Weller 2007, p. 38).

The potential of datascaping to articulate regional difference in Dubai

The question remains to what degree datascaping could assist a Landscape Urbanist in Dubai to produce landscape design that articulates regional difference. I believe datascaping has both potential possibilities and problems in Dubai.

The problems potentially arise from the fact that landscape architects working in Dubai often lack the required information or data to make basic decisions, let alone to construct a datascaping design methodology, which is obviously data reliant. Dubai tends to be, by European standards, an under-regulated building environment, and as such, the planning, building and legislative controls found in Lootsma's Holland do not exist to the same degree in Dubai. What regulatory data that is available in Dubai often derives from internationally accepted standards and thus is less able to contribute to the differentiation of Dubai.

The possibilities spring from data generated by Dubai's extreme climatic, economic and demographic conditions, which should assist in generating alternative landscape design outcomes if given due importance in the design process. Indeed, close attention to technical data such as irrigation requirements could herald, in contrast to the existing Dubai Municipality parks, a vastly reconfigured, xerophytic form of open space.

A problem remains, however, even if all the required data was readily available, it would be unlikely to prepare a Landscape Urbanist for engaging with the complex cultural, societal and pragmatic issues that landscape architects find in Dubai. As Weller notes, 'making form, and crafting its semiotic load, cannot be indefinitely deferred or completely conferred on to mechanisms beyond the author' (Weller 2007, p. 39). Thus, while a privileging of site forces, through datascaping, can bring a landscape designer closer to apprehending the inherent qualities of a site, it does not mean a subjective response to place can be avoided entirely.

Take, for example, the technical data regarding irrigation; even if a Landscape Urbanist in Dubai is cognizant of the extreme irrigation requirements of a palm tree (128 litres per day in summer) and turf (15 litres per square metre in summer), this data will not objectively direct them towards a landscape design. From a broader perspective, this issue then needs to be considered with respect to how much irrigated 'green' landscape is required by the users of landscape either for active or passive recreational pursuits or, perhaps more importantly, to meet Emirati and expatriate cultural expectations for greenery (Ouis 2002), something that is very difficult to reduce to data alone. Any of the objectivity that Maas (1998, p. 49) describes in the design process very quickly becomes mired with a series of necessarily subjective decisions. This is not in itself a problem; it just is not that different from a conventional landscape architectural design process. Indeed, landscape architecture is no stranger to site data. As Weller describes, landscape architecture 'has made site analysis data central to its design process and philosophy for the last three decades' (Weller 2007, p. 39).

Conclusion

The principal conclusion of this chapter is that several of the Landscape Urbanism tenets I have discussed appear problematic when considered in relation to the various environmental, societal and cultural challenges experienced by landscape architecture in Dubai. Undoubtedly, a number of these tenets, such as a 'privileging of site data' and a focus on 'process,' if employed in a reasoned manner, make some sense as a counterbalance to typical Dubai landscape architectural practice. However, the question remains as to what Landscape Urbanism offers in Dubai that is not already on offer as part of a well-practiced, ecologically, societally and culturally aware form of landscape architecture. An attention to process, not merely form, is hardly new to landscape architecture, as is attention to site data (Weller 2007, p. 39).

Further to this, a Landscape Urbanist in Dubai appears to be lacking the kind of tools that provide a bridge between theory and practice. While theories such as New Urbanism provide various tools (for example, the Transect or From Based Codes) by which designers can put the theory of New Urbanism into practice, Landscape Urbanism offers no such props for practitioners in Dubai, leaving them to interpret how theory should be actioned. This is particularly the case where Landscape Urbanism claims 'infrastructure and buildings' (Weller 2006b, p. 67) as being within its sphere of disciplinary influence. Landscape Urbanism literature offers little to Landscape Urbanists in Dubai as to how they would engage with these areas in practical terms. The risk of this general situation being perpetuated is that Landscape Urbanism may become more of a 'planning and literary trope than a guide to physical design' (Dennis & McIntosh 2013, p. 51). Corner himself describes that the complex amalgam of Landscape Urbanism 'is more than a singular image or style; it is an ethos, an attitude, a way of thinking and acting' (Corner 2003, p. 58). While this is legitimate, it diminishes the potential of Landscape Urbanism in a place such as Dubai, where day-to-day practice very much dominates over theory. Ironically, it is such places that are experiencing rapid development that could most benefit from theory informing practice.

With this in mind, the subsequent concluding chapter summarizes the key lessons of the book for practitioners and provides an overview of the implications of continuing current practice in Dubai, as well as exporting the city's urban development model to rapidly urbanizing areas of the globe.

Notes

1 While some Landscape Urbanism literature would appear to suggest otherwise, heavily programmed landscapes such as OMA's proposal for La Villette are also stylized; they are just not naturalistic aesthetics (Thompson 2011).
2 While there is conjecture about the meaning of the German word *Landschaft* as it appears in Corner's writing, this chapter will refer to Corner's interpretation as this pertains directly to the discussion of *Landschaft* in this chapter.

References

Abaza, M 2011, 'Critical Commentary: Cairo's Downtown Imagined: Dubaisation or Nostalgia?' *Urban Studies*, vol. 48, no. 6, pp. 1075–1087.

Andraos, A 2007, 'Dubai's Island Urbanism: An Archipelago of Difference for the 21st Century?' in *Vision Plus Money Plus Historical Circumstance Equals 'Cities from Zero' Unapologetic Expressions of New-Found Economic and Therefore Political-Prowess in the 21st Century*, pp. 47–56, Architectural Association Publishing, London.

Basar, S 2007a, 'Twelve Ultimate Critical Steps to Sudden Urban Success', in *Vision Plus Money Plus Historical Circumstance Equals 'Cities from Zero' Unapologetic*

Expressions of New-Found Economic and Therefore Political-Prowess in the 21st Century, pp. 73–95, Architectural Association Publishing, London.

Basar, S 2007b, 'V+M+HC=CFZ Introduction', in *Vision Plus Money Plus Historical Circumstance Equals 'Cities from Zero' Unapologetic Expressions of New-Found Economic and Therefore Political-Prowess in the 21st Century*, pp. 1–18, Architectural Association Publications, London.

Bolleter, J 2009, 'Para-Scape: Landscape Architecture in Dubai', *Journal of Landscape Architecture*, Spring, no. 4, pp. 28–55.

Bull, C, Weller, R & Bolleter, J 2013, 'The Urban Issue', *Landscape Architecture Australia*, no. 137.

Congress for the New Urbanism 2007, 'Charter of the New Urbanism', in M Larice & E MacDonald, (eds), *The Urban Design Reader*, Routledge, Oxon.

Corner, J 1999, 'Eidetic Operations and New Landscapes', in *Recovering Landscape: Essays in Contemporary Landscape Architecture*, pp. 153–170, Princeton Architectural Press, New York.

Corner, J 2003, 'Landscape Urbanism', in *Landscape Urbanism: A Manual for the Machine Landscape*, pp. 58–62, Architectural Association, London.

Corner, J 2006, 'Terra Fluxus', in *The Landscape Urbanism Reader*, pp. 21–34, Princeton Architectural Press, New York.

Crompton, J 2005, 'The Impact of Parks on Property Values: Empirical Evidence from the Past Two Decades in the United States', *Managing Leisure*, vol. 10, no. 4, pp. 203–218.

Davidson, C 2008, *Dubai: The Vulnerability of Success*, Columbia University Press, New York.

Davis, M 2007, 'Fear and Money in Dubai', *Topos*, pp. 62–70.

Dennis, M & McIntosh, A 2013, 'Landscape and the City', in A Duany & E Talen (eds), *Landscape Urbanism and Its Discontents: Dissimulating the Sustainable City*, pp. 35–56, New Society Publishers, Gabriola Island, BC.

Doherty, G 2008, 'The Landscape of Dubai's Urbanism', in *Instant Cities: Emergent Trends in Architecture and Urbanism in the Arab World*, pp. 103–111, CSAAR, Amman.

Duany, A & Talen, E 2013, 'Looking Backward: Notes on a Cultural Episode', in A Duany & E Talen (eds), *Landscape Urbanism and Its Discontents: Dissimulating the Sustainable City*, pp. 1–16, New Society Publishers, Gabriola Island, BC.

Dubai Municipality 2001, *Recreation Centres in Dubai Map*, in Recreation Centres in Dubai Map, Dubai Municipality GIS Centre, Dubai.

Dubai Municipality 2003, *Ras Al Khor Wildlife Sanctuary*, Brochure, Dubai Municipality. Available from: www.panda.org/who_we_are/wwf_offices/united_arab_emirates/news/?20230/Ras-Al-Khor-Wildlife-Sanctuary.

Elsheshtawy, Y 2004, 'Redrawing Boundaries: Dubai, an Emerging Global City', in Y Elsheshtawy (ed), *Planning Middle Eastern Cities: An Urban Kaleidoscope in a Globalizing World*, pp. 164–187, Routledge, Oxon.

Fainstein, S 2003, 'New Directions in Planning Theory', in S Campbell & S Fainstein (eds), *Readings in Planning Theory*, pp. 173–195, Blackwell Publishing, Malden, MA, and Oxford.

Fishman, R 2003, 'Urban Utopias: Ebenezer Howard, Frank Lloyd Wright, and Le Corbusier', in S Campbell & S Fainstein (eds), *Readings in Planning Theory*, pp. 21–60, Blackwell Publishing, Oxford and Melbourne.

Gallacher, D 2007, 'Overgrazing Their Welcome', *Zawaya*, pp. 30–33.

Gallacher, D & Hill, J 2007, 'Effects of Camel Grazing on Density and Species Diversity of Seedling Emergence in the Dubai (UAE) Inland Desert', *Journal of Arid Environments*, vol. 72, pp. 853–860.

Harvey, D 2002, *Spaces of Hope*, Cromwell Press, Edinburgh.

Harvey, D 2005, *Spaces of Global Capitalism*, Verso, London.

International Federation of Landscape Architects Asia Pacific 2015, *IFLA Asia-Pacific Region Landscape Charter*, International Federation of Landscape Architects Asia Pacific, IFoL Architects Asia Pacific Region.

Johnson, H & Hill, K 2002, 'Introduction: Toward Landscape Realism', in *Ecology and Design: Frameworks for Learning*, pp. 1–28, Island Press, Washington, DC.

Kirchner, M & Rab, S 2007, 'An Arabian Night's Fantasy, and That's OK', *Al Manakh*, vol. 12, no. 7, pp. 18–22.

Kurschner, H 1998, 'Biogeography and Introduction to Vegetation', in S Ghazanfar & M Fisher, (eds), *Vegetation of the Arabian Peninsula*, pp. 63–98, Kluwer Academic, The Netherlands.

Lootsma, B 1999, 'Synthetic Regionalization', in *Recovering Landscape: Essays in Contemporary Landscape Architecture*, pp. 251–274, Princeton Architectural Press, New York.

Maas, W 1998, 'Datascape: The Final Extravaganza', *Daidalos*, no. 69/70, pp. 48–54.

Marsh, W 2005, *Landscape Planning: Environmental Applications*, John Wiley & Sons, Hoboken, NJ.

Office for Metropolitan Architecture, Koolhaas, R & Mau, B 1995, *S,M,L,XL*, Monacelli Press, New York.

Ouis, P 2002, 'Greening the Emirates: The Modern Construction of Nature in the United Arab Emirates', *Cultural Geographies*, no. 9, pp. 334–347.

Parsons Harland Bartholomew 1995, *Structure Plan for the Dubai Urban Area 1993–2012*, Dubai Municipality Planning & Survey Department, Dubai.

Pulliam, H & Johnson, B 2002, 'Ecology's New Paradigm: What Does It Offer Designers and Planners', in *Ecology and Design*, pp. 51–84, Island Press, Washington, DC.

Shannon, K 2008, *Water Urbanisms*, SUN, Amsterdam.

Swaffield, S & Deming, E 2011, 'Research Strategies in Landscape Architecture: Mapping the Terrain', *Journal of Landscape Architecture*, Spring, pp. 34–45.

Talen, E 2013, 'The Social Apathy of Landscape Urbanism', in A Duany & E Talen (eds), *Landscape Urbanism and Its Discontents: Dissimulating the Sustainable City*, pp. 105–114, New Society Publishers, Gabriola Island, BC.

Thompson, I 2011, 'Ten Tenets and Six Questions for Landscape Urbanism', *Landscape Research*, vol. 37, no. 1, pp. 7–26.

Waldheim, C 2002, 'Landscape Urbanism: A Genealogy', *Praxis*, no. 4, pp. 10–17.

Waldheim, C 2006, 'Landscape as Urbanism', in *The Landscape Urbanism Reader*, pp. 35–54, Princeton Architectural Press, New York.

Waldheim, C 2010, 'On Landscape, Ecology and Other Modifiers to Urbanism', *Topos*, no. 71, pp. 20–24.

Waldheim, C & Berger, A 2008, 'Logistics Landscape', *Landscape Journal*, vol. 27, no. 2, pp. 219–246.

Wall, A 1999, 'Programming the Urban Surface', in *Recovering Landscape: Essays in Contemporary Landscape Architecture*, pp. 233–250, Princeton Architectural Press, New York City.

Weller, R 2006a, 'An Art of Instrumentality: Thinking Through Landscape Urbanism', in *The Landscape Urbanism Reader*, pp. 69–86, Princeton Architectural Press, New York City.

Weller, R 2006b, 'Global Theory, Local Practice', *Kerb*, no. 15, pp. 66–71.

Weller, R 2007, 'Between Hermeneutics and Datascapes: A Critical Appreciation of Emergent Landscape Design Theory and Praxis Through the Writings of James Corner 1990–2000', *Landscape Review*, vol. 7, no. 1, pp. 3–44.

Weller, R 2008, 'Landscape (Sub) Urbanism in Theory and Practice', *Landscape Journal*, vol. 27, no. 2, pp. 247–267.

Zaera Polo, A 1994, 'Order Out of Chaos: The Material Organization of Advanced Capitalism', *Architectural Design Profile: The Periphery*, vol. 64, no. 3/4, pp. 24–29.

7   Conclusions

Introduction

Firstly, to refresh reader's memories, a broad overview of the book. In chapter 2, I introduced Dubai in terms of its desert landscape, its evolution as an urban settlement, and finally its powerful development model. This chapter sought to refute two stereotypes about Dubai, namely that it is devoid of a substantive history and is, in environmental terms, a tabula rasa. In chapters 3 and 4 of this book, I discussed the main designed landscape types the urban professions in Dubai deliver and loosely categorized them under the rubrics of parascape, urbscape and xeriscape. I investigated these landscape types for the agendas they embody. In summary, these agendas relate to the political legitimization of the rule of Sheikh Mohammed and the capturing of global capital, amongst others. In chapter 5, I juxtaposed the designed landscapes of the urban professions in Dubai with the goals for sustainability, societal equity and cultural sensitivity in landscape design practice of the United Nations (UN) and the International Federation of Landscape Architects (IFLA). I identified a significant disjunction between these aspirations and landscape design practice in Dubai. Chapter 6 concerned Landscape Urbanism theory and hypothesized about its potential to augment landscape design practice in Dubai. I argued that Landscape Urbanist tenets, such as the 'privileging of site data' and a focus on 'process,' make sense as a counterbalance to prevailing landscape design practice in Dubai; however, I concluded that several key facets of Landscape Urbanism are difficult to reconcile with the environmental, societal and cultural conditions of Dubai.

In this concluding chapter, I set out the main findings of the book and some key learnings that I believe could benefit the urban professions in Dubai and related contexts. Finally, I provide an overview of the implications of the study for both Dubai and the broader region and identify potential future areas for research.

Body

Most importantly, the Dubai experience teaches us that unless the urban professions understand the environmental, societal and cultural context in which they are practicing, they – as the 'handmaidens' of global capital – become complicit in negative forms of development. Moreover, apparently ameliorative and benign practices, such as applying parascape, can compound the environmental, societal and cultural issues that the urban professions claim to be addressing.

Landscape design practice and the environmental context

In Dubai, this lack of understanding manifests itself as a perception that Dubai is a 'fantasy land' in the desert, a landscape that designers need to defeat so that sites can yield 'real' landscape, often in the form of parascape. As chapter 2 of this book indicates, Dubai is far from being a tabula rasa. While Dubai's ecological structures are, in a sense, faint, they do exist and prompt a vastly different form of landscape design practice than in other global cities. Most landscape design in Dubai is a thin veneer over a much older and deeper substrata. The humility that comes with recognizing this substratum, 'from which all goes and from which all comes' (Weller 2006, p. 67), could definitely benefit practice.

The thing is, when you attempt to drown the real place through ignorance or inattentiveness, the real place often comes fighting back. The substantial disconnect between designed and endemic landscapes means that if developers or the Municipality turned the irrigation systems off, most landscape projects would be dead within a week, and the sites returned to the desert landscape to which they belong. As I discussed in chapter 3, Dubai's parascapes 'are often stranger than an equivalent portion of the moon would be in relation to the natural surroundings' (Jensen 2007, p. 119). While it has limitations, renewed attention to site data, as part of a datascaping-driven design process (Lootsma 1999, p. 270), could assist in reconciling design to 'place' and herald novel forms of xerophytic landscapes (as I discussed in chapters 4 and 6).

As I discussed in chapters 3, 4 and 5, some projects the urban professions have delivered in Dubai have worrying environmental dimensions, a situation that they (generally) do not acknowledge. Latent Orientalist values could explain this because they imply that the 'Orient' is in a sense not real and functions primarily as a stage for Western fantasies or entertainment, as I discussed in chapter 5. Edward Said made the observation that 'the European, whose sensibility tours the Orient, is a watcher, never involved, always detached, always ready for new examples of what the Description de l'Egypte called "bizarre jouissance"' (Said 1991) – translating as bizarre pleasures.

In this respect, it is worth contemplating whether the Dubai-based but British-run design practice, who were responsible for the landscaping of the ecologically destructive Palm Jumeirah project (Salahudin 2006, p. 59), would be involved in this project if Nakheel were constructing it in the United Kingdom, perhaps off the coast of Cornwall.[1] This raises the question whether the ethics of design practice are place specific or generic. Because

Sheikh Maktoum authored the diagram of the project in the first place, does that alleviate the complicity of later designers who profit in further elaborating that design? The aspirations of the United Nations for urban development (as I set out in chapter 5) indicate that the answer to such questions is, broadly speaking, no – ethics do not vary in relation to local societal, political or environmental settings. Nonetheless, achieving the environmental aspirations of the UN and IFLA in practice in Dubai is a formidable challenge (as I discussed in chapter 5).

Landscape design practice and the socio-political context

In chapters 3, 4 and 5, I explored how clients – who are generally directly connected to the ruling dynasty – commission landscapes that legitimize the rule of the 'enlightened despot' Sheikh Mohammed (Davis 2007, p. 63). Depending on your perspective, this may or may not pose an ethical issue. It is entirely understandable that Dubai's ruler would seek to consolidate his power and wealth through the various means available to him. Moreover, considered in relation to many other rulers in the Gulf region, his rule is comparatively liberal. Nonetheless, members of the urban professions I met with in Dubai on research trips were extremely uncomfortable with any open criticism of Dubai's ruler, which may reflect his sensitivity to criticism in the press (Davis 2007, p. 63).

Given this restrictive political situation, it is imperative that the urban professions become conversant with the political agendas that drive the projects they are engaged in and, as such, be capable of engaging the fundamental logics behind development – something that has often eluded the urban professions to date. I directed chapters 3 and 4 to elucidating these political agendas. This relative failure of the urban professions is, of course, understandable. In the rush to design, document and construct projects, most design practitioners direct their effort towards delivering design outcomes and avoiding costly mistakes rather than reflecting on the broader socio-political implications of practice.

Nonetheless, Landscape Urbanism theory proposes that through a focus on the processes behind projects – rather than just their spatial form – the urban professions may be able to lobby Dubai's power brokers for more equitable societal outcomes (as I discussed in chapter 6). Furthermore, it identifies that the deployment of a programmed, interactive and inclusive landscape could have the potential to counter the tendency of scenographic parascape to merely legitimize the current regime's rule. Nonetheless, there are limits to what shifts in spatial design can achieve in terms of recasting Dubai's restrictive socio-political structure.

Landscape design practice and the cultural context

The urban professions in Dubai have (sometimes) been responsible for designing projects that trivialize Emirati culture through delivering a caricature of

Dubai's built-form heritage and of Arabic, Islamic urbanism more generally (as I discussed in chapter 4). In these projects, Dubai's built-form vernacular is used by developers to construct a narrative that the authority of Sheikh Mohammed sits in a 'natural line of progress' (Dovey 2016, p. 128) that extends from Dubai's ancient history to the current day. Moreover, by reciting a pastiche of Dubai's built-form heritage, designers are loosely recreating the shell of a historic city; however, the processes, which would lend this form authenticity, have entirely changed – particularly in relation to technology of production, transportation and social organization, amongst other areas.

While members of the urban professions may feel comfortable in the mode of creating (largely) fictitious history, I wonder about the inverse situation – what they might make of an Emirati designer in Australia (for instance), designing fictitious, vernacular-inspired projects. I imagine this would perturb expatriate practitioners. This echoes Edward Said's identification of the implausibility of reversing of the dynamics of Orientalism (1991, p. 50).

In my experience, many landscape designers plan projects without a clear understanding of the needs of Dubai's rich cultural mix and of Emirati culture specifically. This is understandable in that, in many urban projects, developers build under the motto of 'build it, and they will come,' but not knowing whom they may be designing for compromises design. Through not trying to understand who may occupy projects (e.g. Emirati males or females, Indian workers, Western expatriates from Britain or Australia), how they may see the world, or where they may feel comfortable to sit alone or in a group weakens the design of spaces. This understanding is not easy to arrive at. However, a contemporary research project – informed by William Whyte's *The Social Life of Small Urban Spaces* (Whyte 1980) – to analyze how open space is used in Dubai by different cultural groups could provide valuable insights and potentially yield locally distinctive design practice.

In some cases, indifference or arrogance has hampered the design professions' ability to bridge the cross-cultural gulf in Dubai. Bianca Stefano describes how the West has often presumed pre-eminence: 'The unshakeable conviction of their own superiority led certain western thinkers to believe that they had invalidated other, much richer and more meaningful cultural systems' (Bianca 2000, p. 186). As I discussed in chapter 5, design practitioners in Dubai should be wary about perpetuating this mode of operation, which diminishes the potential of landscape design to be culturally enriched and enriching.

The following section sketches out the possible implications of the Dubai development model, both for Dubai in the future and for the regions developers are exporting the model to. I have not countenanced these overarching issues in earlier chapters as they relate to longer-term problems facing Dubai or potentially affect a much broader geographic area.

Implications for the continuation of current practice in Dubai

Given the projected increase of Dubai's population from 3 million today to 5 million by 2027 (Zaatari 2017) and the subsequent urban expansion required, the urban profession's relative inability to address urgent environmental, societal and cultural issues is concerning. Its current role to furnish the city with landscape design that is often ecologically sterile, consumes massive amounts of freshwater, compounds a restrictive political situation and commodifies local culture for global consumption potentially exacerbates these emerging crises.

Societal implications

The continuing influx of immigrants is driving Dubai's projected population growth. This, in turn with a continued predilection for a fragmented urban form, which segregates socio-economic groups often along cultural lines and diminishes the possibility of meaningful social interaction, could lead to socio-political instability over the longer term. As Michele Acuto explains, 'Building a city for users and not inhabitants, alienating an invisible working class and creating an urban order based upon modular liberties might prove to be a socially unsustainable strategy' (Acuto 2010, p. 284). Moreover, the UN also warn us that 'societal inequality can lead to unrest and insecurity' (United Nations 2016).

My concern is that ultimately the segregation of Dubai's population into gated areas could 'breed ignorance, intolerance and homogeneity' (Dovey 2016, p. 175) among Dubai's citizens. The urban professions in Dubai are complicit in creating such a citizenry through its crucial role in designing Dubai's (largely) privatized urban form.

This is important not just for Dubai but also for the broader region. Dubai forms a vital cultural node between the Western, Asian and Arab worlds, facilitating the exchange of information, friendship, material goods, culture, knowledge, insight and skills (Gharipour 2016, p. 3). With ongoing wars in Afghanistan, Iraq and Syria, Dubai's role as a place where diverse cultures can engage with one another on 'neutral ground' becomes crucial. As American sociologist Lewis Mumford attested of the metropolis generally:

> The complexity and the cultural inclusiveness of the metropolis embody the complexity and variety of the world as a whole. Unconsciously the great capitals have been preparing mankind for the wider associations and unifications which the modern conquest of time and space has made probable, if not inevitable.
>
> (1961, p. 561)

Through this reading, a harmonious Dubai that can successfully assimilate and integrate diverse cultures can make a significant contribution towards enriching cultural relationships generally, in an often-troubled region.

Environmental implications

Dubai's projected population growth, endangered biodiversity and stretched water supply all indicate significant environmental challenges ahead. In addition, expected sea level rises over the longer term threaten Dubai's typically low-lying urban fabric. As Mohammad Raouf of the Gulf Research Center warns, given the predicted sea level rises in the next century, Dubai's 'artificial islands will disappear' (Landais 2007). A possible premonition of this is that the ferry company contracted to deliver visitors to The World development has recently sued the developer Nakheel, claiming that the channels have begun to silt up and some islands have begun to sink (Day 2015, p. 91).

Even more concerning than sea level rise are possible wet-bulb temperature events that could affect the Gulf this century. Wet-bulb temperature is a combination of temperature and humidity and is measured using a thermometer covered with a wet wash cloth (Pal & Eltahir 2016, p. 197). A human body can usually adapt to extremes of dry-bulb temperature (referred to as simply 'temperature') through perspiration and the associated evaporative cooling (Pal & Eltahir 2016, p. 197). However, at wet-bulb temperatures above 35 degrees centigrade, the high heat and humidity make it physically impossible for even the fittest human body to cool itself by sweating, with potentially fatal consequences after six hours (Shaheen 2015).

This poses a major issue for Dubai and the Gulf region because extremes of wet-bulb temperature are likely to exceed this critical threshold under a business-as-usual model of greenhouse gas emissions. As Prof. Elfatih Eltahir from the MIT Center for Global Change Science warns, the results 'expose a specific regional hotspot [in the Gulf] where climate change, in the absence of significant mitigation, is likely to severely impact human habitability in the future' (Pal & Eltahir 2016, p. 197). Moreover, the researchers project that fatal wet-bulb temperature extremes could occur every decade or two after 2070 along most of The Gulf coast if the global community does not curb global warming. Readers should note that, in this scenario, wet-bulb temperature events will affect both the region's and Dubai's liveability and viability long before they become lethal. Moreover, using the normal measure of temperature, the study revealed 45 degrees centigrade would become the usual summer maximum in Gulf cities, with 60 degrees centigrade being seen in places like Kuwait City (Shaheen 2015).

The current practice of the urban professions in Dubai exacerbates wet-bulb temperature issues in that parascape (and its irrigated vegetation and expansive water features) can increase the relative humidity of adjacent urban areas by approximately 5 per cent (Taleb 2016, p. 49). At a city-wide scale, climatologists regard that the increased green space and related evaporative losses of water have increased Dubai's humidity and even rainfall. While designers may employ vegetation to mitigate extreme heat events in Dubai, the contribution of vegetation to humidity could instead compound a potentially dangerous wet-bulb temperature situation. Moreover, the urban professions are complicit in creating Dubai's energy and water-hungry landscape, which magnifies Dubai's bloated greenhouse gas emissions, compounds global climate change and might result in potentially lethal wet-bulb temperature events that could threaten the city's liveability and viability over the longer term.

The implications of the Dubai model for developing countries

In chapter 2, I set out the hierarchical structure of Dubai's development model and the regions to which Dubai's developers are exporting this model. By way of summary, in the Gulf region, the Dubai model is spreading to Saudi Arabia, Bahrain (Rizzo 2014, p. 52), Kuwait (Moser, Swain & Alkhabbaz 2015, p. 72) and Qatar (Acuto 2010, p. 283). Farther afield, it is influencing development in China, India (Haines 2011, p. 160), Africa, Jordan, Tunisia, Morocco, Syria, Turkey, Brazil, Baku (Rizzo 2014, p. 52), South Korea, Hong Kong (Al Maktoum 2012, p. 17), Azerbaijan (Rizzo 2014, p. 52) and Lebanon (Abaza 2011, p. 1077). In a particularly overt Lebanese example, real estate company Noor Holding International proposed a 330-hectare land reclamation project named Cedar Island, a regional echo of Dubai's Palm Jumeirah development. The island was to be shaped like the cedar, Lebanon's most patriotic symbol, which is emblazoned on the national flag (Abou-Khalil 2010, p. 451). Despite the use of such symbolism, community hostility caused the project to collapse.

Dubai's urban development model has potential issues wherever developers deploy it; however, it is particularly problematic in what the International Monetary Fund refers to as developing countries, where the Dubai model is seen as marking them as 'having made it in the global economy' (Haines 2011, p. 161). I particularly fear its effects in Africa. Commentators project that 'the future of the world's urbanisation will be in Africa' as the continent's urban population will (almost) triple in the coming 35 years (Van Noorloos & Kloosterboer 2017, p. 2). In Africa, governments and developers are redirecting capital towards the construction of middle- and upper-class-oriented new mega projects rather than meeting the basic needs of urban dwellers – as such, critics fear these developments will lead to new forms of 'spatial injustice' (Van Noorloos & Kloosterboer 2017, p. 14). As a result, van Noorloos claims that these new cities or mega projects will be 'unsuitable for solving Africa's urban problems, and at worst they will increase expulsions and enclosures of the poor, public funding injustice and

socio-spatial segregation and fragmentation' (Van Noorloos & Kloosterboer 2017, p. 1).

Readers can find examples of such Dubai influenced development in
Khartoum in Sudan, Nouakchott in Mauritania (Rizzo 2014, p. 52), Konza
Technology City in Kenya and King Mohammed VI Green City in Morocco
(Van Noorloos & Kloosterboer 2017, p. 5). These mega projects are typically built from scratch as comprehensively planned self-contained enclaves
on the outskirts of existing cities (Van Noorloos & Kloosterboer 2017,
p. 2) and have clear connections with the Gulf states, Dubai in particular,
through their 'urban models, investors and contractors'[2] (Van Noorloos &
Kloosterboer 2017, p. 7). At the heart of the African mega project phenomenon is the attempt to stimulate 'technology, innovation and knowledge,'
which seeks to emulate, at least in part, Dubai's Free Trade Zones (FTZs)
such as Internet City – the Middle East's first electronic FTZ, inaugurated
in 2000 (Al Maktoum 2012, p. 23).

The Dubai model of urban development has also found particular expression in Egypt, in the form of a new capital city, in new master-planned
exclusive communities in the desert surrounding Cairo and in the Dubaification of the existing city of Cairo (Abaza 2011, p. 1075). In these existing
areas, development has resulted in new patterns of spatial segregation created by urban projects advertised as 'islands of luxury' protected by privatized security guards (Abaza 2011, p. 1075). The developers of such projects
seek to facilitate the 'luxurious' lifestyles typical of the Gulf 'oil monarchies'
(Denis 2006, p. 58). For residents of these exclusive urban islands, Cairo has
become a 'complex of unsustainable nuisances against which nothing more
can be done, except to escape or to protect oneself' (Denis 2006, p. 53).

On the desert edges of the city, more than 80 walled and gated communities have proliferated, with lavish landscaping and air-conditioned villas,
connected by highways that are easily accessible to shopping malls (Abaza
2011, p. 1075). One of these is Emaar's flagship Egyptian project, Uptown
Cairo. For those who are familiar with Dubai, the project presents uncan-
nily familiar scenery – 'billboards, impossibly green lawns and those vertical
flags nervously waving on the roadsides . . . palm trees and giant fountains' (Adham & Hossam 2010, p. 472). These luxuriant suburban developments – with names like Allegria, Dreamland, Beverly Hills, Swan Lake and
Utopia – are the home of Egypt's political elite and have required the diver-
sion of freshwater to irrigation, at the same time as many poorer areas of the
city struggle to access drinking water (Piper 2012, p. 2). When protests in
Tahrir Square erupted in 2011, the international media proclaimed a 'social
media revolution' spurred by pro-democracy Egyptians attempting to over-
throw the regime of President Hosni Mubarak. Typically unreported was
the fact that Egypt was also amid a water crisis. As Karen Piper explains, the
January 25 Revolution was not just a revolution of the downtrodden; it was
also a 'Revolution of the Thirsty' (Piper 2012, p. 2). Ironically, while Dubai
has benefitted handsomely from the turmoil of the Arab Spring in terms of

an influx of immigrants and investment, Dubai (to some degree) also triggered the Arab Spring through exporting its exclusive and thirsty models of urban development to Egypt.

In conclusion to this section, while Dubai is (often) viewed by the West as a 'fantasy world in the desert' (Davis 2007, p. 63), in the developing world, which desperately needs socio-ecologically enriching models for urban development, governments are deploying Dubai's model of 'imagineered urbanism.' This is concerning because, as this book has discussed, this powerful model of development comes with significant environmental, societal and cultural impacts (Van Noorloos & Kloosterboer 2017, p. 12) – something that could have dire effects on the African continent (amongst others) already facing formidable challenges around population growth, rural-to-urban migration, slums, climate change, species extinctions and societal segregation.

Future research

This section briefly sets out some related areas for research that have proven beyond the scope of this book yet that are worthy of further exploration.

The urban profession's complicity in the creation of Dubai's often socio-ecologically impoverishing landscape – as I discussed in chapter 5 – highlights the immense challenge of delivering the aspirations of the UN and IFLA in Dubai. The role of the urban professions to straddle the gulf between the ethos advocated by the UN and IFLA and clients who are responsive to Dubai's restrictive political and economic environment is a formidable task. In this respect, the discrepancy between theory and practice invites questioning as to the relevance of the UN- and IFLA-advocated goals in contexts such as Dubai – as well highlighting the need for detailed guidance as to how practitioners may meaningfully deliver these goals in practice. As Williams and Sharro explain: 'Dubai presents a dilemma for urbanists. It represents the antithesis of the contemporary ideas that they are championing, and it does not resemble any of the readymade conceptual models they have developed to understand cities' (Williams and Sharro in Kolo 2016, p. 171). The failure of the urban professions in Dubai to reconcile practice with the 'conceptual models' for urban development of the UN and IFLA means that these conceptual models also need further elaboration and development for such contexts.

Chapter 6 of this book explored Landscape Urbanism theory for its potential to bolster landscape design practice in Dubai. If Landscape Urbanism is going to thrive in contexts such as Dubai, proponents could further develop several components. While Landscape Urbanism theory provides a potentially useful conceptual framework for negotiating some of the challenges that landscape designers face, its application in praxis relies on a large degree of invention by design practitioners. In this respect, Landscape Urbanism proponents need to establish a workable methodology with which practitioners can engage without oversimplification of its nuanced and 'complicated appreciation of ecology and urbanity' (Weller 2008, p. 249). The codification of a New Urbanist planning method is both responsible for its widespread adoption, as well as its collapse into an often overly prescriptive design method. While Landscape Urbanism may avoid this level of codification, its current 'enigmatic' quality (Weller 2008, p. 248) severely limits its influence within everyday design practice in Dubai.

Finally, this book has touched on the effects the Dubai model of development is having on the Gulf region and Africa. Given that I have limited the scope of this book to Dubai, academics could direct future research to understanding in more detail the myriad economic and political interconnections among Dubai's rulers, development companies and the urban projects they are delivering around the world.

Conclusion

I opened this book with a personal aside and will conclude it in the same manner. If I could say one thing to my former 29-year-old self on the eve of departure to Dubai in 2005, it would be to take care.

Take care to understand the Rub al Khali desert and sabkha landscapes, which are as majestic as they are fragile. Grow your designs from these; do not smother them with a veneer of turf. You do not need to defeat the desert.

Take care to remember that what you would consider as deplorable in Australia is equally so in Dubai. If you would not abet a developer in Australia building a palm-shaped megastructure over coral reefs, do not be complicit in such projects in Dubai.

Take care with the people – including the 'invisible underclass' – who do not get to inhabit much of the city they build and service. Lobby for and design landscapes within which they can belong.

Take care to understand the people of the city who are to inhabit your SketchUp renders. As much as you can, imagine yourself in their shoes and be humble enough to consider what your design could offer them. Take care to consider what it might be like to be Emirati, to be numerically marginalized, to feel that you have lost the quieter and simpler city of your childhood. Take care not to trivialize this sense of loss with superficial recitations of the local vernacular.

Take care, reader, and thank you for making it to the end.

Notes

1 This, of course, requires the reader to ignore the impossibility of this occurring due to regulatory or community barriers.
2 This situation is perpetuated by their requiring Islamic-based funding rules.

References

Abaza, M 2011, 'Critical Commentary: Cairo's Downtown Imagined: Dubaisation or Nostalgia?' *Urban Studies*, vol. 48, no. 6, pp. 1075–1087.

Abou-Khalil, R 2010, 'Too Littoral: Gulf Export to Lebanon and the Case of Cedar Island', *Al Manakh- Gulf Cont'd*, vol. 25, no. 2, pp. 451–453.

Acuto, M 2010, 'High-Rise Dubai Urban Entrepreneurialism and the Technology of Symbolic Power', *Cities*, no. 27, pp. 272–284.

Adham, K & Hossam, M 2010, 'Cairo's Boulevard of Dreams: A Visit to Emaar', *Al Manakh- Gulf Cont'd*, vol. 25, no. 2, pp. 472–473.

Al Maktoum, MbR 2012, *My Vision: Challenges in the Race for Excellence*, Motivate Publishing, Dubai.

Bianca, S 2000, *Urban Form in the Arab World; Past and Present*, Thames and Hudson, London.

Davis, M 2007, 'Fear and Money in Dubai', *Topos*, pp. 62–70.

Day, C 2015, 'State of the World', *LA+*, vol. Pleasure, pp. 90–91.

Denis, E 2006, *Cairo as Neoliberal Capital?* American University in Cairo Press, Cairo and New York.

Dovey, K 2016, *Urban Design Thinking*, Bloomsbury Academic, London.

Gharipour, M 2016, *Contemporary Urban Landscapes of the Middle East*, Routledge, London.

Haines, C 2011, 'Cracks in the Façade: Landscapes of Hope and Desire in Dubai', in *Worlding Cities: Asian Experiments and the Art of Being Global*, pp. 160–181, Blackwell, Chichester.

Jensen, B 2007, *Dubai — Dynamics of Bingo Urbanism*, Architectural Publisher, Copenhagen.

Kolo, J 2016, 'Accidental or Envisioned Cities: A Comparative Analysis of Abu Dhabi and Dubai', in G Katodrytis & S Syed (eds), *Gulf Cities as Interfaces*, pp. 161–180, Gulf Research Center Cambridge, Jeddah.

Landais, E 2007, *Climate Change 'Will Hit Coastlines Soon'*. Available from: https://www.pressreader.com/uae/gulf-news/20070305/281655365614486. [22.07].

Lootsma, B 1999, 'Synthetic Regionalization', in *Recovering Landscape: Essays in Contemporary Landscape Architecture*, pp. 251–274, Princeton Architectural Press, New York.

Moser, S, Swain, M & Alkhabbaz, M 2015, 'King Abdullah Economic City: Engineering Saudi Arabia's Post-Oil Future', *Cities*, no. 45, pp. 71–80.

Mumford, L 1961, *The City in History*, Harcourt, San Diego, New York and London.

Pal, JS & Eltahir, EAB 2016, 'Future Temperature in Southwest Asia Projected to Exceed a Threshold for Human Adaptability', *Nature Climate Change*, vol. 6, no. 2, pp. 197–200.

Piper, K 2012, 'Revolution of the Thirsty', *Places Journal*. Available from: https://placesjournal.org/article/revolution-of-the-thirsty/?cn-reloaded=1.

Rizzo, A 2014, 'Rapid Urban Development and National Master Planning in Arab Gulf Countries. Qatar as a Case Study', *Cities*, no. 39, pp. 50–57.

Said, E 1991, *Orientalism*, Penguin Books, London.

Salahudin, B 2006, 'The Marine Environmental Impacts of Artificial Island Construction', Master's thesis, Duke University, Durham, NC, Nicholas School of the Environment and Earth Sciences.

Shaheen, K 2015, 'Extreme Heatwaves Could Push Gulf Climate Beyond Human Endurance, Study Shows', *The Guardian*. Available from: www.theguardian.com/environment/2015/oct/26/extreme-heatwaves-could-push-gulf-climate-beyond-human-endurance-study-shows?CMP=share_btn_tw. [05.11].

Taleb, H 2016, 'Effect of Adding Vegetation and Applying a Plants Buffer on Urban Community in Dubai', *Spaces and Flows: An International Journal of Urban and Extra Urban Studies*, vol. 7, no. 1, pp. 37–49.

United Nations 2016, *Sustainable Cities: Why They Matter*, United Nations. Available from: www.un.org/sustainabledevelopment/wp-content/uploads/2016/08/16-00055K_Why-it-Matters_Goal-11_Cities_2p.pdf. [22.07].

Van Noorloos, F & Kloosterboer, M 2017, 'Africa's New Cities: The Contested Future of Urbanisation', *Urban Studies*, vol. 55, no. 6, pp. 1–19.

Weller, R 2006, 'An Art of Instrumentality: Thinking Through Landscape Urbanism', in *The Landscape Urbanism Reader*, pp. 69–86, Princeton Architectural Press, New York City.

Weller, R 2008, 'Landscape (Sub) Urbanism in Theory and Practice', *Landscape Journal*, vol. 27, no. 2, pp. 247–267.

Whyte, W 1980, *The Social Life of Small Urban Spaces*, Conservation Foundation, Baltimore.

Zaatari, S 2017, 'Dubai Population to Double by 2027?' *Gulf News*. Available from: https://gulfnews.com/news/uae/society/dubai-population-to-double-by-2027-1.2075117. [14.05].

Index

Note: Page numbers in *italic* indicate a figure on the corresponding page.